PHIL VICKERY'S
PUDDINGS

PHIL VICKERY'S
PUDDINGS

EVERY PUDDING YOU HAVE EVER WANTED TO MAKE

PHOTOGRAPHS BY STEVE BAXTER
AND STEVE LEE

SIMON &
SCHUSTER

LONDON • NEW YORK • SYDNEY • TORONTO

FOR MY MUM

There are a few people I'd like to thank, because without their help
this book would not have been possible.

Firstly, Sam Boyce, who set the whole thing up and like me, thank goodness,
believed that great British puddings are the best in the world.

My mother, not only for cooking some of the best puddings and cakes in the land,
but also for putting up with all the mess when I was at college.

My father because I left him out of another book and he has never let me forget it,
and for introducing me at an early age to the great combination of golden syrup
on spotted dick and skin on custard.

Brian Gilham, by far the best 'old school' pastry chef in the land.

Julia Algar, not only for agreeing to re-cook and edit every recipe and doing a fantastic job,
but also for making my food look good on telly.

Billington's sugars for making the job easy and a real pleasure.

For the new edition, thanks to Steve Lee for the extra shots; Francine Lawrence
for overseeing the project and giving up a Saturday; Anna Hitchin for editing so well and
in such detail; and thanks also goes to the almost gangster-like coupling
of John Rush and Luigi Bonomi.

And last, but definitely not least, Fernie, for struggling through doughnut week, Christmas cake
week, ice cream week etc. And for simply being the best wife any man could wish for.

PHIL VICKERY
MAY 2009

*Puddings are my personal passion. I want to take the
fear out of puddings and to show why puddings are
so wonderful to cook, and to eat.*

Phil Vickery

Revised edition published in Great Britain by Simon & Schuster UK Ltd, 2009
A CBS Company

First published in Great Britain by Simon & Schuster UK Ltd as *Proof of the Pudding*, 2003

Simon & Schuster UK Ltd
1st Floor, 222 Gray's Inn Road
London WC1X 8HB

1 3 5 7 9 10 8 6 4 2

Editorial director for the revised edition: Francine Lawrence
Project editor for the revised edition: Anna Hitchin
Copy editors: Deborah Savage; revised edition: Anna Hitchin
Photography: Steve Baxter; Steve Lee: front and back covers and pages 2, 5, 9, 65, 93,
123, 139, 161, 193, 253, 265 and 281
Design: Two Associates
Home economists for photography: Linda Tubby; new recipes: Clare Greenstreet
Stylists for photography: Liz Belton; new recipes: Jo Harris
Printed and bound in China

978-1-84737-683-1

Egg sizes: Eggs are medium-sized unless otherwise indicated.

CONTENTS

WHY PUDDINGS?

I have always been fascinated by puddings, cakes and sweet things. From a very early age I can remember helping my mum to make Victoria sponges, and the best bit was being able to scrape the large Pyrex bowl clean at the end. We were very lucky growing up; my mother only worked part time, so there were always plenty of homemade cakes, puddings, biscuits and even ice cream ready when we got home from school. In hindsight, this probably shaped my chosen career from a very early age.

When we did have shop-bought cakes, it was considered a real treat. I can distinctly remember eating delicious, thick, fudgy fondant icing on a sweet doughnut – it was so satisfying. One day, I looked at the lovely fondant, thinking how do they make that? That was it – off I went and bought a cake-decorating book to discover how to produce this delicious topping. This meant I had to purchase a sugar thermometer and boil sugar, something that 'normal 14 year olds did not do', I remember my mother saying at the time.

Well, the rest is history. From there, I made cakes, buns, rough puff pastry, mastered choux pastry, and even built sugar paste churches by the time I was 15. At college, I was again drawn to the dessert area, winning the pastry chef award in my second year.

I was very lucky to be taught by a brilliant chef called Brian Gilham. He had been the Queen's pastry chef in a former life for many years and scared me to death. His great skill, craft, attention to detail, and most importantly, his knowledge, sealed my love for the pastry kitchen.

After leaving college, I spent the next 30 years working in many great kitchens, mostly in desserts and sweets – something that has been a real joy. It's never been a chore – even now, I really enjoy working on sweet things. I also make an annual pilgrimage to Bruges to work with a friend and chocolate master.

There has been an explosion of Great British Food over the past few years – and it's all very exciting. But our history of making great British puddings goes back many years. Centuries of cooks have cooked and honed the basis of many of the sweet dishes we enjoy today. Great classics such as spotted dick and custard, Grasmere gingerbread, crumbles, possets, flummerys and trifles – they all rightly have a set place in our culinary history.

For the dedicated pastry chef, our islands offer a vast number of unique and highly prized fruits and nuts. Our greengages, for example, are as good as the French mirabelles. West Country cream and apples, Yorkshire forced rhubarb, Scottish raspberries, Kent cob and hazel nuts, Lancashire whimberries – these are what make the British pastry chef's work entirely distinctive. Our mulberries are simply the tastiest fruits in the world, so good in fact that the nursery rhyme must once have evoked all the tastes of summer on that cold and frosty morning.

A French chef once said to me, 'you (British) are only good at roasts and puddings'. I suppose that was faint praise in a way. Mind you, this was the same chef who, after five pints of Shepherd Neame Spitfire bitter, tucked into cod, chips and mushy peas and loved it!

I'm very excited about this book and I've created 18 new recipes for it, to add to my existing favourites. You'll see them labelled throughout and also look out for the orange Techniques pages which have my tips for perfect puddings every time. This book is a condensed version of my 30 years of cooking many sweet things; I hope you enjoy discovering and re-discovering many of our country's classics. Great British puddings, cakes and biscuits are a real joy, and I'm proud to have cooked them, and will continue to do so for many years to come.

Phil V

I love to cook with fresh eggs from my chickens.

MILK AND CREAM PUDDINGS

Milk and cream puddings are the most comforting and satisfying in the world, conjuring up memories of Sunday lunch on cold, rainy days. When I was a child, my family would fight so much over who got the skin off the rice pudding or custard that my dad would have to divide it into tiny portions so that everyone could have a share!

The British love affair with hot, milky puddings began back in medieval times, when large amounts of almonds, imported from Italy, were crushed and mixed with milk and honey to make the first milk puddings.

The quintessential rice pudding came into its own in Victorian times, either boiled or baked, with dried fruits in winter and fresh fruit in summer. Adding spices such as cinnamon and nutmeg was all the rage, and the ultimate fashion accessory for Victorian gentlemen was an ornate silver nutmeg box, so that they could have a whole nutmeg at all times, for grating on to their drinks and puddings.

Cold, baked or boiled rice pudding can be changed dramatically by the addition of candied lemon, lime or even quinces, along with crème fraîche or double cream. Fresh vanilla also works well, as does Yorkshire forced rhubarb and syrup.

Ground and flaked rice are far less popular than they used to be, but both are wonderful. I loved a brand called Creamola rice as a child, hot with jam, and also a pudding made with flaked rice (which is basically a flattened rice grain), cooked and then mixed with summer blueberries and cream. Queen of Puddings is one of my all-time favourites – a classic combination of cake crumbs (best of all Madeira cake), hot milk, meringue, and raspberry and greengage jams.

This chapter is dedicated to real comfort food, and just shows what can be done with the humble grain of rice, piece of cake and pint of milk when you put your mind to it.

RICE PUDDING WITH ROSE-HIP SYRUP AND CRÈME FRAÎCHE

Rose-hips are the fruit of the wild dog rose. They were served in the Middle Ages as a sweet – how they cooked them I do not know – but they do make a very good syrup.

The best time to pick rose-hips is late October, early November when they are starting to soften after the first frost, similar to rowan berries. Any earlier and they are too hard and have not developed their unique flavour. Do not leave it too late, though, or the birds will get there before you. Rose-hips freeze well.

FOR THE ROSE-HIP SYRUP
350 g (12 oz) soft rose-hips
400 g (14 oz) granulated sugar
juice of 1 lemon

FOR THE RICE PUDDING
600 ml (1 pint) whole milk
1 vanilla pod, split
55 g (2 oz) short-grain rice
175 g (6 oz) crème fraîche

juice of 1 lime, to serve

serves 4

To make the rose-hip syrup, wash the rose-hips well and remove any stalks or calyxes. Process in a food processor to a thick purée.

Bring 500 ml (18 fl oz) of water to the boil in a pan, add the purée and then bring back to the boil and simmer for 2 minutes. Remove from the heat and leave to stand for a further 20 minutes. Strain the mixture through a piece of muslin or clean tea towel, reserving both the juice and pulp. Bring another 500 ml (18 fl oz) of water to the boil and add the reserved pulp. Simmer for 2 minutes, then strain again.

Mix the two strained juices together and simmer rapidly in a pan to reduce until you have about 1 litre (1¾ pints). Add the sugar and lemon juice and stir until dissolved. Simmer rapidly until the syrup is deeply coloured and has reduced to about 400 ml (14 fl oz). Strain and then allow to cool. Pour the syrup into a clean jar or bottle and keep in the fridge (this will keep in the fridge for about 3 weeks).

To make the rice pudding, preheat the oven to 180°C/350°F/Gas Mark 4. Pour the milk into an ovenproof pan, scrape in the vanilla seeds, add the vanilla pod and bring to the boil. Sprinkle in the rice, stir, then cover with a lid, transfer to the oven and bake for about 45 minutes, or until thick and creamy.

Remove from the oven and stir well, then replace the lid and allow to cool for 20 minutes. Stir in the crème fraîche and enough rose-hip syrup to flavour the rice. Serve hot or cold, with an additional drizzle of syrup and a squeeze of fresh lime juice over the top.

RICE PUDDING WITH DRIED BANANAS AND BROWN SUGAR

This is very different from the recipe opposite. Here I almost marinate the dried bananas in the pudding and this, along with the evaporated milk, gives it a very caramelly edge.

Just recently, rice pudding has become trendy again. Gone are the days of the thick sludge that we were forced to eat at school; nowadays, it can be eaten hot, cold in a mousse or even as a soufflé as my old pal Paul Kitching does at his Juniper restaurant in Altrincham, which is gorgeous. Flavourings vary from cinnamon, prunes, nutmeg, bananas and stewed apples in the hot version, to clotted cream, crème fraîche, rose- and orange-flower waters, basil, and butterscotch in chilled rice puddings. Either way, rice pudding is a real favourite of mine. The addition of evaporated milk and crème fraîche gives the pudding a really rich twist.

Forget about the calories just this once and enjoy yourself!

410 g can of evaporated milk
about 200 ml (7 fl oz) whole milk
1 vanilla pod, split
55 g (2 oz) short-grain rice
soft brown sugar, to taste
125 g (4½ oz) dried bananas,
    chopped
175 g (6 oz) crème fraîche

serves 4

Preheat the oven to 180°C/350°F/Gas Mark 4. Pour the evaporated milk into a measuring jug. Then top up with the milk until you have 600 ml (1 pint). Pour into an ovenproof, preferably non-stick, thick-bottomed saucepan, add the vanilla pod and bring to the boil very slowly – stir all the time or it will burn.

Once the milk is boiling, rain in the rice and stir well. Cover with a tightly fitting lid, transfer to the oven and bake for about 1 hour, stirring every 10–15 minutes. If the rice becomes too thick or dry during cooking, you can add an extra splash of milk.

When the rice is tender, remove from the oven and stir well. Take out the vanilla pod and add brown sugar to taste; it's up to you how sweet you want the whole thing. Leave to cool for about 5 minutes.

Stir in the chopped dried bananas and crème fraîche and leave again for a few minutes for the bananas to soften; then serve. I think that rice pudding that is too hot is awful, you can't taste it or even eat it, so do leave it to stand for a while before you tuck in.

CHILLED CREAMED RICE WITH CANDIED PINEAPPLE

Chilled creamed rice with pineapple is not a new idea, but it is delicious. You can set the pudding with gelatine, but I tend to like the cooked rice just on its own.

On a trip to Florence, I happened to pop into the central market and found the most wonderful selection of soft, candied fruits. Everything from baby plums to strawberries and even tomatoes were for sale. Candied fruits can be bought all year round now in Britain, and there are some very good ones too: melon, figs and plums can all be found fairly easily. A little goes a long way so don't go mad.

600 ml (1 pint) whole milk
1 vanilla pod, split
55 g (2 oz) pudding rice
100 ml (3½ fl oz) double cream
200 g (7 oz) crème fraîche
heaped 60 ml (4 tablespoons)
    unrefined icing sugar
finely grated zest and juice of
    1 large lemon
100 g (3½ oz) candied or
    semi-dried pineapple, cut
    into very small cubes
30 ml (2 tablespoons)
    chopped fresh mint
My Mum's Shortbread
    (page 278), to serve

serves 4

Preheat the oven to 150°C/300°F/Gas Mark 2.

Bring the milk and vanilla pod to the boil in an ovenproof pan. Rain in the rice and stir well, then cover with a tightly fitting lid, place in the oven and cook for 35–40 minutes, or until thick and creamy. Remove from the oven and allow to cool.

When cool, spoon into a large bowl and break up with a wooden spoon. Add the cream, crème fraîche, icing sugar and lemon zest and juice and mix well. Finally, add the pineapple and mint and fold in together. Chill well, preferably overnight.

Serve in deep bowls, with shortbread.

GOOSEBERRY AND ELDERFLOWER FOOL WITH
CRUSHED MERINGUES

Every year in early summer I used to walk my dog, Max, past some wonderful elderberry trees and each time I thought about the delicious syrup you can make from the elderflowers.

Some chefs deep-fry the flowers to serve with ice cream but I think they are vile. There really are only three ways to use these delicate flowers – as a syrup, added to gooseberries when bottling, and in 'elderflower champagne', now called 'sparkling elderflower apéritif' since the French got funny about the use of the name champagne.

If you are lucky enough to have a nearby tree, you can gather the flowers and make your own cordial; if not, you can buy elderflower cordial now, so why not invest in a bottle and try this sweet – it's simple, very tasty and one of my favourites!

This recipe contains raw or lightly cooked eggs. Because of the slight risk of salmonella poisoning, these should be avoided by the sick, the elderly, the very young, and pregnant women.

225 g (8 oz) gooseberries,
    topped and tailed
2 egg whites (optional)
600 ml (1 pint) double cream,
    softly whipped
about 30–45 ml (2–3
    tablespoons) elderflower
    cordial
2 individual meringues,
    or meringue nests,
    crushed into small pieces
castor sugar, to taste

serves 4

Place the gooseberries in a pan with 50 ml (2 fl oz) of water and bring to a simmer. Reduce the heat and cook gently for about 15–20 minutes, or until the gooseberries have turned to a thick, chunky purée. Remove from the heat and allow to cool.

If using, whisk the egg whites until they form soft peaks; do not over whisk them (see 'Whisking egg whites' on page 127). Place the gooseberry purée in a bowl, add the whipped cream and fold in, and then add elderflower cordial to taste. Finally, fold in the egg whites if using, and crushed meringues. If necessary, add castor sugar to sweeten to taste.

Spoon the fool into glasses and serve straight away.

YORKSHIRE RHUBARB FOOL IN A MUG

A third of the world's supply of new-season (forced) rhubarb is grown in Yorkshire and it makes a delicate and delicious fool. This is a different way of serving fool from the usual wine glasses and I rather like it. Using Savoy sponge fingers adds a little texture.

600 g (1 lb 5 oz) new-season
    rhubarb, cut into 2.5 cm
    (1-inch) pieces
85 g (3 oz) unrefined castor sugar
juice of 1 large lemon
1 vanilla pod, split
about 48 sponge fingers
    (about 275 g/9¾ oz)
300 ml (½ pint) whipping
    cream, whipped to soft peaks
450 ml (16 fl oz) thick custard
    (good-quality ready-made
    custard is quite good for this)

FOR THE RHUBARB SAUCE
225 g (8 oz) new-season
    rhubarb, chopped
100 g (3½ oz) castor sugar
a squeeze of lemon juice

serves 6

Gently cook the rhubarb in a pan with the sugar, lemon juice and vanilla pod for about 4–5 minutes, or until the rhubarb is softened, thick and pulpy. Cool completely and then remove the vanilla pod.

The rest is relatively easy! Line six large, straight-sided tea mugs, about 8 cm (3 inches) in diameter and 300 ml (½ pint) capacity, with cling film – if you wet the inside of the mugs first, it's a lot easier. Then line the sides with sponge fingers.

Carefully fold together the whipped cream, custard and cooled rhubarb. Use the mixture to fill up the mugs, tap down to level and then cover with cling film and chill well (overnight is best if possible).

To make the sauce, gently stew the rhubarb with the sugar and 100 ml (3½ fl oz) of water until soft and stringy. Carefully liquidise and pass through a fine sieve. Add a squeeze of lemon juice and taste; you may need to add more sugar if the sauce is too sour.

Turn out by gently pulling the cling film – the fools will slide out. Serve with a little rhubarb sauce.

BRAMLEY APPLE, CARAMEL AND CUSTARD FOOL

Bramleys are really cheap and great value for money at any time of year. Their unique tartness combined with the dark caramel and custard makes this fool a delicious, light ending to a meal. The secrets are not to add sugar to the stewed apples; to use whipping cream rather than double, its heavier brother, for a light, tasty treat; and to use wine glasses so everyone can see the layers of great colours.

2 Bramley apples, peeled, cored and chopped into 1 cm (½-inch) pieces

finely grated zest and juice of 1 lemon

250 g (9 oz) granulated sugar

450 ml (16 fl oz) custard (make your own, or use a good-quality brand such as Bird's)

600 ml (1 pint) very cold whipping cream, lightly whipped

shortbread or strong coffee, to serve

serves 4

To make the 'apple marmalade', heat the prepared apple in a pan with the lemon zest and juice and cook gently for about 10 minutes, or until the apple is tender – you may need to add a touch of water as the apple cooks if it starts to thicken too much. Once cooked, allow to cool (don't worry too much if there are a few undercooked lumps).

Meanwhile, to make the caramel, place the sugar in a pan and just cover with water. Bring to the boil to make the caramel, and then boil rapidly until the syrup starts to thicken and get darker – keep a careful eye on it as it can burn very quickly indeed (see 'Making caramel' on page 167).

When the caramel is dark brown, carefully tip in 150 ml (¼ pint) of cold water – there will be a lot of spluttering and splashing, so stand back and don't worry about that. Bring the syrup back to the boil and allow any pieces of caramel to melt. Pour into a bowl or jug and leave to cool completely.

To serve, place a little of the apple marmalade in the bottom of four large wine glasses and then pour on some of the caramel syrup. Next, add a spoonful of custard and finally a spoonful of cream. Repeat to fill the glasses. Chill for 15 minutes before serving with shortbread or just on its own with a cup of strong coffee.

CRÈME BRÛLÉE

Every chef seems to have a twist on crème brûlée and there have been some real disasters! Please listen to me, there is, and will only ever be one crème brûlée, made with just egg, cream, sugar, vanilla and a touch of lemon oil from the zest.

The three most common problems with crème brûlée are: overcooked or unevenly cooked custard, mostly due to incorrect oven temperature; using too much egg, so it ends up like an ice hockey puck; and using double cream, which makes the finished crème brûlée heavy.

Oh and by the way, this is another classic example of the French stealing a great British idea (originally called 'Burnt Cream' here), giving it a sexy name and calling it their own.

6 large egg yolks
55 g (2 oz) castor sugar
600 ml (1 pint) whipping cream
zest of 1 large lemon,
    taken off with a peeler
1 vanilla pod, split

serves 4

Preheat the oven to 140°C/275°F/Gas Mark 1. Place the egg yolks and castor sugar in a bowl and gently mix together.

Place the cream, lemon zest and vanilla pod in a pan and slowly bring to the boil. Once boiling, pour on to the beaten egg yolks and sugar, whisk together well and then leave to cool and infuse for 10 minutes.

Strain the mixture through a sieve then pour into four 9.5 cm diameter x 5 cm deep (4-x 2-inch) ramekins. (There has been a trend recently to cook brûlées in very shallow dishes. This is not right in my eyes: the cooked custard should be dense, deep and just a bit wobbly in the middle.) Carefully place in a deep baking tray, and pour boiling water from a kettle into the tray until the water is halfway up the side of the ramekins. Cover the whole tray lightly with foil and bake for 30 minutes, or until just set. Remember the residual heat in the custard will prolong the cooking process for a good 10 minutes or so once out of the oven. Remove from the oven and leave to cool, then chill well, preferably overnight.

When you come to glaze the brûlée, sprinkle a thin layer of castor sugar on top of each, taking care to make sure all the custard is covered (see 'Glazing a custard-filled flan' on page 49). Place under a very hot grill, or (far better) glaze nice and evenly with a blowtorch, and then cool slightly. Repeat the process and then leave to harden before serving. I like to glaze the brûlée just before the start of the meal, then they have time to warm up slightly. There is nothing worse than ice-cold crème brûlée!

ALMOND BLANCMANGE WITH ROSE-PETAL SYRUP

Forget any thoughts of school blancmange, that face-pack-pink, rubbery, tasteless pap we were forced to eat. This is real blancmange: light, creamy and delicious with rose-petal or saffron syrup, a crumbly shortbread biscuit and some sweet English strawberries or raspberries at room temperature.

The whole idea of a blancmange is that the texture should be light and creamy but not too rich, and it must have the essential 'wobble' factor when the plate is moved from side to side. This dessert was part of the meal that won me Chef of the Year a few years ago.

250 g (9 oz) unblanched almonds

600 ml (1 pint) whole milk

125 g (4½ oz) castor sugar

6 egg yolks

4½ gelatine leaves, soaked in cold water (see 'Dissolving gelatine' on page 99)

200 ml (7 fl oz) whipping cream, lightly whipped

Rose-Petal Syrup (page 217), to serve

serves 4

Place the almonds in a food processor and blitz until you have a crumbly powder; alternatively, crush them with a rolling pin. Place in a large heatproof bowl. Boil the milk and pour on to the almonds, cover and leave to infuse for at least 2 hours (or ideally overnight).

After this time, strain the almonds from the milk, pushing all the milk out with the back of a ladle. Measure the milk, and top it back up to 600 ml (1 pint) with fresh milk if necessary – this is very important or the finished blancmange will set too firmly. Discard the almonds.

Place the sugar and egg yolks in a bowl and whisk for about 5 minutes or until light and creamy. Bring the almond milk to the boil and pour on to the sugar and egg mixture; whisk together and return to the pan. Cook over a very low heat, stirring all the time until lightly thickened, but do not overcook – if the mixture thickens too much and looks as though it is starting to separate, pour it into a liquidiser, or use a hand-blender and blitz for a couple of seconds: the mixture will be slightly thinner but still usable. Pass through a fine strainer into a clean bowl.

Next, gently squeeze excess water out of the soaked gelatine, add to the hot custard and stir well until dissolved. Sit the bowl in a large bowl of iced water and stir constantly until the mixture is cool and starting to thicken. Lightly fold the cream into the cooled mixture fairly quickly using a whisk then pour into 150 ml (¼-pint) ramekins, glasses or bowls. Chill until set, for at least 2 hours, before serving with rose-petal syrup.

FERN'S QUEEN OF PUDDINGS

This is one of Fern's favourite puddings. Making it as apprentices, we would finish the top with greengage and raspberry jams: the contrasting colours are essential (Tiptree make a very good greengage jam). The secret is to not overcook the custard. Any cake or breadcrumbs will do but I just love buttery Madeira cake. This and egg custard tart are, I think, the ultimate comfort-food experiences.

600 ml (1 pint) whole milk
1 vanilla pod, split
3 large eggs, separated
25 g (1 oz) castor sugar
85 g (3 oz) Madeira cake crumbs
    or fine breadcrumbs
a pinch of freshly grated nutmeg
finely grated zest of 1 lemon

FOR THE TOPPING
a pinch of cream of tartar
85 g (3 oz) castor sugar,
    plus extra to decorate
85 g (3 oz) icing sugar, sifted
about 45 ml (3 tablespoons)
    greengage or green rhubarb
    jam
about 45 ml (3 tablespoons)
    raspberry jam

double cream, to serve

serves 4-6

Preheat the oven to 160°C/325°F/Gas Mark 3. Lightly grease or oil an 18 cm (7-inch) square x 6 cm (2 ½-inch) deep ceramic baking dish. Put the milk and vanilla pod in a thick-bottomed pan and bring to the boil. Whisk the egg yolks and castor sugar together until pale in colour. When the milk is boiling, pour on to the egg yolks and whisk well. Strain into a large jug and keep warm.

Mix together the cake or breadcrumbs, nutmeg and zest in a large bowl. Pour on the hot milk and whisk together. Carefully pour into the prepared baking dish, cover with foil and bake for about 30 minutes. Take care when cooking: it will set and then curdle very quickly indeed; you want it just set.

When cooked, remove from the oven and cool for 15 minutes (this pudding should be eaten warm, not too hot). Turn the oven up to 220°C/425°F/Gas Mark 7. Next, make the meringue (see page 127). Put the egg whites in a mixing bowl, add the cream of tartar and whisk on half speed. I reckon that if you beat the whites too quickly they tend to separate quicker and cannot hold their own weight (see 'Whisking egg whites' on page 127). When they are thick and foamy, but not separating, add the castor sugar and whisk again on a medium speed until shiny and glossy but take care not to over whisk. Remove the bowl from the machine and carefully fold in the icing sugar.

Fit a piping bag with a 1 cm (½-inch) plain piping nozzle. Fill with the finished meringue. Pipe diagonal lines across the warm custard, leaving a 1.5 cm (⅝-inch) gap between lines, then repeat going in the opposite direction so you end up with diamond-shaped holes.

Fill alternate holes with the two different jams and pipe a nice decoration around the edge. Sprinkle with a little castor sugar and bake in the hot oven for about 7–10 minutes, or until the pudding is a deep beige colour and the meringue is crisp. Serve with a jug of double cream.

STRAWBERRY JUNKET WITH NUTMEG AND CLOTTED CREAM

This is a pudding you either love or hate. I love it, provided it is sweetened and layered with fine English strawberries and topped with clotted cream and nutmeg. An odd combination, I know, but one that works very well.

Junket is a very traditional pudding, especially in the West Country. It's made by very lightly curdling whole milk with rennet at room temperature.

600 ml (1 pint) whole milk
55 g (2 oz) unrefined castor sugar
7.5 ml (1½ teaspoons) rennet
225 g (8 oz) ripe English
    strawberries, hulled and
    thinly sliced
200 g (7 oz) clotted cream
2.5 ml (½ teaspoon)
    grated nutmeg, for dusting

serves 6

Heat the milk and sugar together roughly to blood temperature (99°F/37°C) and then remove from the heat. Pour into a jug, add the rennet and stir well then immediately pour into six 150 ml (¼-pint) ramekins. Leave to set at room temperature. After 1 hour, cover with cling film and chill for about an hour.

To serve, arrange the strawberries on top of the junkets. Finally, carefully top with clotted cream (this can be quite difficult as the junket is very fragile). Dust with a little nutmeg and serve.

New Recipe

BAKED MANGO CREAM

This is one of the tastiest puddings I have ever cooked. It's light, full of flavour and a great end to a heavy meal. Serve it with the Blackcurrant Sorbet (page 192) – it's the most delicious sorbet around.

6 eggs
200 ml (7 fl oz) whipping cream
180 g (6 oz) castor sugar
3 large ripe mangoes,
    skinned and puréed
juice of 2 large lemons
icing sugar, for dusting
Blackcurrant Sorbet (page 192)
    or raspberry sorbet, to serve

makes 6-7 ramekins

Preheat the oven to 180°C/350°F/Gas Mark 4. Break the eggs into a bowl, add the cream, castor sugar and mango purée. Whisk well then whisk in the lemon juice and taste. Add a little more juice, if needed. Finally strain through a fine sieve into a jug.

Lightly oil six ramekins and place in a deep baking tray. Carefully pour in the mango mixture and fill right up to the inner lip. Fill the tray halfway up the ramekin with boiling water. Cover the whole tray with foil and place in the preheated oven. Cook for about 45 minutes until **just** set; the centres should be slightly wobbly.

Remove carefully from the oven lift on to a cool tray, cool and chill well. To serve, dust with icing sugar and a nice large ball of blackcurrant or raspberry sorbet.

BAKED AND STEAMED PUDDINGS

This chapter, probably more than any other, describes what we in Britain are best at. Alexis Soyer writing in his book *The Modern Housewife* (published 1849) once summed up his feelings for the great British steamed puddings by saying, 'There is hardly any of our sex, from childhood to old age but loves this truly English mixture'.

It's true: I don't know anybody who can resist a baked or steamed pudding. Every restaurant, pub or hotel menu these days has some old favourites on the menu. Spotted dick, jam roly poly, gooseberry crumble and steamed suet puddings are all very common. This is great for British food but I do have concerns that these classic puds are being upgraded and refined too far. Every supermarket, food manufacturer or whatever is trying to produce these puddings without, by the looks of it, ever having eaten one or seen an authentic recipe. I have cooked a lot of these puddings for the best part of 30 years. It takes time, care, and above all understanding, to produce them correctly.

A lot of the most famous puddings should be served in or from the baking dish or bowl in which they are cooked. This is a fundamental part of the finished dish. A gooseberry crumble for 6–8 people with all its overcooked toffee edges, should be served at the table and spooned out. This ensures everyone gets the right amount of crumble and filling. Then the custard or cream should be handed round. This is not only the best way to serve a pudding, but also ensures that the whole family eats and chats together.

MY MUM'S SPOTTED DICK

My mother always made her spotted dick this way, and my grandmother used to boil hers in a tea towel, I believe. This recipe is a classic example of a pudding that is best served by turning it out of its bowl at the table and then pouring over hot custard. My father disagrees with the latter tradition, preferring to spoon over golden syrup instead, I have to say that both are perfect accompaniments.

225 g (8 oz) self-raising flour
115 g (4 oz) suet
55 g (2 oz) castor sugar
85 g (3 oz) sultanas
hot custard or golden syrup,
　　to serve

serves 4-6

Half fill a steamer with cold water and bring it to the boil. Grease a 9 cm deep x 17 cm wide (3½ x 6½ inch) pudding basin well.

Place the flour, suet, sugar and sultanas in a bowl and add cold water until you have a dropping consistency, similar to a sponge mix. Do not overwork or the finished pudding will be heavy and chewy to eat. Spoon into the pudding basin then cover well with buttered foil. Place in the steamer and steam for 2 hours, remembering to top up the steamer with boiling water from the kettle periodically.

When cooked, remove from the steamer and turn out on to a hot plate. Cover with hot custard or golden syrup and serve – simple as that and it's very good!

TWICE-BAKED TOFFEE PUDDING

Apart from a steamed chocolate pudding I once encountered that had a calorie-count of 1000 calories per serving, this must be the most fattening pudding ever. That said, it is heaven to eat. I knew a gardener named Percy – he worked at the same hotel – who managed to eat three helpings of this before going to sleep it off in the orchard all afternoon; it takes no prisoners, I promise you!

The only things to eat with this are either vanilla ice cream or thick double cream; the combination of hot and cold is a real joy.

90 g (3¼ oz) unsalted butter

140 g (5 oz) unrefined
    castor sugar

2 large eggs, beaten

225 g (8 oz) self-raising
    white flour

150 g (5½ oz) plump raisins

30 ml (2 tablespoons)
    black treacle

FOR THE SAUCE

115 g (4 oz) unsalted butter

140 g (5 oz) unrefined
    castor sugar

15 ml (1 tablespoon)
    black treacle

275 ml (9½ fl oz) double cream

vanilla ice cream or thick double
    cream, to serve

serves 6-8

Preheat the oven to 180°C/350°F/Gas Mark 4. Butter well an 18 cm (7-inch) square baking tin.

Beat the butter and sugar together with an electric whisk, until white and fluffy. Beat in the eggs, one at a time, and don't worry if the mixture separates. Add the flour and raisins and bring together using the mixer on a low speed. Pour in 275 ml (9½ fl oz) of boiling water and then add the treacle and mix until you have a smooth batter. Immediately pour into the baking tin and bake for about 40 minutes, or until well risen and golden. Remove from the baking tray and cool slightly.

Meanwhile, make the sauce by heating the butter, sugar, treacle and cream together in a pan. Bring to the boil and cook, whisking well, until you have a thick butterscotch sauce.

Run a knife down each side of the cooked sponge and carefully turn out on to a wire rack. Place the sponge, bottom-up, in a baking dish roughly 5 cm (2 inches) larger than the sponge itself. Carefully divide the sponge into six or eight pieces but don't cut all the way down to separate the pieces completely. Spoon over the butterscotch sauce, making sure it gets into the cuts in the sponge.

Turn down the oven to 160°C/325°F/Gas Mark 3 and bake the sponge again for 15–20 minutes, occasionally spooning the sauce over it. You will end up with a thickly-glazed sponge, with plenty of sauce around it.

Remove from the oven and leave to cool slightly before eating as it will be very hot! Alternatively, cool completely and refrigerate for up to a week. Reheat at 160–180°C/325–350°F/Gas Mark 3–4 for about 30 minutes, loosely covered with a piece of foil. You can also warm the whole dish in a microwave, on medium setting for a couple of minutes (but check the manufacturer's instructions); cover with cling film that has been punctured several times.

RUM BABAS

I originally cooked these rum babas when I was at college. My chef at the time was a man called Brian Gilham. A very strict, no-nonsense type of fellow, he would come along and lift the heavily-soaked babas, and would throw them in the bin if they were not soaked correctly – so bear that in mind. Always really soak well, or the inside will be very dry. I like slightly sweetened whipped cream with babas, but vanilla ice cream is always a real treat.

FOR THE DOUGH

2 x 7 g sachets of dried
    quick-acting yeast
125 g (4½ oz) '00' flour (very fine
    pasta flour)
125 g (4½ oz) plain flour
a pinch of salt
15 ml (3 teaspoons) castor sugar
4 eggs, at room temperature
    (this is very important)
50 ml (2 fl oz) warm milk
75 g (2½ fl oz) butter, melted

FOR THE SYRUP

240 g (8½ oz) sugar
150 ml (5 fl oz) dark rum

FOR THE GLAZE

125 ml (8 tablespoons)
    good-quality apricot jam
30 ml (2 tablespoons) water

TO SERVE

10 ml (2 teaspoons) vanilla
    extract
30 ml (2 tablespoons) icing sugar
254 ml pot of double cream

makes 10–12 babas

Place the yeast, flours, salt, sugar, eggs and milk in a food mixer and really beat well in the machine until very soft and gloopy (5–10 minutes). Finally beat in the warm butter until very gloopy and soft, which will take about 5 minutes. Cover and leave to prove in a warm place for 30 minutes until doubled in size. At this point, preheat the oven to 190°C/375°F/Gas Mark 5.

Beat the proved mixture really well with the paddle attachment on the mixer, then pipe or spoon into 8–10 well-buttered dariole moulds or deep muffin tins. Cover with lightly oiled cling film (to prevent the cling film from sticking) until risen by double the volume in a warm place. Remove the cling film and bake in the preheated oven for 15 minutes or so.

When lightly browned, remove from the tins and place on a baking rack on a tray. Continue to bake for 10 minutes until dry and well-browned and coloured. It must be nice and dry and well coloured. Cool, then prick with a needle.

To make the syrup, put the sugar, 400 ml (14 fl oz) water and rum in a saucepan, bring to the boil and then simmer for 30 seconds. Place the babas into the warm syrup one at a time and soak thoroughly. Flip over and lift out when very heavy and well soaked. Drain on a wire rack in a warm place.

Heat the jam and water together over a low heat, stirring well, then sieve the jam and keep warm. Brush the well-soaked babas with the apricot jam to glaze nicely. Place the vanilla and icing sugar in a bowl with the cream and whip together very lightly. Serve the babas with the cream.

BRAMLEY APPLE PUDDINGS

I think apples are one of the most versatile fruits, especially when it comes to hot puddings. The only other fruit that comes close is rhubarb. Here is a small steamed pudding that will keep in the fridge for a week and warms up quickly in the microwave when needed. Just take care not to fill the moulds up too much – or the filling will burst out – and remember to roll the pastry nice and thinly because it will expand when it steams.

about 550 g (1 lb 4 oz) Bramley
    apples, peeled, cored and cut
    into chunks
finely grated zest and juice
    of 1 lemon
60 g (2¼ oz) castor sugar
225 g (8 oz) Sweet Suet Pastry
    (page 39)
beaten egg, for glazing
cream or custard, to serve

serves 4

Butter four 150 ml (¼-pint) pudding moulds and four 15 cm (6-inch) double squares of foil. Place a 24 cm (9½-inch) steamer on top of a pan on the hob, fill with boiling water and keep at a simmer.

Place the apple chunks in a pan, with the lemon zest and juice and toss. Add 15 ml (1 tablespoon) of water and the sugar, and cook gently for about 10 minutes or until thick but not completely broken down. You may need to add a touch more water as the apple cooks, if the mixture looks too dry.

Meanwhile, cut the pastry into four equal pieces. Roll out one piece to about 2.5 mm (¼-inch) thick, trying to keep it as round as possible. Use the pastry to line one of the moulds. It's a bit fiddly, but press the pastry into the side of the mould, smoothing out any creases and leaving the top overhanging.

Fill the lined mould to about three-quarters full with the warm apple mixture. Trim off the top edge of pastry, leaving about 1 cm (½ inch) overhanging. Roll out the cut-off pastry to shape into a small lid and pop on top of the apples. Brush the pastry lid with beaten egg and then fold over the side pastry and press to seal. Fold the double piece of buttered foil in the centre to make a pleat. Place on top of the pudding basin and tightly wrap the pudding. Repeat to make another three puddings, then place in the steamer and cook for 35–45 minutes, or until firm and well risen. The pastry will be nice and tight in the foil top.

When cooked, remove the foil top and turn out carefully. Serve with cream or custard.

WARM LEMON AND LIME PUDDING CAKE
WITH CRANBERRY SYRUP

This is an easy pudding to make and it's very light and refreshing.

3 large eggs
225 ml (8 fl oz) skimmed milk
zest of 1 large lemon
zest of 4 limes
30 ml (2 tablespoons) fresh
    lemon juice
30 ml (2 tablespoons) fresh
    lime juice
20 g (¾ oz) plain flour, sieved
175 g (6 oz) castor sugar
a pinch of salt
a pinch of cream of tartar

FOR THE SYRUP
75 g (2½ oz) castor sugar
80 g (3 oz) cranberries
150 ml (¼ pint) white wine
1 teaspoon (5 ml) arrowroot

double cream (optional), to serve

serves 4–6

Preheat the oven to 190°C/ Gas Mark 5/ 375°F. Whisk together the egg yolks, milk, zests and juices. Add the flour, 115 g (4 oz) of sugar, salt and mix well. Place the egg whites and cream of tartar in a bowl and whisk until foamy and thick. Add the remaining 60 g (2¼ oz) of sugar and whisk on medium speed until glossy and thick. 'Whisk fold' the egg whites into the egg yolk mixture and pour into a 23 cm x 23 cm x 4 cm (9 x 9 x 1½ inch) deep, oiled baking dish. Place the dish in a baking tray and half-fill with boiling water. Carefully place in the oven and bake for 40 minutes, or until well browned and risen.

To make the syrup, put the sugar into a saucepan and add the white wine and cranberries. Bring to the boil and simmer for 1 minute. Mix 30 ml (6 teaspoons) of cold water and arrowroot together. Add the arrowroot mixture to thicken the syrup and boil again. Keep warm. Serve the pudding scooped out into a bowl and spoon over a little syrup. Double cream is nice too.

GOOSEBERRY CRUMBLE

My two favourite crumbles are rhubarb and gooseberry: these puddings cannot be bettered.

875 g (1¾ lb) English
    gooseberries, topped and
    tailed
100–175 g (3½–6 oz) unrefined
    granulated sugar
100 g (3½ oz) cold unsalted
    butter, cubed
a pinch of salt
200 g (7 oz) plain white flour
100 g (3½ oz) castor sugar
clotted cream, to serve

serves 4

Preheat the oven to 190°C/375°F/Gas Mark 5. Place the gooseberries in a stainless-steel saucepan, add the granulated sugar and heat until the fruit starts to burst. Remove from the heat and then tip into a 23 cm (9-inch) ovenproof baking dish; the gooseberries should almost be in a single layer on the bottom of the dish.

Place the cold butter, salt and flour together in a food processor. Pulse until the mixture resembles fine breadcrumbs, then add the sugar and pulse again just to bring together – do not overwork (this ensures that the mixture does not 'cake up', leaving the crumble nice and loose).

Spread the crumble evenly over the cooked gooseberries and bake in the preheated oven for 20–25 minutes, or until golden. Remove from the oven and allow to cool slightly (the secret with crumble is to eat it warm, not hot) and serve with clotted cream.

STEAMED RHUBARB PUDDING WITH BLACKCURRANTS

The success of this pudding relies on one thing and that is to use maincrop rhubarb, which is available from late March until June. The structure and flavour of this deep reddish-green, thick rhubarb suits puddings, jams, chutneys and pickling perfectly. Forced rhubarb available from January is far too delicate and best for poaching, sorbets, sauces and syrups. The addition of a few blackcurrants gives the whole pudding a nice colour and flavour.

Just be sure to keep the pastry nice and thin – remember it will expand considerably when cooked and, if you are not careful, the pudding will become dry and stodgy. Sometimes this pudding will collapse slightly and all the pink juices will flow out but this is quite normal.

400 g (14 oz) maincrop rhubarb,
    cut into 2 cm (¾-inch) pieces
115 g (4 oz) castor sugar
20 g (¾ oz) cornflour
    or arrowroot
100 g (3½ oz) fresh or
    frozen blackcurrants
grated zest of 1 large lemon
¾ quantity Sweet Suet Pastry
    (page 39)
25 g (1 oz) cold unsalted butter,
    cubed
warm custard, to serve

serves 6–8

Your first job is to get the steamer on and rapidly boiling. Next, lightly grease a 9 cm deep x 17 cm diameter (3½- x 5½-inch) pudding basin.

Place the rhubarb, sugar, cornflour, blackcurrants and lemon zest in a bowl and mix well. Roll the pastry out with a rolling pin to the thickness of normal short pastry, roughly double the size of the pudding basin. Remember the pastry will swell slightly when cooked. Carefully lift the pastry and slide it into the bowl. Try to smooth out any folds in the pastry and press into the edge of the bowl lightly. Leave plenty of pastry hanging over the edge.

Spoon the rhubarb mixture into the prepared bowl and then dot with the cold butter. Fold the pastry over the top and cut away a little so you do not have such a thick layer of pastry as the lid. Cover with a double layer of buttered foil and seal well. Place in the steamer and cook for 2 hours, taking care to refill the steamer with boiling water every so often.

When cooked, turn out on to a warm plate and cover with warm custard and serve.

CHRISTMAS PUDDING

As I used to live in Somerset, I know I could be accused of being biased, but I love using cider in my recipes. Here it gives extra moisture and a wonderful flavour to the dried fruits and grated apple in a Christmas pudding. And there's another secret ingredient too – chocolate!

This can be made two months ahead, stored well wrapped in foil and spiked with brandy every month. Reheat over a pan of gently simmering water or in a microwave on medium power. Serve with clotted cream, brandy butter or lashings of custard!

115 g (4 oz) raisins

115 g (4 oz) currants

115 g (4 oz) sultanas

55 g (2 oz) chopped mixed candied peel

115 g (4 oz) carrot, coarsely grated

115 g (4 oz) cooking apple, peeled and coarsely grated

finely grated zest of 1 orange

100 ml (3½ fl oz) cider

2 eggs, beaten

15 ml (1 tablespoon) black treacle

115 g (4 oz) muscovado sugar

115 g (4 oz) plain white flour, sifted

2.5 ml (½ teaspoon) ground mixed spice

2.5 ml (½ teaspoon) grated nutmeg

2.5 ml (½ teaspoon) ground cinnamon

115 g (4 oz) ground almonds

115 g (4 oz) vegetable suet

85 g (3 oz) bitter plain chocolate, roughly chopped

clotted cream, brandy butter or custard, to serve

serves 8
makes a 900 g (2 lb) pudding

Grease a 1.2-litre (2-pint) pudding basin. Cut out a small circle of greaseproof paper and use it to line the base.

Place the dried fruits, chopped peel, grated carrot and apple and orange zest in a large bowl. Pour over the cider and allow to stand for about 10 minutes. Add the beaten eggs, treacle and sugar to the fruits and stir well to combine. Add the flour, spices, ground almonds, suet and chocolate and mix well together. Pour the mixture into the pudding basin and cover with a circle of greaseproof paper.

Place a large piece of foil on top of a large piece of greaseproof paper and then fold in the centre to make a pleat. Place the pleated papers on top of the pudding basin and use a long piece of string to tie the papers tightly just below the rim of the basin. With an extra piece of string, tie a long loop across the top – you can use this as a handle to help lower and lift the pudding in and out of the pan.

Place a heatproof saucer in the bottom of a large saucepan and sit the pudding on top. Fill the pan with enough boiling water to come halfway up the sides of the basin and then cover with a tightly-fitting lid and bring the water to the boil. Reduce the heat and simmer gently for about 7–8 hours. Check the water level every couple of hours and add extra boiling water as necessary to maintain it.

PASTRIES, PIES AND TARTS

Puddings made of pastry and filled with eggs, milk, cream and honey are centuries old. Medieval cooks made a crude pastry with animal grease that they called *croste*. They called a flan tin lined with pastry, a *coffin of paast*. These were filled with all sorts of fruit and nut combinations, but by far the most popular were fillings of eggs, cream and milk.

Pastry is still the basis of many savoury and sweet flans, pies and other puddings. In fact, hardly a day goes by without hearing of a new type of pastry.

Most of the new pastries are variations on the basic theme of flour, fat and liquid, maybe with some sort of flavouring such as nutmeg, citrus zest or cocoa.

I couldn't write this chapter without mentioning bought pastry. Over the years much scorn has been poured on 'ready-made food' – a lot of it quite rightly. But there are exceptions. Frozen peas are a classic and good-quality pastry is another. Ask yourself, 'Can I make it any better?' If you can't, buy it. What's wrong with that? Most chefs can't make pastry to save their lives. The selection of ready-made pastry available today is vast and very good indeed. The only rule I make is to use all-butter puff pastry. This has a far superior flavour than the variety with shortening.

On page 49 there are some tips for making light pastry, filling a pastry case with a liquid filling and glazing a custard-filled flan.

SWEET SHORTCRUST PASTRY AND BLIND-BAKING A FLAN

This is a basic pastry to be used for any dessert work. The method of lining the flan ring is roughly the same for all sizes and shapes.

115 g (4 oz) cold unsalted butter, cubed
225 g (8 oz) plain white flour
a pinch of salt
10 ml (2 teaspoons) castor sugar
1 egg, lightly beaten, plus extra to glaze
half an eggshell full of cold water

makes enough to line a 23 cm (9-inch) diameter, 3 cm (1¼-inch) deep, fluted flan ring

Place the cold butter, flour, salt and sugar together in a food processor. Blitz until you have a fine breadcrumb texture but do not overwork. Add the egg and water and mix well, using the pulse button; again, do not overwork or the pastry will shrink when cooked. Turn out of the processor and knead very gently, just to bring together. Flatten slightly (this makes it easier to roll when chilled) and wrap in cling film, then chill for about 20 minutes.

Lightly flour the surface on which you are going to roll the pastry. Roll the pastry out so you end up with a circle about 4 cm (1½ inches) larger all round than the flan ring. Carefully roll the pastry on to the rolling pin and then unroll over the flan ring, taking care not stretch the pastry too much.

Immediately ease the pastry into the ring and gently push into the bottom and corners; try to make sure that you do not leave any creases in the outside. Use your thumb to push the pastry into the fluted tin, leaving about 1 cm (½ inch) overhanging the top edge then trim off with a sharp knife or roll a rolling pin over the top to remove the excess. Thumb up the top edge again and pinch with your thumb and forefinger to make the edge more decorative; this will also help to stop the pastry from shrinking back into the tin (remember, the higher the rim the more filling you can have in the finished tart, flan or pie). Using a piece of well-floured leftover pastry, push the bottom of the flan into the corners so it's nice and flush. Prick well with a fork and chill for 30 minutes.

To blind-bake the flan, preheat the oven to 200°C/400°F/Gas Mark 6. Cut out a piece of greaseproof paper roughly 4 cm (1½ inches) larger than the flan, scrunch it up, then flatten it out again and carefully place inside the lined flan tin. Fill with baking beans and bake for about 15 minutes, or until the top edge is slightly brown. Remove the paper and beans, turn the oven down to 160°C/325°F/Gas Mark 3 and cook for a further 10 minutes until the pastry is set but has taken no colour. Remove from the oven, brush with beaten egg (this prevents the pastry from getting soggy when you add the filling) and then pop back into the oven for 2 minutes to seal. Cool for a little while before adding the filling.

COCOA PASTRY

This makes a nice change from the ordinary shortcrust pastry used in flans and pies, such as Bitter Chocolate Tart (page 80).

100 g (3½ oz) unrefined
    castor sugar
a pinch of salt
175 g (6 oz) unsalted butter,
    softened
1 egg, lightly beaten
300 g (10½ oz) plain white flour,
    sifted
15 g (½ oz) cocoa powder, sifted

**makes enough to line a 23 cm
(9-inch) diameter, 3 cm
(1¼-inch) fluted deep flan tin**

Cream together the sugar, salt and butter until pale and then gradually beat in the egg. Finally, mix in the flour and cocoa powder, briefly knead the dough into a ball and then flatten it slightly.

Wrap in cling film and chill for 1 hour before using. Unwrap, roll out and use as for Sweet Shortcrust Pastry (opposite).

SWEET SUET PASTRY

This is a lovely, comforting pastry, used for Spotted Dick which is still one of my dad's favourite puddings. Just take care not to overwork the pastry or it will be tough.

225 g (8 oz) self-raising
    white flour
a pinch of salt
115 g (4 oz) suet
55 g (2 oz) castor sugar
1 egg
about 60 ml (4 tablespoons)
    cold water

**makes enough to make
four 150 ml (¼-pint) puddings
or two 15 cm (6-inch) rolls,
for storing**

Place the flour, salt, suet, sugar and egg in a bowl and mix well. Add a little of the water at a time until you have a soft, but not sticky, dough.

Roll out on a lightly floured surface and use straight away as the raising agents start working immediately.

PUFF PASTRY

It took me the best part of two years to make puff pastry successfully but now this, and making croissants, are my two all-time-favourite jobs in the kitchen. There is something really satisfying about producing great pastry – just follow the recipe closely as there really is no margin for error.

415 g (14½ oz) cold,
    unsalted butter
450 g (1 lb) strong white flour,
    plus extra to dust
2 pinches of salt
about 175 ml (6 fl oz) very
    cold water
30 ml (2 tablespoons)
    lemon juice

makes about I kg (2¼ lb)

Cut 115 g (4 oz) of the butter into small cubes and allow the rest of the butter to soften slightly at a cool room temperature (watch out if the kitchen is hot in summer months). Place the flour, salt and cubed butter in a food mixer or processor and make fine breadcrumbs. Add the water and lemon juice and mix to a dough – the dough should be firm but not too firm.

Remove the dough from the machine and knead into a flattened ball. Roll out with a rolling pin to 35 x 45 cm (14 x 18 inches) – this may be a little difficult but persevere. Place on a floured tray, cover with cling film and chill for at least 30 minutes.

Meanwhile, cut out a piece of greaseproof paper roughly 30 x 20 cm (12 x 8 inches). Cut the remaining butter lengthways into six slices and evenly lay out on the greaseproof paper. Use a palette knife to merge the butter together and cover the paper. This process will make the first – and the most critical – rolling-out easier. Leave the butter in a cool place.

Remove the dough from the fridge and check it is soft enough to roll – by this I mean that while the dough was very taut when mixed in the machine, it should have relaxed sufficiently in the fridge that there is little resistance when pulled apart with your fingers. If the dough is too stiff still, just leave it to relax for a little longer. If the dough is too stiff then you will not be able to roll it out easily; on the other hand, if the dough is too slack (due to too much water) the butter will push through when the rolling process starts, losing all the raising layers of butter and pastry.

When it comes to adding butter to the dough for the first time, make sure that they are both the same temperature. Lightly flour a board or worktop and lay the dough on top. Place the spread butter on one half of the dough, by inverting the greaseproof paper on to the dough and peeling it off, then fold the opposite side over the butter to enclose it and seal well. This is very important: I fold the two layers on to themselves making a tight seal – if this seal is broken then the butter will squeeze out and ruin the pastry.

Now carefully roll out the pastry in one direction until it is roughly three times as long as the original piece, making sure all the corners are square and you have a true oblong shape. Dust off excess flour and fold the pastry into three.

Twist the pastry through 90° and mark an arrow in the pastry in the original rolling direction, so you know which direction to roll next time – you must make sure you do this after each turn as this will ensure that the pastry rises evenly when finally cooked. Chill well for 30 minutes to relax.

Repeat the rolling and folding process a further five times, ensuring you dust off excess flour each time; take care to ensure the corners are square and that the pastry is turned and arrowed in the same direction. Between each rolling, cover with cling film and chill for at least 30 minutes.

Roll out the finished pastry and use as required. This will freeze perfectly in its raw state, just wrap well and defrost overnight.

CHOUX PASTRY

I always found this pastry difficult to make but then, one day, I think I found out the reason. When you boil the water, if the butter is in large cubes you tend to get quite a bit of evaporation before the fat is completely melted. This changes the proportion of water to butter; you end up with the wrong balance so the cooked pastry will not fully rise when cooked. So make sure the butter is cut into very small pieces and you should be fine!

115 g (4 oz) unsalted
    butter, cubed
a pinch of sugar
a pinch of salt
140 g (5 oz) plain white
    flour, sifted
3–4 large eggs, beaten

**makes enough for
about 70 baby éclairs**

Bring the butter and 300 ml (½ pint) of cold water to the boil in a pan. Add the sugar and salt, and then straight away add the flour and beat well until the mixture comes away from the pan. Allow to cool completely (more egg is absorbed when the mixture is cold).

Gradually add three of the beaten eggs to the cooled pastry, a little at a time (if you can, it's best to do this in a food mixer, or food processor) and then beat small amounts of the last egg into the mixture until you get the right consistency. The reason for only adding three of the eggs at the start is that the mixture needs to be quite tight; if you add too much egg the end product will not rise correctly and, of course, you can always add the extra egg but you can't take it out. If the paste is to be used for fritters or beignets then it has to be fairly tight. The finished paste should just fall off the paddle on the machine. It's best to use choux dough straight away but it will keep for a couple of days in the fridge.

SHORTBREAD PASTRY PÂTE SABLÉ

This pastry is suitable for flans, fruit pies, Bakewell tarts, biscuits and even very rich mince pies. It's a very rich and crumbly pastry that can be quite temperamental to handle but is really good for some desserts, such as sponge-filled tarts. Stick to shortcrust when you have a large amount of liquid filling, such as an egg-custard tart.

200 g (7 oz) unsalted butter

a pinch of salt

100 g (3½ oz) golden,
    unrefined castor sugar

1 large egg yolk

250 g (9 oz) plain white flour

makes enough for two 23 cm (9-inch) diameter x 4 cm (1½-inch) deep flan rings

With a wooden spoon, beat the butter, salt and castor sugar together in a bowl until just soft. Add the egg yolk and flour. Mix to make a stiff dough. Remove from the bowl. Wrap in cling film. Chill for 20 minutes.

Roll out as for Shortcrust Pastry (page 38). Do take care to roll out quickly as the butter rapidly warms up, making it difficult to work with. Always cook in a fairly hot oven so the butter sets sharpish or the pastry will collapse.

MELON AND MINT TART

A very refreshing tart that has to be eaten fairly quickly. The best thing is to chill it very well and serve with cream. This is a good pudding to serve after a heavy meal, or it's just fine with a cup of tea.

1 ripe Galia or 2 Charentais
    melons, about 1.1 kg (2 lb 7 oz)
    total weight
100–200 ml (3½ –7 fl oz)
    Sauvignon Blanc white wine
20 ml (4 teaspoons) castor sugar
2 pinches of citric acid powder
8 fresh mint leaves, finely
    chopped (optional)
2½ gelatine leaves, soaked
    in cold water
23 cm (9-inch) diameter x 4 cm
    (1½ -inch) deep Sweet
    Shortcrust Pastry case, baked
    blind (page 38)
cream, to serve

serves 4–6

Cut the melon or melons in half and scoop out the seeds with a spoon. Next, using a 2 cm (¾-inch) melon baller, scoop out as many melon balls as possible and keep to one side.

Scoop out all the flesh that is left on the skin and place in a liquidiser, along with 100 ml (3½ fl oz) of the white wine, the castor sugar, citric acid and mint leaves, if using. Blitz until smooth and then pass through a fine sieve and pour into a measuring jug. You will need 400 ml (14 fl oz) in total – if you have slightly less just top up with a little more white wine.

Remove the gelatine from the water and shake off any excess, then place in a small pan and gently heat until melted.

Quickly stir the melted gelatine into the melon purée, add the melon balls and stir well. Pour into the cooked flan case, arrange the melon balls so the rounded sides are uppermost and then chill for about 2 hours, or until set.

Cut into wedges and serve with cream.

GOOSEBERRY TART

Fresh gooseberry purée is an absolute joy; gooseberry is the first of the glorious summer berries and gets you in the mood for what's to come. The fact that gooseberries are only around for a few weeks makes them all the more special. I used to bottle my own, a job that takes a little time but is well worth the effort. Canned gooseberries in syrup are actually quite a good substitute for a tart like this, but do make sure you buy a good-quality brand – I find Hartley's is the best.

2 x 300 g cans of gooseberries or
    400 g (14 oz) freshly poached
    gooseberries, well drained
4 large eggs plus 2 large egg yolks
140 g (5 oz) castor sugar
225 ml (8 fl oz) whipping cream
juice of 1 small lime
25 cm (10-inch) diameter x 4 cm
    (1½-inch) deep Sweet
    Shortcrust Pastry
    case, baked blind (page 38)
vanilla ice cream, to serve

serves 6–8

Preheat the oven to 160°C/325°F/Gas Mark 3. Blitz the gooseberries in a liquidiser until you have a thick purée. Press through a fine sieve.

Whisk the eggs and egg yolks in a bowl with the sugar and cream until smooth. Add the gooseberry purée and whisk carefully – the mixture will thicken but don't worry, if you continue to whisk the mixture will let itself down again. Finally add the lime juice and then pour into the cooked pastry case (see 'Filling a pastry case with a liquid filling' on page 49). Bake for about 40–45 minutes, or until just set.

Leave to cool to room temperature. Slice and serve with ice cream.

EGG CUSTARD TART WITH BLACKCURRANT SAUCE

This is probably the most frequently cooked and eaten dessert I have ever made; it was always a real winner with diners.

500 ml (18 fl oz) whipping cream

1 vanilla pod, split

6 egg yolks

85 g (3 oz) castor sugar

5 ml (1 teaspoon) arrowroot

5 ml (1 teaspoon) rose-water

19 cm (7½ -inch) diameter x
    5 cm (2-inch) deep Sweet
    Shortcrust Pastry case, baked
    blind (page 38)

10 ml (2 teaspoons) grated
    nutmeg

icing sugar, sifted, to decorate

FOR THE BLACKCURRANT SAUCE

300 g (10½ oz) frozen
    blackcurrants

100 g (3½ oz) castor sugar

a squeeze of lemon juice

serves 6-8

Preheat the oven to 160°C/325°F/Gas Mark 3. Pour the cream into a small pan, add the vanilla pod and bring to the boil.

Meanwhile, whisk the egg yolks and sugar together for 1 minute, and then whisk in the arrowroot. Pour on the boiling cream and stir well, add the rose-water and strain the whole mixture through a fine sieve.

Pour the cream and egg mixture into the pastry case (see 'Filling a pastry case with a liquid filling' on page 49) and carefully place in the oven. Cook for about 30 minutes, or until just set and still slightly wobbly (the custard can suddenly overcook so keep an eye on it). When cooked remove from the oven, sprinkle over the nutmeg and leave to cool. Chill well, preferably overnight.

To make the blackcurrant sauce, liquidise the blackcurrants with the sugar, lemon juice and about 75 ml (5 tablespoons) of cold water to make a smooth sauce, adding a touch more water if needed. Pass through a fine sieve to remove any seeds.

To serve, cut the tart into 6–8 nice wedges, dust with icing sugar and pour over a little blackcurrant sauce.

GLAZED PASSION-FRUIT AND ORANGE TART

This is one of my favourite puddings, fairly simple to prepare and delicious to eat. It's an afternoon-tea favourite but also fits well into any dinner or lunch party. I quite like to serve this tart with some freshly picked English strawberries or raspberries at room temperature.

The glazing is best done with a small, powerful blowtorch. It's very difficult to glaze this kind of pastry tart with a creamy, just-set filling under the grill without curdling the custard; so if you do not own a blowtorch, just dust with unrefined icing sugar.

12 ripe passion-fruit, halved
8 eggs
250 g (9 oz) castor sugar
a pinch of cornflour
600 ml (1 pint) double cream
finely grated zest of
    1 large orange
25 cm (10-inch) diameter x 4 cm
    (1½-inch) deep Sweet
    Shortcrust Pastry case, baked
    blind (page 38)
sifted golden icing sugar, to glaze
double cream, very lightly
    whipped, to serve

serves 6-8

Preheat the oven to 180°C/350°F/Gas Mark 4. Scoop out all the flesh and pulp from the passion-fruit. The next step is to remove the juice from the pips – I use a hand blender set on the lowest speed so all the flesh comes away very easily. The trouble with a liquidiser is that the high speed breaks up the seeds so you end up with a custard with black specks; you can avoid this to some extent by using the pulse setting. Failing all of these, push the passion-fruit pulp through a fine sieve. Place the passion-fruit juice and flesh in a measuring jug – you should end up with just over 200 ml (7 fl oz) of juice (top it up with orange juice if it's a bit short).

Put the eggs, sugar and cornflour in a large bowl and whisk well but do not overwork. Pour in the double cream, passion-fruit juice and orange zest and mix well (the mixture will slightly curdle but don't panic, just keep on gently whisking and it will thin out again).

Pour the filling into the pastry case (see 'Filling a pastry case with a liquid filling' on the page opposite) and cook for about 45 minutes or until the custard is just set but still wobbly – it's very difficult to put an exact time on this so keep an eye on the tart as it will overcook very quickly indeed and 'soufflé' up at the edges. Carefully remove from the oven and cool on a wire rack.

To serve, dust with a small amount of sifted golden icing sugar and glaze with a blowtorch, then repeat this process to ensure a nice, even glaze (see 'Glazing a custard-filled flan', opposite). Cut into wedges and serve with a large blob of very lightly whipped double cream.

This tart will keep for one day in a fridge but is best eaten fresh at room temperature within a couple of hours of cooking.

TECHNIQUES

PASTRY-MAKING, FILLING A PASTRY CASE AND GLAZING A FLAN

PASTRY-MAKING

1 Firstly, as long as the fat is cold and you work quickly, there is no problem. Chill the finished pastry before rolling.

2 Secondly, sifting flour makes absolutely no difference whatsoever to the lightness of the finished pastry.

3 Finally, for light pastry, you need the correct proportion of fat to flour, you need the steam which the liquid provides and, most importantly, you mustn't overwork the dough in the way you would for bread. And never roll out the finished pastry more than twice.

FILLING A PASTRY CASE WITH A LIQUID FILLING

1 When you are filling a flan with a liquid filling, to avoid slopping filling over the side by filling it too much or overcooking a filling and making it dry because the filling was too shallow, put the flan case, still in its tin and resting on a baking sheet, in the preheated oven and carefully pull out the oven shelf. Fill the pastry three-quarters full with the filling and gently slide the shelf back into the oven. Finally, use an egg cup to fill the flan up to the very top with the rest of the mixture.

2 Remember not to overcook these types of flans; the filling should still be slightly wobbly in the centre. It's very difficult to put a time on this as ovens vary, so keep an eye on the tart as it will overcook very quickly indeed and soufflé (puff up) at the edges.

GLAZING A CUSTARD-FILLED FLAN

Glazing a custard-filled flan under the grill is difficult, because the heat of the grill can overcook the filling causing it to become grainy. The best way is to use a culinary blow torch. When the flan is cool, sprinkle with a fine layer of icing sugar through a sieve and glaze with the blowtorch. For a nice, even glaze, repeat this process. (The same method can, of course, be applied to crème brûlées of all sorts.)

BLIND-BAKING A FLAN: see page 38

PLUM TART

A nice way to use plums not often seen these days. My old pastry chef used to cook a version of this using the small mirabelles from France and serve it as an afternoon-tea fancy.

375 g (13 oz) Puff Pastry (page 40) or a 375 g sheet of 'all-butter' ready-rolled puff pastry
1 large egg yolk
50 g (1¾ oz) white bread (about 2 slices), crusts removed and crumb made into fine breadcrumbs
600 g (1 lb 5 oz) ripe plums (about 10), halved and stoned
20 g (¾ oz) castor sugar
45 ml (3 tablespoons) apricot jam
Earl Grey tea, to serve

serves 4–6

Preheat the oven to 200°C/400°F/Gas Mark 6. Lay the pastry out on a non-stick baking sheet and trim so you end up with a sheet measuring 23 cm (9 inches) x 30 cm (12 inches).

Break up the egg yolk with a pastry brush and brush a 3 cm (1¼-inch) border of egg all around the edge of the sheet. Don't let the egg spill over the cut edge as it can impede the rising of the pastry.

Then, with a sharp knife and going only halfway through the thickness of the pastry, not all the way through, make an incision marking out a 2 cm (¾-inch) border all around the pastry – this will allow the sides to rise up around the plums. Prick all over the centre of the pastry with a fork.

Spread the breadcrumbs over the pastry but keep them off the border. Lay the halved plums on top of the breadcrumbs, again keeping inside the incision. Sprinkle the sugar over the plums.

Bake for 30 minutes, or until well risen and golden. Remove from the oven and leave to cool.

Mix the jam and 15 ml (1 tablespoon) of water together and then bring to the boil. Brush the whole tart with the warmed apricot jam and cut into slices. Enjoy with a large cup of Earl Grey tea.

SEMOLINA AND LAVENDER TART WITH APRICOTS AND PINE NUTS

It's not often you see semolina used in this way: most people remember it as the awful, sticky gunge dished out at school mealtimes. This is a novel and interesting way to use this forgotten-about sixties pudding staple. The inclusion of lavender is up to you. I pick ours each year, dry it, and then store it in an airtight container. It keeps very well.

115 g (4 oz) unrefined castor sugar

115 g (4 oz) unsalted butter

2 large eggs, beaten

25 g (1 oz) potato flour

115 g (4 oz) semolina

finely grated zest of 1 large lemon

30 ml (2 tablespoons) dried lavender (optional)

24 cm (9½ -inch) diameter x 4 cm (1½-inch) deep Sweet Shortcrust Pastry case, baked blind (page 38)

100 g (3½ oz) pine nuts

2 x 410 g cans of apricot halves, drained

icing sugar, to decorate

TO SERVE

200 g (7 oz) greek-style yogurt

Earl Grey tea

serves 6–8

Preheat the oven to 180°C/350°F/Gas Mark 4. Cream the sugar and butter together until light and fluffy and then add the eggs, a little at a time, until fully incorporated. Fold in the potato flour, semolina, lemon zest and lavender, if using, but do not overwork. Spoon into the blind-baked pastry case and spread out evenly.

Sprinkle over the pine nuts and arrange half the apricots evenly over the top, keeping the rounded side uppermost. Bake in the oven for 30–40 minutes or until set and well risen.

Remove from the oven and allow to cool. Dust heavily with icing sugar and carefully glaze under a hot grill or with a blowtorch (see 'Glazing a custard-filled flan' on page 49). Roughly chop the remaining apricots, add to the yogurt and stir well. Serve a large wedge of the flan with the yogurt and a cup of Earl Grey tea.

PEACH AND ALMOND TART

This tart must be eaten at room temperature to get the best flavour; all you will need to go with it is a little very thick cream.

85 g (3 oz) flaked almonds

4 large, ripe peaches

23 cm (9-inch) diameter x 3 cm (1¼ -inch) deep Sweet Shortcrust Pastry case, baked blind (page 38)

2 large egg yolks

200 ml (7 fl oz) double cream

60 g (2¼ oz) unrefined castor sugar

30 ml (2 tablespoons) brandy, preferably peach-flavoured

unrefined icing sugar, to decorate

thick cream, to serve

serves 6-8

Preheat the oven to 180°C/350°F/Gas Mark 4 and bake the almonds for about 5–6 minutes until lightly browned. Bring a small pan of water to the boil. Once boiling, drop the peaches in, one at a time, leave for 10 seconds and then straight away lift out with a slotted spoon and plunge into a bowl of iced water. You will find the skins should come away now very easily; if not, just repeat the process.

Place the browned almonds in the bottom of the cooked tart case. Cut each peach into twelve slices and arrange on top of the almonds.

Whisk the egg yolks, cream, castor sugar and brandy together and pour over the sliced peaches. Sit the pastry case on a baking sheet and cook in the oven for about 30 minutes, or until the custard is just set. Remove from the oven and leave to cool.

Just before serving, dust with a little unrefined icing sugar and glaze under a hot grill or with a blowtorch (see 'Glazing a custard-filled flan' on page 49). Serve at room temperature, with thick cream.

MACADAMIA NUT TART

The macadamia nut is synonymous with Australia but in fact is now grown in the United States and other countries. I believe it is one of the world's most expensive nuts and is very high in natural fats, something like 70 per cent. Nevertheless, macadamias are absolutely gorgeous. The only way to eat them, I think, is in a warm tart with honey and brown sugar.

325 g (11½ oz) macadamia nuts
85 g (3 oz) golden castor sugar
50 ml (2 fl oz) double cream
50 ml (2 fl oz) acacia honey
 or golden syrup
a pinch of salt
finely grated zest of 1 lemon
10 ml (2 teaspoons) vanilla
 powder or extract
3 large egg yolks
85 g (3 oz) unsalted butter,
 melted and warm
24 cm (9½ -inch) diameter x
 4 cm (1½-inch) deep Sweet
 Shortcrust Pastry case, baked
 blind (page 38)
ice cream or crème fraîche,
 to serve

serves 6–8

Preheat the oven to 200°C/400°F/Gas Mark 6 and toast the macadamias for 6–8 minutes or until lightly browned. Turn the oven down to 160°C/325°F/ Gas Mark 3. Roughly chop the toasted macadamias, but not too small.

Stir together the castor sugar, cream, honey or syrup, salt, lemon zest, vanilla powder or extract and egg yolks. Stir in the warm melted butter and bring together.

Pour into the blind-baked pastry case and bake for 35 minutes, or until just set. Allow to cool before slicing and serve with a little ice cream or crème fraîche.

BAKED RASPBERRY TART

I don't, as a rule, like to cook summer berries – to me they are just perfect on their own, served at room temperature with cream. But here we have a nice summer lunchtime dessert that's a little different and very simple.

500 g (1 lb 2 oz) fresh ripe
    summer raspberries
70 g (2½ oz) unrefined castor
    sugar
juice and finely grated zest of
    1 large lemon
25 cm (10-inch) diameter x 4 cm
    (1½-inch) deep Sweet
    Shortcrust Pastry case, baked
    blind (page 38)
5 ml (1 teaspoon) ground
    cinnamon
crème fraîche, to serve

serves 6–8

Preheat the oven to 190°C/375°F/Gas Mark 5. Place the raspberries, sugar, lemon juice and zest in a pan. Heat just to bring to the boil, stirring occasionally but trying not to break up the fruit too much.

Immediately pour the cooked raspberries into the tart case, which they should fill right to the brim. Sprinkle over the ground cinnamon and bake for 35 minutes, or until thick and just set. Remove from the oven and allow to cool completely.

Serve at room temperature, cut into thick slices, with a nice blob of crème fraîche.

RHUBARB AND ALMOND CRUMBLE TART

This recipe uses maincrop rhubarb, the deep red, olive-green-tipped variety. This is grown outside and most gardens have a few crowns. Ready to eat from March right through to May and a lot more stringy than forced rhubarb, it is nevertheless perfect for this tart. You could use the indoor, forced variety for this but it has such a delicate flavour that it might get lost in the sponge.

175 g (6 oz) granulated sugar

300 g (10½ oz) maincrop
   rhubarb, washed well and cut
   into 2.5 cm (1-inch) pieces

FOR THE SPONGE

115 g (4 oz) very soft
   unsalted butter

115 g (4 oz) castor sugar

2 eggs, beaten

25 g (1 oz) plain white flour,
   sifted

115 g (4 oz) ground almonds

23 cm (9-inch) diameter x 4 cm
   (1½-inch) deep Sweet
   Shortcrust Pastry case, baked
   blind (page 38)

FOR THE CRUMBLE

115 g (4 oz) plain white flour

140 g (5 oz) cold unsalted butter,
   cubed

85 g (3 oz) granulated sugar

55 g (2 oz) Jordan's Original
   Muesli

55 g (2 oz) porridge oats

cream or custard, to serve

serves 4-6

Preheat the oven to 180°C/350°F/Gas Mark 4. Dissolve the sugar in 175 ml (6 fl oz) of cold water and then add the rhubarb and bring to the boil. Once boiling, turn the heat right down and simmer very gently for about 1 minute – do not overcook; the rhubarb needs to be kept whole. Cover and leave to cool completely.

To make the sponge, cream the butter and sugar together until thick and creamy. Slowly add the eggs, beating all the time. When fully incorporated gently fold in the flour and almonds.

Spoon the mixture into the prepared pastry case and then top with the strained, cooled, poached rhubarb. Bake for about 25 minutes.

Meanwhile make the crunchy, crumble topping. Pop the flour and butter into a food processor and blend into fine breadcrumbs. Then add the sugar and mix well. Add the muesli and porridge oats and pulse briefly just to mix together.

When the tart is starting to brown and just set, fill the tart with the crumble topping. Pop into the oven again and continue to cook for about a further 20 minutes. The topping will turn golden brown and nice and crunchy.

Remove from the oven and leave to cool for 15–20 minutes. I think it's best to leave until just warm. Serve with cream or custard.

FRESH STRAWBERRY, MINT AND PISTACHIO TART

There is something very attractive about this flan; the deep red of the strawberries and the glaze, contrasted with the deep green of the pistachios looks stunning. Just remember to use ripe, room-temperature English strawberries.

250 g (9 oz) cream cheese

30 ml (2 tablespoons)
  unrefined castor sugar

grated zest and juice of 1 small
  orange

15 ml (1 tablespoon) chopped
  fresh mint

23 cm (9-inch) diameter x 2.5 cm
  (1-inch) deep Sweet
  Shortcrust Pastry case, baked
  blind (page 38)

500 g (1 lb 2 oz) small English
  strawberries, hulled

90 ml (6 tablespoons)
  strawberry jam

60 ml (4 tablespoons) chopped,
  peeled pistachios

double cream, lightly whipped,
  to serve

Beat together the cream cheese, sugar and orange zest and then carefully mix in the orange juice and mint. Spread the cheese mixture over the bottom of the pastry case. Top with the strawberries, packing them tightly together.

Heat the strawberry jam with 45 ml (3 tablespoons) of cold water, stirring all the time. Sieve the jam mixture and then carefully spoon over the strawberries making sure it covers them all. Sprinkle with the chopped pistachios and leave to cool. Serve with lightly whipped double cream.

PECAN PIE

This is one of the better things to come out of America and it is a truly great dessert. I often wonder how anyone came to invent this pie: it has to have been a mistake because, when you look at how the thing is put together, you think it surely can't work! But work it does and it's a marvel when it is made properly.

The American versions I have tasted have always been tooth-achingly sweet; my version is less sweet.

175 g (6 oz) pecans (or walnuts, it's up to you)

25 g (1 oz) bitter chocolate, grated

2.5 ml (½ teaspoon) vanilla powder or extract

2 pinches of salt

175 g (6 oz) good-quality maple syrup

2 large eggs

150 g (5½ oz) golden granulated sugar

55 g (2 oz) butter, melted

24 cm (9½ -inch) diameter x 4 cm (1½-inch) deep, Sweet Shortcrust Pastry case, baked blind (page 38)

cream or a large pot of tea, to serve

serves 8

Preheat the oven to 160°C/325°F/Gas Mark 3. Place the nuts, chocolate, vanilla, salt and maple syrup in a bowl.

Beat the eggs together and stir into the nut mixture, with the sugar. Finally, add the melted butter and stir well.

Pour into the prepared pastry case and bake for 40–50 minutes or until set in the middle. Allow to cool completely before trying to cut. Just serve with cream or on its own with a cup of tea.

PRUNE AND BRANDY MERINGUE PIE

A great combination using canned prunes, this pie is very tasty and a complete change from the normal lemon meringue pie.

420 g can of prunes in syrup,
    drained and stoned
30 ml (2 tablespoons) brandy
    or Armagnac
2 large eggs plus 2 large egg yolks
300 ml (10 fl oz) whipping cream
50 g (1¾ oz) castor sugar
a squeeze of lemon juice
24 cm (9½ -inch) diameter
    x 4 cm (1½-inch) deep Sweet
    Shortcrust Pastry case, baked
    blind (page 38)

FOR THE MERINGUE

3 large egg whites
a pinch of cream of tartar
85 g (3 oz) castor sugar
85 g (3 oz) icing sugar
granulated sugar, to decorate

serves 6–8

Preheat the oven to 180°C/350°F/Gas Mark 4. Place the stoned prunes and brandy or Armagnac in a liquidiser and blitz to make a very thick purée. Spoon the purée into a bowl, add the eggs and yolks and mix well. Add the cream, sugar and lemon juice and whisk until smooth.

Pour into the blind-baked pastry base (see the last paragraph on page 38). Place on a baking sheet and cook in the oven for about 35 minutes or until just set – the pie should be slightly wobbly right in the centre when the pie is tapped; this is perfect as the residual heat will finish off the pie. Do not let the pie overcook or 'soufflé' or it will separate. When cooked, remove from the oven.

Turn up the oven to 220°C/425°F/Gas Mark 7. Make the meringue by whisking the egg whites and cream of tartar on a moderate speed until thick and creamy (see 'Whisking egg whites' on page 127). Add the castor sugar and continue to whisk until thick and glossy. Add the icing sugar and whisk well.

Pipe the meringue decoratively on to the top of the pie. Sprinkle over a little granulated sugar and bake in the hot oven for a few minutes until the meringue is firm to the touch and lightly browned.

COCONUT TART

This is a variation of my all-time-favourite pudding, egg custard tart. It is very difficult to get people to eat coconut – most are put off by being force-fed Auntie Betty's coconut buns, or rock-hard macaroons, when they were small children. I can't really blame them, desiccated coconut isn't the nicest thing to eat. But if it is used carefully and with a little thought, as with most 'difficult' ingredients, the results can be very good.

This creamy tart is very moreish and perfect on a summer's day with a little fresh fruit and a coconut or mango sorbet (page 188 or 186).

2 x 50 g sachets of creamed coconut

600 ml (1 pint) whipping cream

8 egg yolks

115 g (4 oz) castor sugar

45 ml (3 tablespoons) Malibu coconut liqueur

24 cm (9½ -inch) diameter x 4 cm (1½-inch) deep Sweet Shortcrust Pastry case, baked blind (page 38)

100 g (3½ oz) desiccated coconut, toasted in the oven until crunchy

serves 6–8

Preheat the oven to 160°C/325°F/Gas Mark 3. Pour 300 ml (½ pint) of boiling water on to the creamed coconut and stir to dissolve.

Pour the cream into a saucepan and bring to the boil. Meanwhile, whisk together (by hand so the egg does not froth up too much) the egg yolks and sugar. Pour on the boiling cream and mix well. Add the Malibu and coconut milk and mix well.

Place the flan case on a baking sheet and pour in the filling (see 'Filling a pastry case with a liquid filling' on page 49). Cook for about 30 minutes, checking occasionally that the filling is not puffing up and spoiling – if this starts to happen you may need to turn the oven down a touch.

When cooked the tart must still have what we call 'the wobble factor'. This means it just wobbles when the side of the tray is tapped. Remove from the oven and place on a wire rack.

Sprinkle over the toasted coconut very carefully and then cool completely. Chill well, if possible overnight. Cut into large wedges to serve.

TWICE-COOKED RHUBARB TART

The only way to cook rhubarb tart this way is to pre-cook the rhubarb, or you end up with too much juice and soggy pastry. This is a very simple pudding but very tasty and quick to prepare. It is best to use new-season rhubarb for this dish as maincrop rhubarb would be too stringy.

225 g (8 oz) Puff Pastry (page 40)
   or 225 g (8 oz) sheet of
   all-butter ready-rolled puff
   pastry (25 cm/10-inch disc)
450 g (1 lb) new-season rhubarb,
   trimmed and cut into 5 cm
   (2-inch) pieces
juice of 1 large lemon
200 g (7 oz) castor sugar
55 g (2 oz) unsalted butter
cream or ice cream, to serve

serves 4

Roll out the pastry very thinly to a 30 cm (12-inch) circle and chill for 30 minutes. Preheat the oven to 220°C/425°F/Gas Mark 7. Place the rhubarb, half the lemon juice and 85 g (3 oz) of the sugar in a pan and gently cook for about 4–5 minutes, or until the rhubarb is just soft but still whole. Carefully strain through a colander.

Next, prick the puff pastry well with a fork. Place the remaining 115 g (4 oz) of castor sugar in an ovenproof 25 cm (10-inch) diameter non-stick frying pan. Heat the sugar until it turns to a light caramel and then stir in the butter – at this point it looks like the whole thing is separating but don't panic, this is quite normal. Add the rest of the lemon juice and stir; the sauce will start to thicken again.

Arrange the well drained rhubarb in the hot pan and then immediately lay the pastry on top of the bubbling, buttery caramel and rhubarb mixture. Using a round-bladed knife, tuck the edges of the pastry down the sides of the pan. Let the pan bubble away for about 2–3 minutes and then put the pan in the hot oven and cook for about 12–14 minutes, depending on the thickness of the pastry. When the pastry is well risen and a nice golden colour, remove from the oven and leave to set for 3 minutes before attempting to turn it out. This allows the sauce to thicken and it will hold its shape better.

Carefully turn out by placing a plate on top of the pan and invert quickly; be careful of any hot sauce which may spill out. Cut into wedges and serve with cream or ice cream.

MINCE PIES

There are numerous ways of making mince pies – in patty tins, on baking sheets and using shortbread, shortcrust or even puff pastry. My favourite method and, I think, the most delicious, is using patty tins and the pastry recipe below – they're crumbly, buttery and a perfect treat for teatime on Boxing Day.

I really think that, if you are too busy to make your own mincemeat, buying a good-quality product is fine; there are some very good ones around these days.

Because of the high proportion of butter to flour, this pastry is very short and crumbly. At room temperature the dough is rather fragile and will soften quickly, so it is important that it is well chilled before you attempt to work with it. When rolling out, handle only the amount of pastry you need at that time and leave the remainder in the fridge. For the same reason, allow the mince pies to cool before removing from the tins so the butter has a chance to firm up.

400 g (14 oz) unsalted butter,
    softened

a pinch of salt

2.5 ml (½ teaspoon) ground
    mixed spice

200 g (7 oz) castor sugar

finely grated zest of 2 oranges

3 large egg yolks

500 g (1 lb 2 oz) plain white flour,
    sifted

450 g (1 lb) luxury mincemeat

1 large egg, beaten, to glaze

brown sugar, to sprinkle

TO SERVE

clotted cream

brandy

makes 20–24

Place the softened butter in a large mixing bowl with the salt, mixed spice, castor sugar and orange zest. Stir until the ingredients just come together. Add the egg yolks and flour and mix to make a firm dough. The pastry will be even better if you make it in the food processor. Remove the dough from the bowl and wrap tightly in cling film then chill in the fridge for about 1 hour.

Preheat the oven to 200°C/400°F/Gas Mark 6 and grease patty tins.

Roll out half the dough on a floured surface to a thickness of about 5 mm (¼ inch) and use a cutter to cut out pastry discs which will line the bases of the patty tins. Carefully line the tins with the pastry and then spoon in enough mincemeat to only fill three-quarters full.

Brush a little beaten egg around the inside rim of the pastry. Roll out the remaining pastry and cut out smaller circles to make lids for the pies. Place on top of the mincemeat and pinch around the edges to seal. Lightly brush across the lids to glaze and sprinkle over a little brown sugar, then use a sharp knife to make a small hole in the centre.

Bake in the oven for about 12–15 minutes, or until the pastry is golden brown and crisp. Allow the mince pies to cool before removing from the tins.

To enjoy at their best, follow my lead and serve with clotted cream and a glass of brandy!

TANGY LIME AND LAVENDER TART

As an apprentice, I had to make a Lancaster lemon tart – soft sponge drizzled with lemon icing – for afternoon tea; it was delicious. Here I have adapted the recipe to use lime and lavender instead. This, along with Lavender Shortbread (page 273) are two very nice ways of incorporating an unusual culinary ingredient. Moroccan and French cooks still use lavender in their cooking, but only occasionally, and then very cautiously. In this recipe I use fresh lavender, as dried can taste like old socks, unless you have dried it yourself.

FOR THE PASTRY

115 g (4 oz) salted butter

225 g (8 oz) plain white flour

1 large egg, plus ½ eggshell full
    of water

10 fresh lavender heads (about
    20 heaped/4 ml teaspoons)

juice and finely grated zest of
    1 large lime

FOR THE SPONGE

115 g (4 oz) unsalted butter,
    softened

115 g (4 oz) castor sugar

2 eggs, beaten

115 g (4 oz) self-raising flour

175 g (6 oz) blackcurrant or
    blueberry jam

FOR THE ICING

about 115 g (4 oz) icing sugar,
    sifted

double cream, to serve

serves 6–8

Preheat the oven to 180°C/350°F/Gas Mark 4. To make the pastry, rub the butter into the flour to resemble fine breadcrumbs. Crack in the egg, then add the water and lavender with half the lime juice. Mix lightly with a fork and then gently knead to make a dough – do not overwork or the pastry will lose shape and blister when cooked.

Use the pastry to line a greased 23 cm (9-inch) diameter, 4 cm (1½-inch) deep fluted flan tin; do not roll out the pastry too thickly or it will not cook in the same time as the sponge mixture. Trim off the excess pastry and thumb up the edge. Prick the base all over using a fork and chill for about 30 minutes.

To make the sponge, beat the butter and sugar together until pale. Add about a quarter of the egg and beat well using your hand (the heat of your hand really is beneficial as it helps to prevent the mixture from separating). Gradually beat in the rest of the egg and then add the flour and fold in again with your hand. Lightly stir in the lime zest, being careful not to overwork the mixture.

Spread the jam evenly over the base of the chilled pastry case and then spoon the sponge mixture on top. Spread out evenly, place on a baking sheet (the added heat from the tray helps the pastry to cook the bottom of the tart) and cook in the oven for about 25 minutes or until the sponge is well risen, nicely brown and firm to the touch – if the sponge begins to come away from the sides it is starting to overcook. Allow to cool on a cooling rack.

Prick the cooled sponge all over with a skewer. Gradually mix enough icing sugar into the remaining lime juice to make a soft icing, then spread evenly over the sponge and leave to set. Serve in thick slices, with double cream.

New Recipe

LANCASHIRE CHEESE APPLE PIE

I really like the old-fashioned pairings of sweet and savoury items. Eccles cakes with Lancashire cheese is another example of lovely textures and flavours working really well together. I'm also partial to Christmas cake with a thin slice of mature Montgomery's Cheddar on top. I adore Bramley apples; they are simply the best cooking apple in the world. When I cooked this recipe on the This Morning *programme on television, many people wrote and emailed, with fond memories of their earlier years.*

50 g (1¾ oz) unsalted butter

4 large Bramley apples, peeled and roughly chopped, not too small

30 ml (2 tablespoons) soft brown sugar

a pinch or two of black pepper

5 ml (1 level teaspoon) mixed spice

2 x 24 cm (9½-inch) discs of dessert pastry (ready-rolled)

250 g (9 oz) Lancashire cheese, thinly sliced

5 ml (1 teaspoon) fresh sage, chopped

1 egg, lightly beaten

makes a 24 cm (9¹/₂-inch) pie

Preheat the oven to 190°C/375°F/Gas Mark 5. Heat a saucepan, add the butter and melt. Add the chopped apples, sugar, black pepper and spice and then cook to a thick, chunky pulp, with the lid on the pan. Tip out into a bowl to cool.

Line a 24 cm (9½-inch) loose-bottomed baking tin with one of the discs. Lay over the cheese and fresh sage. Add the apple and really fill up the base then lightly egg the top edge. Top with the other disc of pastry. Brush the top with egg and then place into the preheated oven. Cook for 35–40 minutes or until well golden. Cool slightly and turn out before cutting.

FRITTERS AND
FRIED PUDDINGS

British cooks have always fried things. Fritters have been made here for centuries. Elizabethan cooks were probably the first to cook fruit fritters using apples, cherries and quinces. They viewed all raw fruit with great suspicion, cooking some apple and quince dishes for as long as six hours.

Like many other aspects of cooking, deep-frying is a great skill; it takes time to learn. Oils, cooking temperature, coatings, draining – all play a vital role in getting the end product absolutely perfect.

In this section I cook a few great favourites of mine. One of them is doughnuts – I cooked doughnuts for a whole week, perfecting the recipe (my next-door neighbour is sick of the sight of them). Another of my favourites is the Five-Spice Choux Fritters and you'll love these with a cup of strong coffee and a brandy.

PINEAPPLE FRITTERS WITH HOT BITTER CHOCOLATE SAUCE

Pineapple is one of my favourite fruits; it's very refreshing and versatile and good value for money. The best way to tell if a pineapple is ripe is to make sure it has a wonderful deep aroma – I don't think the method of checking ripeness by pulling out the leaves is as reliable. The pineapple should have a golden colour and not be green and hard.

Deep-frying is a great way of preparing this gorgeous fruit, especially with a wicked bitter chocolate sauce. If you want to go the whole hog, a big scoop of vanilla ice cream with it is pure decadence.

1 baby pineapple, 'Del Monte' variety if possible
2.5 ml (½ teaspoon) finely grated lemon zest
2.5 ml (½ teaspoon) lemongrass powder
45 ml (3 tablespoons) dark rum

FOR THE SAUCE
85 g (3 oz) good-quality cocoa powder
175 g (6 oz) castor sugar
40 g (1½ oz) cold unsalted butter, cubed

FOR THE BATTER
225 g (8 oz) self-raising flour
about 425 ml (¾ pint) sparkling mineral water
2.5 ml (½ teaspoon) ground allspice
vegetable oil, for deep-frying

TO SERVE
castor sugar, for sprinkling
ground allspice, for sprinkling
ice cream (optional)

serves 4–6

Remove the top from the pineapple with a sharp knife and then cut off the bottom as well. Carefully cut down the sides to remove the skin, taking care not to remove too much flesh. Lay the fruit on its side and cut into 1 cm (½-inch) slices; then cut each slice into six wedges, leaving the core in. Place the pineapple wedges in a bowl and sprinkle over the lemon zest, lemongrass powder and dark rum. Leave to marinate for 1 hour.

Meanwhile, make the chocolate sauce. Bring 300 ml (½ pint) of cold water, the cocoa powder and sugar to the boil in a pan. Simmer for 2 minutes and then take off the heat and whisk in the butter until melted. Strain through a sieve and keep warm.

Finally, make the batter. Sift the flour into a large bowl and then whisk in enough fizzy water to make a thick batter (about the same consistency as Yorkshire pudding batter). Mix in the allspice and allow to stand for 5 minutes.

Fill a deep-fryer or a deep pan one-third full with oil and heat to 180°C/350°F. Pat dry the pineapple on kitchen paper and then dip in the batter to coat. Cooking in batches, drop the pineapple carefully into the hot oil and cook until golden and crisp. Drain well on kitchen paper and sprinkle with castor sugar and allspice.

Pour a pool of hot chocolate sauce into shallow bowls and arrange a few fritters on top. Serve immediately, with ice cream if you like.

FIVE-SPICE CHOUX FRITTERS

These simple fritters are great with coffee and the kids will love them. They are easy to make and cook very quickly indeed. I use five-spice to flavour my fritters but other good variations for flavouring are grated nutmeg, ground cinnamon or green cardamom seeds.

vegetable oil, for deep-frying
15 ml (1 tablespoon) five-spice
    powder
30 ml (2 tablespoons)
    castor sugar
1 quantity Choux Pastry
    (page 42)

serves 4

Heat the vegetable oil in a deep-fryer or wok to 185°C/365°F. Sift the five-spice powder and sugar together.

Put the choux pastry into a piping bag fitted with a 1.5 cm (⅝-inch) nozzle. Pipe small lengths of the choux pastry into the hot oil, cutting the paste off with a small knife and very carefully dipping the knife into the hot oil occasionally to stop it sticking to the mixture. Do not overload the fryer or the temperature will drop and the fritters will not brown. Cook for a few minutes, stirring occasionally, until the fritters are puffed up and crisp. Carefully remove with a slotted spoon and drain on kitchen paper.

Roll in the sugar and five-spice mixture and serve straight away, piping hot.

New Recipe

LACY PANCAKES WITH LEMON CURD YOGURT

I first cooked these many years ago. Not too long ago, I cooked them again for a leaflet for the supermarket Aldi (where you can buy the lemon curd yogurt), and the response was huge. And when I recently launched my online cookery academy for schools, the response to this recipe was, again, wonderful. It is basically a twist on the original pancake and very simple and effective.

2 eggs

a pinch of castor sugar

a pinch of salt

100 g (3½ oz) plain flour

150–200 ml (5–7 fl oz) milk,
    approximately

25 g (1 oz) melted butter

30 ml (2 tablespoons)
    vegetable oil

2 x 150 g tubs of lemon
    curd yogurt

runny honey, for drizzling

icing sugar, for dusting

serves 4

First make the pancakes. Break the eggs into a bowl and add the sugar, salt, and flour. Whisk well then add ¾ of the milk until you have a thick batter. Add more milk if needed - the batter should have a thick double cream consistency. Finally, add the melted butter and whisk in.

Heat a non stick frying pan with a tablespoon of vegetable oil, until slightly smoking.

Using a tablespoon, spoon the mixture around the pan, then backwards and forwards to make a web pattern. Cook over a high heat until nicely browned, flip over and brown on the other side. Lift out and cool on greaseproof paper. Repeat the process, until all the mixture is used up.

Fold the pancakes into four, leaving them fairly open. Spoon over a little curd, then top with another pancake, and finally top with more curd. Drizzle with honey and dust with icing sugar, then serve.

New Recipe

TANGY LEMON CURD

I love lemon curd. The shop bought stuff can be pretty good and the one from Wilkin & Sons is very good, however it's fun and quite satisfying to make your own. Just remember to cook the mixture until well thickened. You will have to whisk all the time or the eggs will curdle and the butter will not come together perfectly.

4 eggs, at room temperature

350 g (12 oz) castor sugar

finely grated zest and juice of
    5 large lemons (about
    300 ml/10 fl oz)

a pinch of citric acid

250 g (9 oz) unsalted butter,
    cut into very small pieces

a pinch of arrowroot or cornflour

Place the eggs, sugar, lemon zest and juice, citric acid, butter and arrowroot or cornflour into a large heatproof bowl, and whisk together well.

Place over a pan of gently simmering water and whisk gently, until the mixture has heated and cooked. This will probably take about 15–20 minutes. Keep an eye on the mixture because it will thicken considerably. You will know when the curd is cooked when it thickens and resembles whipped cream. At this point, cook for a further 1 minute.

Then cool the curd and pour into 150 g (5½ oz) sterilised jars.

DOUGHNUTS

These, as we all know, are delicious. I like to roll them in unrefined icing sugar for a nice caramel edge, and a little cinnamon.

The secret of a feather-light doughnut is the mixture of bread and soft flours, and very slightly 'over-proving' the dough: when they are double in size, leave them for a further 10 minutes and then pop them into the hot fat four or five at a time – they will puff up straight away. I use a wok half-filled with sunflower oil with a sugar thermometer, or a free-standing fryer fitted with a thermostat.

50 ml (2 fl oz) whole milk

200 g (7 oz) strong white bread
flour, sifted

100 g (3½ oz) plain white flour

7 g sachet fast-acting dried yeast

40 g (1½ oz) unrefined
castor sugar

3 pinches of salt

1 large egg, beaten

35 g (1¼ oz) unsalted butter,
melted

vegetable oil, for deep-frying

TO DECORATE

unrefined icing sugar

ground cinnamon

**makes about 25 small
doughnuts**

Warm the milk and 100 ml (3½ fl oz) of cold water together to blood temperature. Mix both the flours with the yeast, sugar, salt and egg.

Add the melted butter to the flour mixture and then add about half the warm milk and water – as strong flours vary greatly in absorption capacity you might not need all the liquid. Mix to a dough, adding a little more liquid at a time if necessary. The mixture must be very soft and pliable but not too sticky. Tip on to a lightly floured work surface and knead lightly; then return to the bowl, cover with cling film and leave in a warm place to prove for 30 minutes or until doubled in size.

When fully risen, remove the cling film (there will be a sweet, warm smell) and gently knead on a lightly floured surface to 'knock back'. The dough will be very soft but not sticky. Mould into small balls the size of a small apricot (remember they will rise substantially). Place on an oiled baking sheet, cover with cling film and then prove again for 20–30 minutes or until almost doubled in size.

Heat the oil in a deep-fryer until the temperature reaches 190°C/375°F. Drop three or four doughnuts into the hot oil and cook for about 2 minutes or until nicely browned, then flip over and cook for a further 3 minutes. Remove from the hot oil and drain on kitchen paper. Repeat the process, making sure the oil comes back to the right temperature each time.

Sprinkle the cooked doughnuts with unrefined icing sugar and ground cinnamon and eat warm.

APPLE TURNOVERS WITH CRUNCHIE ICE CREAM

5 Granny Smith apples
grated zest and juice of 1 lemon
grated zest and juice of 1 orange
4 filo pastry sheets,
    measuring about 29 x 23 cm
    (11½ x 9 inches)
1 egg, beaten
icing sugar, to decorate

FOR THE ICE CREAM
400 g (14 oz) good-quality
    vanilla ice cream
4 Crunchie bars, chopped

serves 4

Peel, core and chop the apples into small pieces and then place in a heavy-bottomed pan. Add the zest and juice from both the lemon and orange. Cook for about 35–40 minutes or until soft and dry. Place in a sieve and leave overnight if possible to drain and dry further – you should end up with a dry, tight stew.

Cut one of the filo sheets in half lengthways. Lightly brush beaten egg over the top half of each piece and then fold up the bottom halves so they are on top. Place a small spoonful of the apple mixture in one corner, brush egg along the edges and then fold in half on the diagonal and seal well. Repeat to make eight turnovers.

Take the ice cream out of the freezer and allow to soften slightly. Fold in the Crunchie pieces and re-freeze. Deep-fry the turnovers in batches in hot oil (170°C/340°F) for 3–4 minutes or until golden brown and crisp. Drain on kitchen paper and then dust with icing sugar. Serve the hot fritters with the ice cream.

CUSTARD BRIOCHES

This is one of my favorites – a gorgeous creamy dessert. The secret is to cook the brioches very slowly so the outside is set and just browned and the inside soft and jelly-like.

2 large all-butter brioche
    buns, about 9 cm (3½ inches)
    diameter and 7.5 cm
    (3 inches) deep
2 large eggs
100 ml (3½ fl oz) double cream
50 ml (2 fl oz) whole milk
55 g (2 oz) soft light brown sugar
2.5 ml (½ teaspoon)
    vanilla extract
Caramel Pecan ice cream
    (page 170) or vanilla ice
    cream, to serve

serves 4

Place the brioches on a chopping board, slice about 1 cm (½ inch) off the bottom and then cut them in half horizontally.

Mix together the eggs, cream, milk, sugar and vanilla thoroughly. Sit the brioche, cut-side down, in a shallow dish, making sure they sit nice and tightly together. Pour over the egg mixture and leave to soak for the best part of 1 hour (or overnight in a fridge is better), carefully turning occasionally. As they soak up the mixture the brioche will become heavy and soggy.

Preheat the oven to 160°C/325°F/Gas Mark 3. The secret to cooking the brioches is to cook them in a completely dry, un-oiled pan. Just warm up an ovenproof frying pan on the hob and then pop in the brioches, cut-side down, and gently cook for a few minutes until the bottoms are slightly brown and set. Turn the brioche over, pop the pan into the oven and bake for about 15–20 minutes or until they are just cooked, so you end up with a soft, but set centre. Remove and keep warm. Serve with ice cream on each brioche half.

TECHNIQUES

DEEP-FRYING AND MAKING BATTER

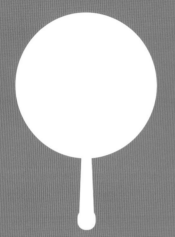

DEEP-FRYING

1 First rule: the new oil must be heated to a temperature of 185°C/365°F and cooled, and then re-heated. This process I call proving. It makes sure that the oil will brown the food slightly and the food will taste better. New oil cooks without colouring, so people overcook the food because they cannot see any colour. Sounds bizarre, but it's true.

2 Second rule: cut whatever you're cooking into smallish pieces. Not only do they cook quicker, they also cook more evenly.

3 Third rule: make sure the temperature of the oil is spot on. The batter or coating has to seal straight away, otherwise the oil will seep into the food and spoil it. Don't overload the fryer, as this can cause the temperature of the oil to drop by as much as 20°C/70°F. Cook a little at a time.

4 Fourth rule: get the consistency of the batter right; too thin and it will fall away in the hot oil and expose the food (remember the batter or coating is there to protect the food from the hot oil); too thick and you end up with a leaden stodge.

5 Fifth and final rule: never fill the pan more than one-third full with oil. This ensures that the oil doesn't rise over the rim of the pan when the food is added.

MAKING BATTER

For me there are really only two ways to make a batter. The first is a Japanese tempura-style batter made with egg whites and cornflour, great for vegetables and fish. The other is a great all-round batter which I use all the time.

1 To make the all-round batter, I make it with lager or sparkling water, self-raising flour and a touch of flavouring.

2 Remember not to overwork the flour when adding the liquid as this makes the batter very heavy and leaden.

3 Make the batter at the last moment to ensure a light, crisp, airy result.

CHOCOLATE DESSERTS AND CAKES

No puddings book could be written without including chocolate. In Britain we consume about 11 kg per person per year, making us serious chocoholics. It is probably the most important ingredient for puddings and desserts, apart from sugar.

Over the years I have really enjoyed cooking with chocolate – and I still do. I find it such a satisfying ingredient because you always, and I mean always, end up with something spectacular for your guests. It might be a rich-tasting mousse with coffee sauce, a visually stunning Easter egg wrapped up in ribbon, or a professional-looking hot bitter chocolate and chilli soufflé. You simply cannot go wrong.

Chocolate has come a very long way since it began to be cultivated in South America around 500 BC. It wasn't until Christopher Columbus was given some beans in 1502 that anybody had really seen cacao beans in the northern hemisphere. The Spanish brought the beans back home about 30 years later; they then kept the whole chocolate thing a secret for the best part of 40 years.

The chocolate we eat every day really isn't chocolate at all, as the amount of cocoa solids is very small indeed. The cocoa solids are mixed with milk powder, vegetable fat and sugar to end up with the creamy confection we all love. The rest of Europe's thoughts on our chocolate are well documented: they detest it.

Couverture is a different thing altogether; it contains a much higher percentage of cocoa solids. The cocoa solids are mixed with sugar and formed into large blocks. We chefs use couverture for desserts because it is chocolate in its purest form. It has a very deep, slightly bitter flavour and a smooth, velvety feel on the tongue and mouth.

I have tried to give a cross-section of chocolate recipes, from the ever-popular chocolate tart and chocolate pudding to simple frozen chocolate torte and roulade. All will, I hope, inspire you and never fail to impress.

STEAMED HOT CHOCOLATE PUDDING
WITH CHOCOLATE FUDGE SAUCE

This pudding can be made the day before if kept chilled; the next day, cut it into portions and reheat in the microwave for 2–3 minutes on full power; take care it doesn't burn.

3 large eggs

125 g (4½ oz) castor sugar

100 g (3½ oz) plain white flour, sifted

25 g (1 oz) cocoa powder, sifted

100 g (3½ oz) unsalted butter, melted

125 g (4½ oz) bitter chocolate, 70% minimum cocoa solids, finely chopped

FOR THE SAUCE

85 g (3 oz) unsalted butter

140 g (5 oz) soft brown sugar

300 ml (½ pint) double cream

85 g (3 oz) bitter chocolate, 70% minimum cocoa solids, chopped

double cream, to serve

serves 6-8

Butter well a 2-litre (3½-pint) heatproof bowl and a piece of foil (big enough to cover the dish).

Place the eggs and castor sugar in the mixing bowl of a food mixer and whisk on a high speed for 15 minutes or until very thick and foamy (see the second paragraph of the method for Basic Light Sponge on page 256). When ready, remove the bowl from the machine and carefully fold in the flour and cocoa powder – take care not to over mix or the sponge will be tough and leaden. Next, add the melted butter and chopped chocolate, again folding in carefully.

Spoon the mixture into the prepared bowl, cover with the buttered foil and cook in a steamer for about 1 hour, or until cooked – the sponge will be very soft and spongy. Do not overcook or the sponge will be leaden.

Meanwhile, make the sauce. Heat the butter and sugar together in a pan until melted, stirring occasionally. Add the cream and chocolate and bring to the boil, stirring all the time so the sauce does not stick. When completely melted, you can pass the sauce through a fine sieve if you like. Cover the sauce with cling film and keep warm.

Turn the pudding out while it's still warm and pour over plenty of the sauce. A nice spoonful of double cream over the pudding is completely over the top but absolutely gorgeous.

BITTER CHOCOLATE TART

The secret here is to not refrigerate the tart; it must be eaten at room temperature once cooled. If you have to chill it, make sure you take it out of the fridge at least an hour before eating. For a real chocolate-addict's version, use chocolate-flavoured pastry for the flan case.

150 g (5½ oz) bitter chocolate,
    70% minimum cocoa solids
150 g (5½ oz) milk chocolate
2 large eggs, plus 2 large egg
    yolks, at room temperature
60 g (2¼ oz) castor sugar
150 g (5½ oz) unsalted butter,
    melted
23 x 3 cm (9- x 1¼ -inch) Sweet
    Shortcrust Pastry (page 38)
    or Cocoa Pastry case (page
    39), baked blind
icing sugar, to decorate

TO SERVE
Coffee Bean Syrup (page 216)
clotted cream (optional)

serves 6-8

Preheat the oven to 220°C/425°F/Gas Mark 7. Melt the two chocolates together in a heatproof bowl over a pan of gently simmering water (see 'Melting chocolate' on page 89).

Place the eggs, yolks and sugar in the bowl of a food mixer and whisk at high speed until very thick (see 'Whisking egg whites' on page 127). Remove the bowl from the machine and carefully stir in the melted chocolate, taking care not to knock too much air out from the eggs. Finally, fold in the melted butter, again very carefully.

Place the baked-blind flan case on a baking sheet, pour the chocolate mixture into the pastry shell and cook in the oven for 7–8 minutes or until just set – do not let the edges of the tart soufflé up. Remove from the oven and leave to cool on a wire rack.

Eat at room temperature, cut into wedges, dusted heavily with icing sugar and with a little fresh coffee syrup. I also like to serve a little clotted cream, but that is entirely optional.

CHOCOLATE CUP CAKES

An all-time-favourite of mine, these are great for Sunday afternoon tea. The kids will love the mini eggs.

115 g (4 oz) unsalted butter,
softened
115 g (4 oz) castor sugar
3 large eggs, beaten
a pinch of vanilla powder
115 g (4 oz) self-raising flour
10 g (¼ oz) cocoa powder
55 g (2 oz) bitter chocolate,
chopped

FOR THE CHOCOLATE ICING
175 g (6 oz) bitter chocolate,
chopped
175 ml (6 fl oz) whipping cream
20 ml (4 teaspoons)
liquid glucose
2.5 ml (½ teaspoon) instant
coffee
10 ml (2 teaspoons)
cocoa powder
24 chocolate mini eggs

a pot of tea, to serve

makes 12

Preheat the oven to 180°C/350°F/Gas Mark 4. Line a twelve-hole patty tin with paper cases. Beat the butter and castor sugar together until pale and creamy. Gradually add the eggs until incorporated, then add the vanilla powder, flour, cocoa and chopped chocolate; do not overwork the mixture.

Spoon the chocolate cake mixture into the paper cases, making sure you leave a small indentation in the middle so the buns rise evenly – only fill up the cases one-third to one-half full so that you end up with enough space on top of the cooked buns to hold the icing. Bake in the preheated oven for about 25 minutes, or until well risen and firm to the touch. Remove from the oven, and leave to cool on a wire rack.

Meanwhile, make the icing. Melt the chocolate in a heatproof bowl over a pan of gently simmering water (see 'Melting chocolate' on page 89).

Bring the cream, glucose, coffee and cocoa powder almost to the boil in a small pan. Pour the cream mixture on to the melted chocolate and whisk well until smooth. Leave to cool slightly, whisking occasionally to prevent a skin from forming.

When the icing is starting to thicken, pour or spoon on to the cooked sponges, filling up to the top of the foil case. Top the cakes with mini eggs. Pop in the fridge and leave until just set. Enjoy with a large cup of tea; I bet you can't eat just one!

ICED GLAZED CHOCOLATE TORTE

As an apprentice, I had to make torten all the time. In those days they were all filled and decorated with butter cream, these have, sadly, become a bit unfashionable. So, with this in mind, I have crossed a parfait with a torte and ended up with a very rich and scrummy dessert.

FOR THE SPONGE

3 eggs

100 g (3½ oz) unrefined
    castor sugar

90 g (3¼ oz) plain white flour,
    sifted

10 g (¼ oz) good-quality cocoa
    powder, sifted

chocolate liqueur or brandy

FOR THE FILLING

double-quantity of Basic
    Meringue (page 122)

275 g (9¾ oz) good-quality
    bitter chocolate, melted but
    not too hot (see 'Melting
    chocolate' on page 89)

200 ml (7 fl oz) double cream,
    lightly whipped

FOR THE GLAZE

2½ gelatine leaves

85 g (3 oz) good-quality cocoa
    powder

85 g (3 oz) unrefined castor sugar

25 g (1 oz) unsalted butter

pouring cream, to serve

serves 6–8

Preheat the oven to 180°C/350°F/Gas Mark 4. Grease and base-line a 25 cm diameter x 6 cm deep (10 x 2½ inch) spring-form cake tin.

To make the sponge, whisk the eggs and sugar together, preferably in a food mixer, and whisk at a medium speed until they are very thick and holding their own weight (see the second paragraph of the method for Basic Light Sponge on page 256). Carefully fold in the sifted flour and cocoa and mix well. Spoon into the greased cake tin. Place in the oven and cook for about 20 minutes, or until well risen and springy to the touch. When cooked, cool slightly, run a knife around the edge to release, then open the tin. Cool.

Remove the sponge from the bottom of the tin and wash the tin well. Re-assemble the tin and line with cling film. Invert the sponge and replace in the lined tin (it should come just under halfway up). Sprinkle with chocolate liqueur or brandy.

To make the filling, make the meringue and whisk until very stiff. Fold in the melted chocolate carefully and finally add the cream and mix well, but do not over mix. Spoon into the tin and cover with cling film. Freeze overnight.

To make the glaze, put the gelatine leaves to soak in cold water (see 'Dissolving gelatine' on page 99). Place all the other ingredients, except the gelatine, in a small pan with 275 ml (9¾ fl oz) of cold water and heat gently to dissolve the sugar. Increase the heat and bring to the boil and then simmer for 20 seconds, stirring all the time. Remove from the heat and stir in the softened gelatine. Cool to setting point.

Meanwhile, remove the torte from the freezer, undo the outside ring and carefully lift out of the mould, peel off the cling film and place on a wire rack with a tray underneath so it's ready for the glaze to go on as soon as the glaze begins to set.

Quickly pour over the setting glaze and spread over the torte, taking care to cover the whole thing including the sides; the glaze will set very quickly. Chill again for 20 minutes. Carefully place on a large plate and cut into large wedges. Serve with pouring cream.

HOT AND COLD CHOCOLATE MILK SHAKE WITH COOKIES

This is a very easy and simple thing to create; the trick is to get the two milk shakes ready at the same time, so you end up with the hot and cold mix.

3 large egg yolks

45 ml (3 tablespoons) castor sugar

60 ml (4 tablespoons) Tia Maria

4 small scoops of good-quality chocolate ice cream

250 ml (5 fl oz) very cold milk

175 ml (6 fl oz) double cream

5 ml (1 teaspoon) cocoa powder

Chocolate Chip Cookies or Brandy Snaps (page 268 or 271), to serve

serves 4

First, place the egg yolks, castor sugar and Tia Maria in a heatproof bowl and sit it over a pan of gently simmering water. Whisk quickly until you have a thick foam, taking care not to scramble the eggs. Keep warm and covered.

Next, put the ice cream, milk, cream and cocoa powder in a liquidiser or processor and pulse until you have a thick shake – don't over-pulse the shake.

Divide the cold milk mixture between four chilled glasses, only filling them two-thirds full, and then immediately top with the warm foam. Serve with the cookies.

BITTER CHOCOLATE MOUSSE

This recipe came from a very talented chef, Allan Garth, who gave me a job at Gravetye Manor in 1985. I think the only reason he took me on was that I had just left the Lake District, where he had been brought up. He always ribbed me about 'the scruffy letter' I had written to him asking for a job! In the end I spent, on and off, the best part of four years there, which was probably the happiest time I had as a young chef, learning the art of being a pastry chef.

This mousse is very rich and dense and the only way to eat it is in large scoops similar to eating ice cream, with lightly whipped double cream and fresh coffee sauce. Just make it and let it set in a large bowl; it's not to be mucked about with!

2 large eggs, plus 2 large egg yolks

350 g (12 oz) extra-bitter chocolate, broken into small pieces and melted (see 'Melting chocolate' on page 89)

550 ml (19 fl oz) whipping cream, lightly whipped

50 ml (2 fl oz) dark rum

TO SERVE
Fresh Coffee Sauce (page 225)
double cream, lightly whipped

serves 6–8

Whisk the eggs and egg yolks in a heatproof bowl over a pan of gently simmering water, until thick and cooked; this will take about 15 minutes – I find the best thing to use is an electric hand whisk. Take care the eggs do not overcook or scramble. Remove the bowl from the pan and whisk for a couple of minutes to cool slightly.

This is the important stage: pour the whisked egg mixture into the hot melted chocolate and whisk well and very quickly: you can be quite brutal here. The mixture will look as though it is starting to separate but persevere. When halfway incorporated, add half the cream, and quickly whisk well. The reason you have to move a bit sharpish here is that the temperature of the cold cream can set the chocolate and egg very quickly indeed, but you should end up with a very smooth texture. Panic over, finally whisk in the rest of the cream and add the rum. Pour into a bowl, cover and chill overnight.

Using a hot spoon, scrape off large curls of mousse and serve in glasses, pouring over a little Fresh Coffee Sauce and double cream.

CHOCOLATE CHESTNUT ROULADE

This was a real hit in the late seventies; people seemed strangely attracted by the fact that this cake had no flour. Everybody made roulades then, from spinach, courgette and Swiss cheese to chestnut and almond. Some were pretty vile, I have to say.

Nevertheless, when made correctly, roulades are very good. This recipe is deliciously moist and perfect at Christmas time as an alternative to Christmas pudding.

15 g (½ oz) cornflour

15 g (½ oz) good-quality
cocoa powder

3 large eggs, separated

175 g (6 oz) unrefined
castor sugar

finely grated zest of 1
large orange

200 g (7 oz) unsweetened
chestnut purée

2 pinches of cream of tartar

FOR THE FILLING

300 ml (½ pint) double cream,
lightly whipped

30 ml (2 tablespoons) cocoa
powder, sifted

60 ml (4 tablespoons) icing sugar,
sifted

a pinch of ground cardamom

finely grated zest of 1 large lemon

TO DECORATE

75 g (2¾ oz) extra bitter
chocolate

icing sugar, sifted

serves 6

Preheat the oven to 200°C/400°F/Gas Mark 6. Line a 21 cm x 30 cm (8½-2½-inch) Swiss roll tin with baking parchment and brush well with melted butter. Sift together the cornflour and cocoa powder.

Place the egg yolks in a mixer with 125 g (4½ oz) of the unrefined castor sugar and the orange zest and whisk on a high speed until very thick (see the second paragraph of the method for Basic Light Sponge on page 256). Add the chestnut purée and whisk again to incorporate thoroughly. Finally, fold in the cornflour and cocoa powder.

Whisk the egg whites and cream of tartar together on a medium speed or by hand until thick and foamy. Add the remaining unrefined castor sugar and whisk again to just incorporate – the meringue must be soft and silky, not too stiff.

Carefully fold the two mixtures together. Spoon into the prepared Swiss roll tray and spread out evenly. Bake in the oven for 15 minutes, or until springy to the touch and well risen. Turn out on to lightly sugared baking parchment to cool.

To make the filling, fold the whipped cream, cocoa powder, icing sugar, cardamom and lemon zest together. Spread on to the sponge and carefully roll up, swiss-roll style, using the parchment to help. If the roulade splits slightly, don't worry, it's all part of the appeal of this unique cake. Transfer to a long plate and chill for 30–40 minutes.

Just before serving, melt the chocolate (see 'Melting chocolate' on page 89). Drizzle the melted chocolate over the roulade and dust with icing sugar.

CHOCOLATE BREAD AND BUTTER PUDDING

A wickedly rich pudding that will satisfy the most indulgent chocoholic. Adjust the recipe to your liking, by adding more or less chocolate. You can even experiment with milk chocolate but in that case reduce the sugar as milk chocolate is sweeter than plain. Those with nut allergies should avoid Nutella.

500 ml (18 fl oz) milk
600 ml (1 pint) double cream
finely grated zest of 1 lemon
85 g (3 oz) bitter chocolate,
     chopped
175 g (6 oz) Nutella or Belgian
     chocolate spread
400 g (14 oz) fruited loaf, cut into
     1 cm (½ -inch) slices
8 egg yolks
55 g (2 oz) castor sugar
5–10 ml (1–2 teaspoons)
     freshly grated nutmeg
icing sugar and cocoa powder,
     sifted together, to decorate
double cream, to serve

serves 6–8

Preheat the oven to 160°C/325°F/Gas Mark 3. Boil the milk, cream and zest together, then add the grated chocolate. Remove from the heat and leave to infuse for 10 minutes

Next, spread the chocolate spread over the slices of bread and arrange, overlapping, in a baking dish roughly 30 x 20 x 5 cm deep (12 x 8 x 2 inches).

Whisk together the egg yolks, castor sugar and nutmeg. Pour on the hot chocolate and milk mixture and whisk well. Pour this mixture over the bread and leave to soak for 10 minutes, pressing down occasionally with a potato masher so the bread is well soaked.

Cover the dish with foil and place in a deep baking or roasting tin. Place in the oven then carefully half fill the tin with boiling water. Cook for about 50 minutes, or until just set in the middle – the custard will still be slightly runny.

Remove from the oven, lift off the foil and dust with a little icing sugar and cocoa powder. Serve warm, but not hot, with cream.

WHITE CHOCOLATE MOUSSE WITH COFFEE SYRUP

We often see bitter chocolate mousse so it's nice to ring the changes. White chocolate isn't actually chocolate at all – it contains cocoa butter rather than cocoa solids, and is normally packed with milk powder and extra sugar. Some brands use vegetable oil as well, so check when buying. Take care when melting white chocolate as it has a tendency to thicken for no reason at all.

250 g (9 oz) good-quality
    white chocolate
2 large eggs, plus 2 large egg yolks
2 gelatine leaves, soaked in
    cold water
375 ml (13 fl oz) double cream,
    lightly whipped
15 ml (1 tablespoon) white rum

TO SERVE
Coffee Bean Syrup (page 216)
    plus a few beans from
    the syrup
'cigarette' biscuits

serves 6

Melt the white chocolate in a heatproof bowl over a pan of gently simmering water (see 'Melting chocolate' on the opposite page). Whisk the eggs and yolks in a heatproof bowl over another pan of gently simmering water, until thick and hot. Add the softened gelatine and whisk until dissolved then remove from the heat and continue whisking to cool. For a lighter mousse, add half a leaf of gelatine and set in glasses rather than moulds.

This is the tricky part – pour the chocolate into the eggs and whisk well; the mixture will thicken and start to look strange but don't worry. Immediately add half the cream and whisk well.

When fully incorporated, add the rest of the whipped cream and the rum, and carefully fold in. Pour into six very lightly oiled 150 ml (¼-pint) pudding moulds and chill well, overnight if possible.

To serve, dip the moulds into hot water, then turn the mousses out and surround with Coffee Bean Syrup. Decorate with a few of the beans from the syrup. It's also nice to serve this with 'cigarette' biscuits.

TECHNIQUES

COOKING WITH CHOCOLATE

CHOOSING CHOCOLATE

I recommend you use chocolate with the highest percentage of cocoa solids you can buy (you hear chefs say this all the time). Most supermarkets or delis now stock dark bitter chocolate with about 70 per cent solids and I believe you can now also buy a chocolate with an incredible 90 per cent cocoa solids, although I have not cooked with it.

RULES FOR COOKING WITH CHOCOLATE

When it comes to cooking with chocolate, the rules are very simple.

1 Do not overheat the chocolate or it will thicken and turn lumpy. If this happens it's best to throw it away and start again.

2 Probably the most important rule is to remember that the slightest drop of water or condensed steam will thicken and ruin chocolate very quickly indeed. Again, the only thing to do is to throw it away and start again, so be careful.

MELTING CHOCOLATE

1 Put a pan about half full of water on to heat. Break the chocolate into chunks. Place the chunks in a heatproof bowl and sit the bowl over the pan. Keep the water at a simmer and stir occasionally while the chocolate melts.

2 Make sure that the simmering water doesn't touch the bottom of the bowl or that steam doesn't get into the chocolate as either of these can cause the chocolate to 'seize': it becomes thick and grainy and the texture of the finished dish will be spoiled.

3 You can melt chocolate in the microwave but use low power and keep checking to see whether it is soft: the chunks hold their shape more than if melted over water and it's easy to think that they aren't ready because they look solid and this leads to overheating them.

4 If you're adding alcohol or orange juice to flavour the chocolate, it's best not to do this until the chocolate has melted.

GLAZED CHOCOLATE CAKE

Everybody likes a chocolate cake, however bad it is for your teeth and your waistline. My view is: everything in moderation. Don't eat this cake every day; just enjoy it when you do. It's quite a long recipe but well worth the effort and time, I promise. Try the chocolate decorations too if you can.

FOR THE CAKE

100 g (3½ oz) ground almonds

25 g (1 oz) cocoa powder

100 g (3½ oz) plain white flour

100 g (3½ oz) extra-bitter chocolate, chilled well

5 eggs, separated

150 g (5½ oz) castor sugar, plus 30 ml (2 tablespoons) castor sugar

30 ml (2 tablespoons) amaretto liqueur

chocolate decorations (optional)

FOR THE FILLING

125 g (4½ oz) extra-bitter chocolate

125 g (4½ oz) double cream, plus 225 ml (8 fl oz) double cream, lightly whipped

22.5 ml (1½ tablespoons) liquid glucose

45 ml (3 tablespoons) raspberry jelly

1 quantity Sweet Shortcrust Pastry or Shortbread Pastry (page 38 or 43)

FOR THE CHOCOLATE GLAZE

225 g (8 oz) extra-bitter chocolate

250 ml (5 fl oz) double cream

chocolate decorations (optional)

serves 6–8

Preheat the oven to 220°C/425°F/Gas Mark 7. Grease a 25 cm diameter x 5 cm deep (10-x 2-inch) springform cake tin, line with greaseproof paper and then lightly re-grease.

Roughly grate the chilled chocolate and then sift together with the ground almonds, cocoa powder and plain flour. Place the egg yolks, 150 g (5½ oz) of castor sugar and amaretto in a mixing bowl and whisk until very thick and creamy (see the second paragraph of the method for Basic Light Sponge on page 256). Whisk the egg whites until foamy but not grainy (see 'Whisking egg whites' on page 127). At this point, add the 30 ml (2 tablespoons) of castor sugar and whisk until thick, but not too thick or it will be difficult to fold into the egg yolks easily. Fold the flour mixture into the egg yolks and then carefully fold in the meringue. Pour into the prepared baking tin and bake for about 20–25 minutes, or until the cake is fully risen and firm to the touch. Allow to cool in the tin then turn out.

Next, make the filling by melting the chocolate in a heatproof bowl over a pan of gently simmering water (see 'Melting chocolate' on page 89). Place the 125 ml (4½ fl oz) of cream and liquid glucose together in a small pan and bring to the boil.

Remove the bowl of chocolate from the pan of water, add the hot cream and glucose to the chocolate and whisk well. Leave to cool in a cool part of the kitchen until the mixture thickens and will hold its own weight.

Slice the sponge in half with a long, sharp knife. Spread the raspberry jam or jelly over the shortbread or pastry disc, then sit the bottom half of the sponge on top of the jam. Press down lightly. Carefully spread the chocolate filling on to the bottom layer of the sponge, then add the whipped cream. Sit the remaining piece of sponge on top, lay a wire cooling rack on top and press down slightly. Tidy up any excess filling which may have come out and use to fill in any gaps: you will end up with a chocolate and cream sandwich. Chill for 2 hours.

To make the glaze, mix the chocolate, cream and 100 ml (3½ fl oz) water together in a bowl and place over simmering water. Stir until melted. Remove the chilled sponge from the fridge and carefully place on a wire cooling rack with a piece of greaseproof paper underneath. Pour over the glaze and, using a palette knife, spread it all over nice and evenly, covering the sides as well. Leave to cool in a cool place until the glaze is set and shiny. Try not to put the cake in a fridge at this point or the glaze will lose its shine and may attract condensation. Add the chocolate decorations (see the instructions below), if using, and serve in very large wedges!

To make chocolate decorations (optional)
Melt some bitter chocolate (70% cocoa solids). Use a small piping nozzle to pipe small shapes on to baking parchment. Freeze until hard and set, then use to decorate the cake just before eating.

CHRISTMAS FRUIT CHOCOLATE TIFFIN

Chocolate and soft raisins combined with digestive biscuits are a classic combination and make a simple and tasty Christmas idea with a delicious, deep flavour.

225 g (8 oz) unsalted butter,
    melted
115 g (4 oz) raisins
50 g (1¾ oz) brown sugar
45 ml (3 tablespoons)
    cocoa powder
45 ml (3 tablespoons)
    Golden Syrup
5 ml (1 teaspoon) ground
    mixed spice
300 g (10½ oz) digestive biscuits,
    crushed
150 g (5½ oz) bitter chocolate,
    melted
strong tea, to serve

**makes 28 little squares
or 14 triangles**

Melt the butter in a large saucepan, then add the raisins and mix well. Stir in the sugar, cocoa, Golden Syrup, spices and finally the biscuits and mix well. Spoon into an 18 cm x 28 cm (7-inch x 11-inch) baking tray lined with baking parchment and spread out evenly. Chill well.

Once chilled, spread the melted chocolate over evenly. Using a serrated spatula or a fork, quickly make tight, wiggly lines across the top and then chill well. Cut into small pieces when chilled. Serve with strong tea.

COLD MOUSSES
AND
CHEESECAKES

I do not know anybody who does not like a mousse or cheesecake. In a way, that makes it very easy to write a chapter like this. The only problem is that I have so many recipes it's very difficult to whittle them down.

There are a few interesting flavours here for you to try – marzipan for instance. Marzipan was probably one of the first dessert ingredients to be used in this country. Medieval cooks loved marzipan, albeit a very crude version made by mixing ground almonds with honey, spices and sometimes marigold petals to get the deep yellow colour. This paste was used to flavour curds, flummery, possets and even cheesecakes. Later the honey was replaced with sugar, when it became affordable and readily available, to form a thick paste roughly similar to the marzipan we know today. Nowadays it is usually reserved for cake decoration, but it makes a great mousse or charlotte. Blood oranges are another flavour not often used. They are at their best between January and March, and make a simple, well-flavoured mousse.

I must confess that I have a real weakness for chilled cheesecakes: ever since my mum made the packet variety in the early seventies, I have been hooked. Vanilla cheesecake with pecans is one of my favourites and, let me tell you, it was a close second to the egg custard as the best-selling pudding on the menu when I was at The Castle Hotel in Somerset.

PASSION-FRUIT MOUSSE WITH PASSION-FRUIT JELLY AND GLAZED BANANAS

This is a very light mousse set in a glass or bowl. It has something of an old-fashioned syllabub consistency, so you cannot turn it out successfully – the idea is to get a fresh, light mousse packed with flavour. Passion-fruit are ideal; this small fruit does not yield too much juice but, boy, does it pack a punch! Make sure every last seed and drop of juice is removed from the skins. If you want to be really posh, make the jelly as suggested below, pour on top of the chilled mousse and allow to set again.

I found that the more wrinkled (ripe) the fruits, the more juice you seem to get; also the fruit seems a little sweeter, but these are just my thoughts. I really love this fruit; whether in a hot soufflé in their own shells (page 112), or in a frozen mousse or sorbet, passion-fruit have such a unique flavour.

FOR THE MOUSSE

250 ml (5 fl oz) whole milk

4 egg yolks

70 g (2½ oz) castor sugar

2 gelatine leaves, soaked in
    cold water

10 passion-fruit

300 ml (½ pint) whipping
    cream, lightly whipped

FOR THE JELLY

juice and seeds from
    5 passion-fruit

25 g (1 oz) castor sugar

1 gelatine leaf, soaked in cold
    water (see page 99)

FOR THE BANANAS

3 ripe bananas

castor sugar, to taste

serves 6

To make the mousse, bring the milk to the boil. Meanwhile, whisk the egg yolks and sugar together for about 2 minutes until slightly pale. Pour the boiling milk over the egg and sugar mixture, stir well and pour back into the pan. Cook over a low heat, stirring continuously, until the custard thickens and lightly coats the back of a wooden spoon. Remove the custard from the heat, add the gelatine and stir until dissolved, then strain into a clean bowl and allow to cool.

Meanwhile, cut the passion-fruit in half and scoop out the flesh using a teaspoon (make sure you get every last seed). Blitz in a food processor or using a hand blender until all the flesh and juice has been removed from the seeds. Take care not to break up the seeds too much or you will end up with tiny black dots in the finished mousse – I find it best to 'pulse' the machine.

Push all the juice through a fine sieve using a large spoon. Measure the juice: you should end up with 200 ml (7 fl oz); if slightly under, just top up with a little fresh orange juice. At this point, remove the whipped cream from the fridge if necessary. Leave at room temperature for 10 minutes to take off the chill and ensure the mousse doesn't set too quickly, allowing you to spoon into wine glasses.

Either place the custard in the fridge, stirring occasionally or carefully sit it in a bowl of iced water and stir constantly until the mixture is at setting point and is starting to thicken – take care the custard really is at setting point or the finished mousse will separate. Add the passion-fruit juice and stir carefully. Finally, add the whipped cream and stir until fully incorporated – you may have to speed up so the mousse does not set on you. Immediately spoon into glasses and chill well.

Meanwhile, make the jelly – blitz the passion-fruit seeds and juice together as before and then pass through a fine sieve, discarding the seeds. Gently heat the sugar and 100 ml (3½ fl oz) of cold water together to dissolve, then remove from the heat and cool slightly. Stir in the softened gelatine until dissolved and allow to cool.

Once cool, add the passion-fruit juice (not adding the juice until this point ensures that the finished jelly has the freshest possible taste). Pass through a fine sieve or piece of muslin into a jug. Pour a thin layer over the chilled mousses and chill for 20 minutes, or until set.

The glazed bananas are very simple to do – peel the bananas and slice at an angle, place on a non-stick baking sheet and sprinkle with a little castor sugar. Glaze with a blowtorch (see 'Glazing a custard-filled flan' on page 49) or place under a hot grill. Repeat the process (this is the secret to even glazing) and then leave to cool.

Stand the mousses on plates, surrounded by slices of glazed banana.

STRAWBERRY MOUSSE

We used to make this recipe all the time in the early eighties. It's the best flavoured mousse I know and also the simplest: the secret is to get the mousse at the right setting point, without knocking out too much air. This recipe can be used for all summer fruits – blackberry is my other favourite. The eggs are uncooked, so do take care to whom you serve this.

280 g (10 oz) ripe English
    strawberries
2 gelatine leaves, soaked in
    cold water
2 large eggs plus 2 large egg yolks
175 g (6 oz) castor sugar
150 ml (¼ pint) double cream,
    very lightly whipped

TO SERVE
Raspberry Sauce (page 227)
Meringue 'Asparagus' (page 135)

serves 4–6

First, make the strawberry purée: liquidise the strawberries and then pass through a fine sieve to remove the seeds. You may need to add a touch of water, say 1 tablespoon, to get the whole thing going but do not dilute the purée more than absolutely necessary.

Remove the gelatine from the water, shake off any excess, place in a small pan and gently heat until melted (see 'Dissolving gelatine' on the page opposite). Whisk the eggs and yolks with the castor sugar until the mixture is very thick and foamy and holding its own weight (see the second paragraph of Basic Light Sponge on page 256).

Add the melted gelatine to the egg and sugar mixture and stir through very carefully. Carefully stir in the strawberry purée – do not over mix or all the air you have put in during the whisking process will be lost and you will end up with a heavy, dull mousse.

Finally, add the lightly whipped cream. The mousse should start to thicken quite quickly now but, especially in the summer months, you may need to sit the bowl over a larger bowl of iced water at this point and stir the mixture to encourage the setting process. Just as the mixture is beginning to set and hold its own weight, pour it into a large mould or individual glasses and chill until set.

Serve with raspberry sauce and meringue 'asparagus' spears.

TECHNIQUES

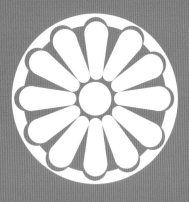

ADDING GELATINE TO MOUSSES AND CHEESECAKES

I once made a caramel mousse for a very well known food critic. I followed the recipe to a 'T'. Unfortunately the recipe was incomplete. It said nothing about chilling the mixture which is crucial. I poured what I thought was a finished mousse into the wetted mould and popped it into the fridge. Came to turn out the mousse later on, and to my horror it had split into egg froth, cream and jelly! The food critic's party was ready for their dessert, so I had no choice but to serve it. Thank goodness the chef did not see. There was no comeback until the end of the meal, when the food critic declared it an outstanding success, even singling out the caramel mousse for special praise as 'one of the nicest things I have ever eaten'. Phew! In spite of my lucky escape, I still maintain the important thing with mousses is to follow the recipe very carefully.

ADDING GELATINE

Be sure to chill the mixture over a bowl of ice before adding the gelatine – this is very important, as the cooled gelatine has to be suspended in the egg and cream froth – to avoid what happened to my caramel mousse!

DISSOLVING GELATINE

1 Leaves of gelatine are better than sachets because they dissolve more easily. Soak the leaves in cold water to cover for about 15 minutes, until they are completely soft all over and rubbery and pliable. If they are not soaked enough now they won't dissolve properly and mix with the other ingredients. Then remove them from the soaking water and shake off any excess water. Heat is now needed to dissolve them completely so, if the gelatine is added to a cold mixture, put them in a small pan with 10 ml (2 teaspoons) of cold water and very gently heat them until completely dissolved. Be very careful not to overheat. You can strain the gelatine through a fine sieve to remove any undissolved lumps, if necessary. Keep warm until needed. If the gelatine is to be added to a warm or hot mixture, it doesn't need to be melted.

2 Either way, once added, whisk well until you are sure that no lumps of gelatine remain in the mixture, which would be unpleasant in itself and might prevent it from setting properly.

RHUBARB TIRAMISÙ

Tiramisù is the best Italian sweet by far; a perfect combination of cream, mascarpone and coffee. I have spent a long time trying to get it right and I think that you will enjoy this rhubarb version. The combination seems to work really well and is a great way to end a heavy meal. Oh, and by the way, we actually got rhubarb from the Italians in the eighteenth century.

425 g (15 oz) new-season
    rhubarb
175 g (6 oz) granulated sugar
12 sponge fingers
2 large eggs
heaped 45 ml (3 tablespoons)
    plus 30 ml (2 tablespoons)
    castor sugar
250 ml (5 fl oz) double cream
350 g (12 oz) mascarpone cheese
cocoa powder, to decorate
strong coffee, to serve

serves 4–6

Wash the rhubarb well in plenty of cold water and then cut into 1 cm (½-inch) cubes. Pop into a pan with the granulated sugar and 225 ml (8 fl oz) of cold water and gently bring to the boil. As soon as the liquid starts to boil, remove from the heat and carefully place a piece of greaseproof paper directly on top of the syrup and rhubarb. Leave to cool for at least 5–6 hours.

When the rhubarb is cooled, carefully strain into a colander, keeping all the gorgeous pinkish syrup. Arrange the sponge fingers in a suitable dish or glass bowl - I use a dish that measures about 28 x 23 x 25 cm deep (11 x 9 x 2 inches). Spoon over about half of the rhubarb syrup and leave to soak in – within about 15 minutes most of the syrup will have disappeared. You can add a little more syrup if you want to; it's up to you but I prefer it not to be too soggy. Chill well.

Next place the eggs and heaped 45 ml (3 tablespoons) of castor sugar in a heatproof bowl and gently whisk over a pan of simmering water until they are thick and creamy and cooked; this will take a few minutes. In a mixer, whisk at high speed until thick and cool.

In a separate bowl, whip the double cream until it just makes peaks. Do take care as double cream over whips very quickly. Keep at room temperature. Finally – you need plenty of bowls for this pudding! – whisk the mascarpone and heaped 30 ml (2 tablespoons) of castor sugar together until loose and creamy.

Next is the easy bit, I promise! Fold together the mascarpone and double cream, and then carefully fold in the egg mixture to lighten the whole thing. Remove the dish with the soaked sponge fingers from the fridge and sprinkle the poached rhubarb evenly over the top. Spoon over the egg and cream mixture, flatten out with a palette knife and chill well. That's it, dust with cocoa powder and serve with a strong cup of coffee.

CRUNCHIE CHOCOLATE CHIP CHEESECAKE

The crunchy honeycomb keeps its texture due to the coating of chocolate.

FOR THE BASE

175 g (6 oz) digestive biscuits,
    ground in a food processor
25 g (1 oz) unsalted butter, melted
22.5 ml (1½ tablespoons) clear,
    runny honey
15 ml (1 tablespoon) freshly
    grated nutmeg

FOR THE CHOCOLATE-COATED
HONEYCOMB

3 x 40 g Crunchie bars
150 g (5 oz) bitter chocolate,
    melted (see page 89)

FOR THE FILLING

250 g (9 oz) Philadelphia
    full-fat, soft cream cheese
140 g (5 oz) castor sugar
200 ml (7 fl oz) whipping cream,
    very lightly whipped and not
    too cold
2 leaves of gelatine, dissolved
    (see page 99)
2 egg whites
a pinch of cream of tartar
15 ml (1 tablespoon) castor sugar
grated zest and juice of 2 limes

TO SERVE

a few English strawberries, at
    room temperature
a little double cream

serves 6–8

Add the biscuit crumbs to the melted butter, honey and nutmeg. Mix well. Turn out into a 23 cm x 4 cm (7 x 1½-inch) loose-based flan ring. Press lightly into the bottom with a teaspoon. Chill well. Next, cut the Crunchie bars into small pieces, say 5 mm (¼ inch); this is rather tricky as the texture of honeycomb shatters very easily. Salvage as many small pieces as possible, then eat the rest. Carefully place three or four pieces in the warm, melted bitter chocolate and individually re-coat well, then remove with a fork and place on baking parchment or greaseproof paper separately. Once all the honeycomb is coated, chill well.

The next point is quite important – the cheese must not be too cold so make sure it is at room temperature. Otherwise, when you add the gelatine, either it will set too quickly or you will end up with lumps of jelly. So, remove the cream cheese from the fridge about 20 minutes before you start. Beat the cream cheese and sugar together, on a slow speed, until light and soft, about 10 minutes. Lightly whip the cream, and leave out of the fridge for 10 minutes. Melt the gelatine in a small pan (see page 99) and keep warm. Lightly whisk the egg whites with the cream of tartar, add the sugar and beat to soft foam – do not let them turn grainy (see 'Whisking egg whites' on page 127).

The next stages need to be carried out as quickly as possible, or the cheesecake will set before you have time to get it into the flan base. So, remove the base from the fridge, quickly beat the hot melted gelatine into the cream cheese, add the cream and blend quickly. Remove the bowl from the machine, fold in the egg whites and lime juice and zest. You do not need to be too careful as this is a cheesecake not a mousse. Finally, fold in the chocolate honeycomb pieces and spoon into the prepared biscuit base. Chill for 2 hours.

To serve the cheesecake, remove from the fridge. Uncover and pop out of the flan ring. Cut in wedges using a knife dipped in very hot water. Serve with a few room temperature fresh English strawberries and a little double cream.

CARAMEL MOUSSE

I have cooked this mousse for many years. It's very light and is a perfect way to end a rich, heavy meal. A few strawberries and Rich Lemon Curd Ice Cream (page 168) are just the perfect accompaniments.

250 g (9 oz) granulated sugar

5 large eggs, plus 2 large egg yolks

25 g (1 oz) castor sugar

4½ gelatine leaves, dissolved
    in cold water (see 'Dissolving
    gelatine leaves' on page 99)

300 ml (½ pint) whipping
    cream, lightly whipped

finely grated zest of 1
    small lemon

serves 6–8

Place the granulated sugar in a thick-bottomed saucepan and cook gently until you have a nice dark caramel (see 'Making caramel' on page 167). Carefully add 150 ml (¼ pint) of cold water – don't worry about the noise and spitting, just stand back and be careful. Immediately remove the pan from the heat and pour the contents into a bowl to cool.

Whisk the eggs, yolks and castor sugar together in a large heatproof bowl over a pan of gently simmering water until thick and foamy (see the second paragraph of the method for Basic Light Sponge on page 256). Remove from the heat, then very carefully sit the bowl of egg froth mixture over a bowl of iced water and stir until cool. Add the cool caramel syrup and fold in carefully.

Lift the leaves of gelatine out of the water and shake off any excess water. Place in a small pan and gently heat to melt the gelatine (see page 99) and then stir into the cooling egg and caramel mixture.

When completely cool, add the whipped cream and lemon zest and continue to stir until the mixture thickens; at this point very quickly pour the mousse mixture into tall glasses or a nice mousse mould before it sets. The mould will need to be wetted or very lightly oiled. Chill for about 4 hours and then, if you have set the mousse in a mould, invert on to a serving plate, and carefully turn out.

MARZIPAN CHARLOTTE

Crude versions of marzipan have been around for centuries. It was probably one of the first confections ever made, either discovered by accident, or invented as an ingenious way of keeping almonds from spoiling (the natural oils in almonds turn rancid fairly quickly).

You either love or loathe marzipan: my mother hates the stuff but I adore the deep, sugary almond paste – so much so that I invented this delightful pudding.

There are two points to make regarding this recipe. The first one is that you must use the natural-colour product, and not the ghastly bright yellow rubbish – believe me, it's awful compared with the real thing. The other is, when you are melting the marzipan, take your time and stir constantly or it will catch. The rest is easy.

20–25 sponge fingers, weighing about 140 g (5 oz) in total
250 ml (5 fl oz) whole milk
200 g (7 oz) natural-colour marzipan, cut into small cubes
5 egg yolks
25 g (1 oz) castor sugar
2½ gelatine leaves, dissolved in plenty of cold water (see 'Dissolving gelatine leaves' on page 99)
30 ml (2 tablespoons) amaretto liqueur
300 ml (½ pint) double cream, lightly whipped

TO SERVE
blueberries
poached forced rhubarb

serves 6–8

Brush a little water inside a 17 cm diameter x 7 cm deep (6½-x 3-inch) soufflé dish and then line with cling film. Place a sponge finger against the side and then snip off the top so it is flush with the rim. Repeat the process until the dish is completely lined; the last finger should be nice and tightly in place (you may need to trim it slightly to fit exactly) so the ring of fingers hold their own weight – this can be a little tricky, so take your time. Alternatively, the finished mousse can just be poured into a nice serving dish and spooned out to serve – the choice is yours.

Place the milk and marzipan in a pan and warm over a low heat until the marzipan is completely melted. Meanwhile, place the egg yolks and castor sugar in a bowl and whisk together. Pour the milk and marzipan mixture on to the eggs, whisk well and then pour back into the pan and cook over a low heat until thickened and creamy, stirring continuously. Do not overcook. Pour into a clean bowl.

Squeeze excess water out of the gelatine and add to the hot custard (see step two of 'Dissolving gelatine' on page 99) along with the amaretto and stir well until dissolved. Fill a large bowl with iced water and then sit the bowl with the mousse mixture inside it. Stir until cold and starting to thicken, then remove from the bowl of iced water and carefully fold in the whipped cream. You should end up with a thick, cold mousse that is still pourable.

Pour or spoon into the prepared soufflé dish, cover with cling film and chill well, overnight if possible. Carefully turn out on to a large plate, remove the cling film and serve. A few blueberries or a little poached forced rhubarb is a perfect accompaniment.

NEW YORK STYLE CHEESECAKE

I didn't like the flavour or the texture of this type of cheesecake when I first tasted it but, after numerous trips to the States, it has rather grown on me. I was put off by the heavy, cloying texture and rather bland taste. In this recipe, I have tried to sort out these problems by lightening the mixture considerably and by adding rum, vanilla and plenty of lemon.

225 g (8 oz) Sweet Shortcrust Pastry (see page 38), or ready-rolled shortcrust pastry
700 g (1 lb 9 oz) full-fat cream cheese
350 g (12 oz) castor sugar
45 ml (3 tablespoons) vanilla extract
45 ml (3 tablespoons) dark rum
3 pinches of salt
284 ml carton of sour cream
grated zest and juice of 2 large lemons
3 eggs, at room temperature, separated
a pinch of cream of tartar
icing sugar, to decorate
Rich Lemon Curd Ice Cream (page 168) or a little Blackcurrant Sauce (page 46), to serve (optional)

serves 8-10

Preheat the oven to 190°C/375°F/Gas Mark 5. Take a 24 cm x 7 cm deep (9 ½ inch x 3 inch) springform cake tin and grease the base well. Roll out the pastry or, if using ready-rolled pastry, lay it on a lightly floured board or work surface.

Place the tin on top and carefully cut around the base. Lift off the tin, carefully place the pastry inside the tin and press to the edges. Prick well with a fork and cook in the preheated oven for 20 minutes, to set and very lightly brown. Turn the oven down to 160°C/325°F/Gas Mark 3. Remove the cake tin from the oven and leave the pastry to cool. Then grease the sides of the tin.

Beat the cream cheese, sugar, vanilla, rum and salt together until thick and creamy; this will take about 5 minutes in a food mixer. You can use a wooden spoon and beat it by hand, but this will take a little longer. Add the sour cream, lemon zest and egg yolks and beat well.

Place the egg whites and cream of tartar in a separate bowl and whisk until the whisked whites will just hold their own weight, ribbon fashion; do not over-whisk (see 'Whisking egg whites' on page 127). Place the whites and lemon juice in the cheese mixture and fold in with a large spoon. Pour the mixture into the lined baking tray and smooth out.

Bake in the preheated oven for 45–55 minutes until just set. The outside will soufflé very slightly and the inside will be very slightly runny but this is fine: once cooled and chilled, the cheesecake will set perfectly. The top of the cheesecake may also crack slightly when cooling but don't worry, this is quite normal.

Once chilled, dust heavily with icing sugar and cut into large wedges. This is nice with Rich Lemon Curd Ice Cream (see page 168) and a little Blackcurrant Sauce (page 46).

MAPLE SYRUP CHEESECAKE WITH CARAMEL PECANS

This is one of the tastiest cheesecakes around; the subtle maple syrup flavour is delicious. Just remember to use the best quality maple syrup – maple syrup is like olive oil: generally speaking, the higher the price, the better the quality.

200 g (7 oz) Philadelphia full-fat cream cheese, at room temperature
175 g (6 oz) digestive biscuits
25 g (1 oz) unsalted butter, melted
5 ml (1 teaspoon) grated nutmeg
22.5 ml (1½ tablespoons) clear, runny honey
175 g (6 oz) best-quality maple syrup
2 gelatine leaves, soaked in cold water
2 large egg whites
2 pinches of cream of tartar
15 ml (1 tablespoon) castor sugar
200 ml (7 fl oz) whipping cream, lightly whipped and not too cold

FOR THE CARAMEL PECANS
175 g (6 oz) granulated sugar
115 g (4 oz) pecan halves
15 ml (1 tablespoon) lemon juice

crème fraîche, to serve

serves 6–8

Remove the cream cheese from the fridge about 20 minutes before you start (it must not be too cold – otherwise, when you add the gelatine, it will set too quickly or you will end up with lumps of jelly). Place the biscuits in a food processor and grind into fine breadcrumbs. Add the melted butter, nutmeg and honey and pulse the food processor to mix well.

Turn the crumb mixture out into a 23 cm diameter x 4 cm deep (9-inch x 1½ -inch) loose-based cake tin and press into the bottom with a teaspoon. Don't push the crumbs down too tightly or you will end up with a heavy, sodden base. Chill well.

Beat the cream cheese and maple syrup together in a food mixer on a slow speed for about 10 minutes, or until light and soft. Lift the gelatine out of the water and heat to dissolve (see 'Dissolving gelatine' on page 99). Keep warm. Lightly whisk the egg whites with the cream of tartar, then add the castor sugar and beat to a soft foam but do not let them turn grainy (see 'Whisking egg whites' on page 127).

The next stages need to be carried out as quickly as possible, or the cheesecake will set before you have time to get it in the flan base. Remove the base from the fridge. Quickly beat the hot melted gelatine into the cream cheese, add the lightly whipped cream and blend quickly. Fold in the egg whites – you do not need to be too careful as this is not a mousse. Immediately pour into the prepared base, tap the tin to settle the mixture and chill well, if possible overnight. When the mixture is just set, carefully cover with cling film.

To make the caramel pecans, oil a non-stick baking tray well. Place the sugar in a heavy-bottomed saucepan and add enough cold water just to cover the sugar. Cook on a high heat; the syrup will thicken and start to turn a very pale amber (see 'Making caramel' on page 167). The sugar will also give off a slight caramel aroma – now this is the time to take care.

I think that the soufflé must have
by mistake. I cannot see anybod
making a soufflé. My theory is th
a chef or cook must have accide
egg tart (very popular with mec
or whisked sponge too long in
result was probably a very sorr
burnt thing – but well risen, wh
thought in the cook's mind.

There really is no secret to a g
process is a very simple one, ir
bubbles of air are trapped and
high heat so that they expand
steam – and, hey presto!– a w

Soufflés are very easy to make
you follow the recipe carefully
also very easy to get wrong. I
once cooking 120 banana sou
important New Year's Eve di

Continue to cook the caramel until you have a dark amber mixture (the lighter the colour the sweeter the taste) then add the nuts, take off the heat and stir with a wooden spoon to coat. The nuts will brown fairly quickly in the caramel as it is about 170°C/340°F. When the nuts are ready add the lemon juice and stir well, then immediately pour out on to the oiled tray and spread out using a wooden spoon. Leave to cool completely.

To serve the cheesecake, remove from the fridge. Uncover and pop out of the flan ring and then cut into wedges. Break the caramel pecans up into small pieces, place in a food processor and process until you have a chunky powder, not too fine. Sprinkle over the cheesecake and serve. It's also quite nice to serve a little crème fraîche with the cheesecake.

HOT

SC

MERINGUES

MERINGUES

BAKED VANILLA SOUFFLÉ PUDDING

It's not often you see a baked soufflé pudding like this any more, but they are a really nice change and very light. I cooked these at college years ago but I've updated the recipe, making the soufflé light and with the all-important 'wobble factor'. All you need to do is turn the soufflé out and pour over warm Caramelised Apricot Sauce.

55 g (2 oz) unsalted butter
55 g (2 oz) plain white flour
300 ml (½ pint) whole milk
75 g (2¾ oz) castor sugar
15 ml (1 tablespoon) vanilla
    extract or powder
3 large eggs, separated
a pinch of cream of tartar
warm Caramelised Apricot Sauce
    (page 226), to serve

serves 6

Preheat the oven to 190°C/375°F/Gas Mark 5. Butter a 20 cm (8-inch) diameter, 11 cm (4½-inch) deep soufflé dish or Pyrex bowl. Mix the butter and flour together to make a soft paste. Bring the milk to the boil, add the butter and flour mixture and whisk to bring back to the boil, then turn the heat down and stir over a low heat for 1 minute to cook the flour. Add 55 g (2 oz) of the castor sugar and the vanilla and stir well. Cover and leave for 20 minutes.

Whisk the egg whites with the cream of tartar on a medium speed until thick and foamy. Add the remaining 20 g (¾ oz) of castor sugar and continue to whisk until glossy and firm (see 'Whisking egg whites' on page 127).

Quickly stir the egg yolks into the milk mixture. Whisk half the meringue into the thick egg and milk mixture and then carefully fold in the remaining meringue. Spoon into the buttered dish.

Place the dish in a deep baking tray and fill the pan with enough cold water to come halfway up the side of the dish. Bake for 35–40 minutes or until well risen and golden brown on the top. Remove from the oven, turn out carefully on to a large, warm serving plate and pour over the warm apricot sauce.

TECHNIQUES

MAKING THE PERFECT SOUFFLÉ

Soufflés are perfect for the home cook; they are quick, easy and very simple to get together, provided you follow some basic rules.

WHISKING, GREASING AND COOKING SOUFFLÉS

1 Use very clean utensils: any speck of grease or yolk will break down the egg white. Always use egg whites at room temperature.

2 Whisk meringue with the tiniest pinch of cream of tartar on a medium speed. This ensures a soft, malleable meringue, easy to stir into custards and purées.

3 Don't over whisk — it prevents the soufflé from rising, making it heavy and firm.

4 Grease the dishes carefully. This helps the soufflé to rise evenly.

5 Always check the oven temperature; the finished soufflé must be well risen, nicely coloured and warm in the centre.

BANANA SOUFFLÉS

This soufflé base can be used for all sorts of flavourings. It's a lot more stable than the egg-yolk variety, by which I mean that, once removed from the oven, it should stand for a good couple of minutes before starting to collapse.

250 ml (5 fl oz) whole milk
3 large eggs, separated
120 g (4¼ oz) castor sugar
40 g (1½ oz) plain white flour
2 bananas, finely mashed with
    a fork
a pinch of cream of tartar
icing sugar, to decorate

serves 4

Preheat the oven to 220°C/425°F/Gas Mark 7. Butter four 200 ml (7 fl oz) ramekins.

Pour the milk into a pan and bring to the boil. Meanwhile, whisk together the egg yolks and 35 g (1¼ oz) of the castor sugar until thick and creamy, then whisk in the flour. Pour the hot milk on to the egg mixture and whisk well, then return the custard to the pan and cook over a low heat until the mixture comes to the boil, stirring all the time. Remove from the heat, pour into a clean bowl and cover with cling film. Leave to cool to room temperature – the mixture must be cool but not cold.

Add the mashed banana to the cooled custard and whisk well. Place the egg whites and cream of tartar in a very clean mixing bowl and whisk on a medium speed until the egg whites are thick and foamy (see 'Whisking egg whites' on page 127). Add the remaining 85 g (3 oz) of castor sugar and continue to whisk until glossy and fairly thick; do not over whisk or the finished soufflé will be hard and solid. Fold the meringue into the banana custard mixture.

Divide the mixture between the ramekins, place on a baking sheet and bake for 12–15 minutes, they will rise slowly at first but can then shoot up and overcook, so take care. Remove from the oven, dust with icing sugar and serve straight away.

HOT PASSION-FRUIT SOUFFLÉ PUDDING

Passion-fruit in any way, shape or form are delicious. This is a simple, very old-style pudding, that I was taught many years ago. The original soufflé pudding was a heavy, flour-based one. Here I have updated it and made it lighter so the pudding is a really nice treat.

zest and juice of 1 large orange

juice from 10 passion-fruits

70 g (2½ oz) castor sugar

15 ml (3 teaspoons) arrowroot

60 g (2¼ oz) unsalted butter

4 egg yolks, whisked together
   briefly

4 egg whites, at room
   temperature

a pinch of cream of tartar

80 g (3 oz) castor sugar

45 ml (3 tablespoons)
   passion-fruit or orange curd

icing sugar, for dusting

double cream, for pouring

serves 4

Preheat the oven to 200°C/400°F/Gas Mark 6. Place the orange and passion-fruit juices, orange zest and castor sugar in a bowl. Heat in the microwave to dissolve and cook for 30 seconds.

Stir in the arrowroot, until nicely thickened. Whisk the butter into the warm mixture and allow it to melt and then leave to cool slightly before adding the yolks. Stir well.

Pop the egg whites and cream of tartar into a mixing bowl and whisk on medium speed until they form a peak. Add half of the castor sugar and whisk until they form soft peaks, not too stiff. Remove the bowl from the mixing machine and fold in the last of the sugar. Spoon the curd into the bottom of a 20 cm (8-inch) baking or soufflé dish and spread out evenly.

Place the thickened juice and egg yolk mixture into a large mixing bowl, add half the egg white mixture and whisk well. Then add the rest of the whites and fold in carefully. Spoon into the baking dish and pop into the oven. Cook until nicely browned and slightly risen, about 20 minutes.

The secret to this pudding is to make sure that the middle is soft and the outside is nice and brown. Dust with a little icing sugar and serve with some double cream.

LIME SOUFFLÉ PANCAKES

Tony Tobin, a good friend of mine, gave me the idea for this. The good thing about this pudding is it's up to you how much lime you add so if you want it really limey, then just add more juice and take away some of the sugar. You can also substitute lemon for lime, or even orange.

FOR THE PANCAKES

2 eggs

a pinch of castor sugar

a pinch of salt

100 g (3½ oz) plain white flour, sifted

about 200 ml (7 fl oz) whole milk

25 g (1 oz) cold unsalted butter, melted

vegetable oil, for frying

FOR THE FILLING

finely grated zest and juice of 2 large limes

60 g (2¼ oz) castor sugar

heaped 7.5 ml (1½ teaspoons) arrowroot, soaked in cold water

2 eggs, separated

40 g (1½ oz) unsalted butter, cut in small cubes

FOR THE SAUCE

juice of 2 limes

30 ml (2 tablespoons) castor sugar

15 g (½ oz) cold, unsalted butter, cut in small cubes

icing sugar, for dusting

TO SERVE

icing sugar, for dusting

ice cream

serves 4

First, make the pancakes. Break the eggs into a bowl, add the sugar, salt and flour and whisk well. Add enough milk to make a thin batter. Add the melted butter and whisk in. Cover and leave to cool.

Heat a little oil in a frying pan. Spoon in enough batter to cover the bottom and cook over a high heat until nicely browned, then flip over and brown on the other side. Lift out and cool on greaseproof paper. Repeat to make four pancakes slightly thicker than the usual crêpes.

Preheat the oven to 220°C/425°F/Gas Mark 7. To make the filling, place the lime juice, zest and 25 g (1 oz) of the castor sugar in a pan and bring to a gentle simmer. Add the arrowroot and bring to the boil, stirring. Take off the stove, and leave to cool for 3 minutes.

Add the egg yolks and butter and whisk in until melted and thickened. Keep warm. Whisk the egg whites until they become thick and foamy, but not grainy. Add the remaining 35 g (1¼ oz) of castor sugar and whisk until the whites form soft peaks, but do not over whisk them or they will not expand in the oven (see 'Whisking egg whites' on page 127).

Whisk half the meringue into the warm curd mixture, then carefully fold the remaining whites in with a whisk. Divide the mixture between the four pancakes and fold the pancakes in half to enclose. Place on a non-stick baking sheet and bake for 8–10 minutes, or until well risen and nicely browned.

Now make the sauce. Bring the lime juice, 15 ml (1 tablespoon) of cold water and the sugar to a simmer in a pan. Whisk in the butter to thicken. This is a very powerful sauce, so you'll only need a small spoonful over each pancake.

Using a fish slice, transfer the pancakes on to warm serving plates, spoon over a little of the sauce and dust with icing sugar. Serve with ice cream.

PASSION-FRUIT SOUFFLÉ IN THE SHELL

I need to put the record straight here: this is an idea that I once cooked and which Ainsley Harriott stole and put in one of his books – we have a good laugh about it but, strangely enough, he still can't remember where the idea came from!

It's a nice way to end a heavy meal, and all the preparation can be done well in advance.

8 passion-fruit

2 large eggs, separated

a pinch of cream of tartar

55 g (2 oz) unrefined castor sugar

55 g (2 oz) unrefined icing sugar,
   sifted, plus extra to decorate

serves 2

Preheat the oven to 220°C/425°F/Gas Mark 7. Cut the passion-fruit in half and use a teaspoon to remove as much of the pulp and juice as possible. Keep the empty shells. Using a hand-blender on the slowest setting, whizz the passion-fruit pulp and seeds together until very runny and loose. If you do not have a hand-blender then just break up well with a whisk or fork. Strain well through a fine sieve, take care to get as much juice as possible out of the seeds.

Place the egg yolks in a large bowl, add the passion-fruit juice and mix well. Whisk the egg whites with the cream of tartar on a medium speed until they are thick and foamy (see 'Whisking egg whites' on page 127). Add the castor sugar and continue to whisk on a medium speed until thick and glossy but do not over whisk – the mixture should be soft and silky. Finally, add the icing sugar and mix well again.

Spoon half the meringue into the egg-yolk-and-passion-fruit mixture and whisk together well by hand. Finally, carefully fold in the rest of the meringue.

Spoon into the passion-fruit shell halves, making sure the mixture stands nice and proud. Sit on a baking sheet or in small patty tins, dust with a little icing sugar and bake for about 8 minutes, or until lightly browned. That's it, simple. Serve straight away.

BITTER CHOCOLATE AND CHILLI SOUFFLÉS

The combination of chilli and chocolate is not a new one but the combination of olive oil and dark chocolate is not only fairly new but absolutely perfect, if the olive oil is wonderfully perfumed. Try it, it's beautiful.

100 g (3½ oz) extra-bitter
    chocolate, broken into small
    pieces
2.5 ml (½ teaspoon) de-seeded
    and very finely chopped fresh
    red chilli
30 ml (2 tablespoons) fragrant
    extra-virgin olive oil
4 large eggs, separated
a pinch of cream of tartar
115 g (4 oz) castor sugar
icing sugar, for dusting
lightly whipped double cream,
    to serve

serves 4

Preheat the oven to 220°C/425°F/Gas Mark 7. Butter four 200 ml (7 fl oz) ramekins. Place the chocolate in a heatproof bowl, sit it over a pan of very gently simmering water and gently melt (see 'Melting chocolate' on page 89).

Place the chilli and olive oil in a small pan and cook gently for 5 minutes to soften. Keep warm. To make the meringue, using a medium speed, whisk the egg whites and cream of tartar together until thick and foamy. Add the castor sugar and continue to whisk until firm and very glossy, but do not over-whisk (see 'Whisking egg whites' on page 127).

Remove the chocolate from the simmering pan, add the olive oil and chilli and stir in, then stir in the egg yolks. Add about half the meringue to the chocolate and egg mixture and whisk well by hand until incorporated, then add the remainder and fold in carefully.

Spoon the mixture into the buttered ramekins, place on a baking tray and bake for 12–14 minutes, or until well risen and set. Dust with icing sugar and serve with lightly whipped double cream.

HOT RASPBERRY SOUFFLÉS

This is the quick method for making a soufflé, which needs to be eaten straight away or it will collapse. The way to make a soufflé that will hold its shape for a few minutes is to use crème pâtissière or 'confectioner's custard', basically, a custard thickened with cornflour to make it more stable – as in Banana Soufflés (page 116). Both are very nice to eat. Soufflés are a spectacular way to end a meal, but do take a little practice.

500 g (1 lb 2 oz) fresh raspberries
4 large eggs, separated
100 g (3½ oz) castor sugar

serves 4

Preheat the oven to 220°C/425°F/Gas Mark 7. Carefully butter four cappuccino cups, measuring 10 cm (4 inches) in diameter by 6 cm (2½ inches) deep, paying particular attention to the sides. Chill for 30 minutes. Butter the cups again.

Purée the raspberries and then pass through a fine sieve to remove the seeds. You should have about 400 ml (14 fl oz) of thick purée, so only add enough water (if any) to make it up to that amount. Mix together 200 ml (7 fl oz) of the raspberry purée and the egg yolks.

To make the meringue, whisk the whites either with a hand-held electric whisk or in a food mixer (see 'Whisking egg whites' on page 127). When the whites are thick and foamy but not grainy, add half the sugar and continue to whisk until thick and glossy. Finally, add the rest of the sugar and whisk in.

Put half of the meringue into the egg yolk and purée mixture and whisk well, then carefully fold in the remaining meringue, until thoroughly mixed.

Pour into the cups, tap down gently and place on a baking sheet. Cook for about 8–10 minutes, but check them after 8 minutes – if they are rising nicely but browning too quickly then turn the oven down a touch. Cook until well risen.

Carefully remove from the oven and serve with the remaining raspberry purée. Eat straight away.

I think that the soufflé must have been invented by mistake. I cannot see anybody thinking of making a soufflé. My theory is this: years ago a chef or cook must have accidentally left an egg tart (very popular with medieval cooks) or whisked sponge too long in the oven. The result was probably a very sorry-looking, split, burnt thing – but well risen, which sparked a thought in the cook's mind.

There really is no secret to a good soufflé. The process is a very simple one, in which minute bubbles of air are trapped and subjected to high heat so that they expand with a little steam – and, hey presto!– a well risen soufflé.

Soufflés are very easy to make provided you follow the recipe carefully, but they are also very easy to get wrong. I remember once cooking 120 banana soufflés for a very important New Year's Eve dinner. The pastry chef at the time had everything ready, but neglected to whisk the meringue to the correct consistency. The weight of the banana and pastry cream caused the meringue to collapse and we ended up with risen soufflés that fell over the edge of the dish! Needless to say, it was me who had to change my jacket and enter the ballroom and explain to the rather merry bunch that we would have to start again. Since then I have never trusted anybody else when it comes to making soufflés.

I have tried to give a good variety of soufflés in this chapter, from the old-fashioned pudding soufflés that were popular in the fifties and sixties, through soufflé pancakes (very trendy in the late sixties), to some very modern soufflés like tamarillo, chocolate and chilli, and passion-fruit in its own shell.

There are many stories about the origin of meringues. The best one I have heard is that they were created in the early 1700s, quite by accident, by a baker who gently beat egg whites with a little sugar until they were thick and firm. He came from Meiringen in Switzerland – hence the name.

These 'drop scone' type meringues were often coloured very brightly with saffron or cochineal (crushed beetles) and they were greatly enjoyed throughout Europe and apparently by Marie Antoinette and the French court. It seems ironic that only a few hundred years earlier the French had declared sugar a poisonous and evil ingredient, and viewed it with great suspicion. Later on, the piping bag was used to shape the meringue and all sorts of wonderful decorations were created for banquets and state occasions.

The basic recipe is still the same – egg whites and sugar. The only addition I make is a little cream of tartar; this helps to stabilise the basic structure of the meringue. If you don't have any cream of tartar, a little lemon juice is a good alternative. Add the cream of tartar or lemon juice to the egg whites at the very beginning, before you add the sugar. It ensures that the foam will not split or become grainy.

Sugars vary. I like to use a mixture of castor and icing sugar for basic meringues; this gives the end product a smooth crumbly texture. Use Billington's unrefined sugars to give the meringue a slightly caramelly edge.

In this chapter you'll find (don't sneer) directions for using packet meringue mixture (very handy if you are in trouble). I defy anybody to taste the difference once it's cooked or added to a mousse.

New Recipe

BASIC MERINGUE

Follow this recipe for lovely meringues every time.

2 large egg whites (70 g/2½ oz)
    at room temperature
a pinch of cream of tartar
70 g (2½ oz) castor sugar
70 g (2½ oz) sieved icing sugar

Place the egg whites and cream of tartar in a machine bowl and whisk on a medium to three quarter speed until they are thick and creamy, what we call 'break'. Add the castor sugar and whisk on medium to three quarter speed until firm, but silky and shiny. Finally, remove the bowl from the machine, and carefully fold in the sieved icing sugar. Pipe or mould accordingly on to a baking tray lined with baking parchment or greaseproof paper. Bake at 120°C/250°F/Gas Mark ½ for 4 hours or until dry and firm to the touch. Remove from the oven and leave to cool.

MACAROONS

Nice to eat with ice creams, mousses and as petits fours with a cup of strong coffee.

3½ large egg whites
115 g (4 oz) castor sugar
115 g (4 oz) icing sugar
150 g (5½ oz) ground almonds
35 g (1¼ oz) ground rice
rice paper
flaked almonds, to decorate
ice cream, mousse or strong
    coffee, to serve

**makes about 30 small
macaroons**

Set the oven to 140°C/275°F/Gas Mark 1. Whisk the egg whites until they are thick and foamy, whisk in the castor sugar and continue to whisk until you have a glossy meringue (see 'Whisking egg whites' on page 127). Fold in the icing sugar, ground almonds and ground rice.

Spoon into a piping bag fitted with a plain 1 cm (½-inch) diameter nozzle and pipe the mixture into small mounds, about the size of a 10p piece, on to rice paper, and top each with a flaked almond. Bake for about 4 hours until set, but slightly chewy inside. Cool and remove from the rice paper. Store in an airtight container for a couple of weeks. Enjoy with a cup of coffee or with some ice cream or mousse.

PACKET MERINGUE

The reason I mention this very good product is that it removes all problems with uncooked eggs because it's pasteurised, it's stable and works every time, and it's a very good substitute for Italian meringue. In Italian meringue, a boiling sugar syrup is whisked into egg whites, rather than just sugar and then the meringue is cooked so it sets firmly. This makes it safer for babies, the elderly and pregnant women to eat but, if you don't want to go to all the trouble of making your own, this product is a very good substitute in puddings and mousses.

Not many 'ready-made' products are of a really high quality, but this meringue, and good-quality pastry, are extremely good. Let the purists protest, I bet they couldn't taste the difference when cooked.

275 g sachet of Supercook
    Whisk and Bake Meringue
    Mix
25 g (1 oz) unrefined castor sugar
2.5 ml (½ teaspoon) vanilla
    powder

Pour the sachet into a food mixer, add the sugar and whisk on a high speed for 15 minutes. Remove the bowl from the machine and fold in the vanilla powder. Pipe or mould accordingly on to a baking tray lined with baking parchment or greaseproof paper. Bake at 120°C/250°F/Gas Mark ½ for 4 hours or until dry and firm to the touch. Remove from the oven and leave to cool.

That's it, simple, and stable.

JAPONAISES

When I was an apprentice, the pastry chef would make me make these soft, delicious biscuits every other day as my first job. He said I needed the practice with a piping bag. The consistency should be soft and chewy, a cross between a macaroon and the inside of a correctly cooked pavlova.

The mixture can be eaten with ice cream or piped into small discs and sandwiched with Real Buttercream (page 230) or crème chantilly (double cream sweetened with icing sugar and softly whipped). Larger discs can be sandwiched with ice cream and frozen, for an unusual ice-cream cake. I also like to layer strips in blackcurrant or caramel parfaits.

150 g (5½ oz) egg white at
    room temperature (about 4
    large egg whites)
a pinch of cream of tartar
150 g (5½ oz) unrefined castor
    sugar
50 g (1¾ oz) unrefined icing
    sugar
150 g (5½ oz) ground almonds
25 g (1 oz) cornflour

makes about 16 biscuits

Preheat the oven to 150°C/300°F/Gas Mark 2. Fit a piping bag with a 1 cm (½-inch) plain piping nozzle. Lightly grease two or three baking trays. Cut a piece of greaseproof paper or baking parchment to fit each tray perfectly and then, using a mould or tea cup as a guide, mark out sixteen 7 cm (2¾-inch) diameter circles with a pencil. Turn the paper over and press on to the tray.

In a very clean mixing bowl, whisk the egg white and cream of tartar on a medium speed until thick and foamy (see 'Whisking egg whites' on page 127). Add the castor sugar and continue to whisk on a slightly higher speed until very thick and glossy. Carefully fold in the sifted icing sugar, almonds and cornflour.

Fill the piping bag with the mixture and pipe out sixteen discs, using the pencil circles as a guide. Bake for 12–15 minutes, or until the meringues are lightly browned and soft to the touch. Remove from the oven and cool before storing in an airtight container.

CHOCOLATE AND PEAR MERINGUE GÂTEAU

This is the kind of pudding that nobody can really resist. You can poach your own pears, by placing 225 g (8 oz) of granulated sugar and 300 ml (½ pint) of cold water and a good squeeze of lemon in a saucepan. Bring to the boil, add four ripe, peeled pears and simmer for 1 minute, covered with a disc of greaseproof paper, then leave to cool in the syrup. Once the pears are cooked, place an inverted saucer on top of the greaseproof paper to keep the fruit suspended in the syrup and to prevent the pears from discolouring.

double-quantity of Basic
  Meringue (page 122) or
  2 x 275 g sachets of
  Supercook Whisk and
  Bake Meringue Mix
20 ml (4 teaspoons)
  vanilla powder
50 g (1¾ oz) castor sugar
juice of ½ small lemon
8 small tinned Bartlett pear
  halves, drained
300 ml (½ pint) double cream,
  very lightly whipped
100 g (3½ oz) bitter chocolate,
  grated
30 ml (2 tablespoons)
  good-quality cocoa powder,
  sifted
Bitter Chocolate Sauce,
  to serve (page 225)

serves 6–8

Preheat the oven to 120°C/250°F/Gas Mark ½. Mark out four 18 cm (7-inch) diameter circles on two sheets of parchment paper . Very lightly grease two baking sheets. Stick the papers down on to the sheets, with the side you drew on facing downwards. Fit a 1.5 cm (⅝-inch) piping nozzle on to a large piping bag.

If using sachets, whisk the meringue mixtures together on high speed until thick and glossy. Add the vanilla powder, castor sugar and lemon juice to the meringue (sachet or home-made) and whisk again. Spoon the meringue into the piping bag. Pipe a ring of meringue around the edge of two of the marked circles, then top each ring with another layer to make the rings about 3 cm (1¼ inches) high.

Next, completely cover another of the circles with more piped meringue to make a solid base for the dessert. Pipe two rings of meringue, one on top of the other on the outside edge of this solid base, so you end up with a 5 cm (2-inch) wall to the base.

Finally, pipe a lid on the last circle – the design's up to you! I like to pipe from the edge to the centre of the circle to form a dome effect. You should have ended up with two rings, a base with a side wall and a lid. Bake for about 2–3 hours, or until firm and set. When cooked, leave to cool completely before attempting to remove from the paper.

The easy part is to assemble it: chop the pears into small chunks and add to the whipped cream with two-thirds of the grated chocolate and lightly fold together. Carefully place the two meringue rings on top of the wall on the base, then spoon the cream and pear mixture into the centre, making sure all the meringue sticks together nicely. Add the lid, dust liberally with cocoa powder and sprinkle with the remaining grated chocolate. It's best to chill the whole gâteau for 1–2 hours so the meringue starts to soften. Serve with the chocolate sauce.

TECHNIQUES

MAKING THE PERFECT MERINGUE

WHISKING EGG WHITES

1 First of all, it's important to make sure that the bowl you are going to use and the whisk or beaters are spotlessly clean and dry, without a trace of grease, which can prevent the egg whites from whisking properly. The important thing is to pick a bowl that is big enough to whisk the requisite number of whites without bits of whisked mixture flying out everywhere.

2 You can use a food mixer, a hand-held electric beater or a hand whisk, either rotary or a balloon whisk. If you're using a mixer or electric beater, then whisk on a medium speed – it takes slightly longer, but the whites won't separate so quickly. Generally, avoid over-whisking egg whites, to the point at which they turn grainy. This is called 'break'.

TIPS ON INGREDIENTS AND BAKING MERINGUES

1 There are three things to remember about egg whites when making meringues. The first is that they should always be at room temperature because this helps to whip in the air, as the bubbles are a lot more stretchy. Secondly, if whisking on a machine, always whisk on no more than ¾ of the total speed to produce a soft, shiny meringue, especially for soufflés and piping. And thirdly, always weigh the egg whites, then allow double the amount of sugar, so 100 g (3½ oz) egg white with 200 g (7 oz) sugar.

2 Adding a pinch of cream of tartar to the whites helps to get the whites whisking up as well. Resist the temptation to add more cream of tartar. A pinch is all you need. It looks like nothing, but it will work, I promise. Too much cream of tartar will give the finished meringue a metallic aftertaste.

3 Measure the sugar carefully and add it at the correct point in the recipe. Many a recipe has been spoiled due to lack of attention to this.

4 The oven temperature must be correct for each recipe; too hot and the sugar will leach out and the meringues will darken; too cold and the meringues will collapse and take forever to dry out.

CHEAT'S PASSION-FRUIT PAVLOVA

Over the years I have struggled with meringues and pavlovas. They are notoriously fickle things. Egg whites tend to have a mind of their own; if you took identical egg whites, sugar, and the same bowl and made meringue twice, the two lots could be completely different. Why? I'm not sure exactly but I think I have narrowed it down to the weather and how old the whites are.

One chef even told me that frozen and then defrosted whites made far better meringues; it does seem that older whites are better but who knows? Anyhow, using meringue mix for this is a great cheat and I defy anybody to tell the difference.

275 g sachet of Supercook Whisk and Bake Meringue Mix or 1 quantity of Basic Meringue (page 122)
10 ml (2 teaspoons) cornflour
15 ml (1 tablespoon) white wine vinegar
6 ripe and withered passion-fruits, seeds and pulp scooped out
600 ml (1 pint) double cream, very lightly whipped
Champagne, to serve

serves 4–6

Preheat the oven to 110°C/225°F/Gas Mark ¼. Line a baking sheet with baking parchment. Whisk the meringue mix to very stiff peaks. Carefully fold in the cornflour and vinegar.

Next, pile the meringue on to the lined baking sheet, roughly into a 20 cm (8-inch) cake shape – don't worry too much about the shape being exact as the meringue will expand in the oven. Leaving about a 5 cm (2-inch) border, scoop out the top half of the meringue from the centre and pile it on to the edge. Tidy up the edge with a palette knife and pop the pavlova into the oven for 4 hours. As it is cooking, the pavlova will take on a little colour and expand and may even crack but don't worry, this is normal.

After 4 hours, increase the oven temperature to 160°C/325°F/Gas Mark 3 and cook for a further 10–12 minutes; watch the meringue as it will colour slightly more. Remove from the oven and leave to cool completely. The pavlova will be slightly toffeeish, marshmallowy and sticky on the inside still – this is perfect. If you are making this on a rainy day, take care to eat fairly swiftly as a damp atmosphere will soften the meringue very quickly indeed.

To serve, quickly fold the passion-fruit seeds and pulp into the cream but do not overwork or the acid in the juice will thicken and separate the cream. Pile into the centre of the pavlova shell and chill for about 30–45 minutes. Serve very cold, with a glass of Champagne.

BAKED ALASKA

One of my all-time favourites, the best ever, and it reminds me of my mum!

3 large eggs, at room temperature
75 g (2¾ oz) castor sugar
75 g (2¾ oz) plain white flour, sifted
25 g (1 oz) unsalted butter, melted

FOR THE FILLING

410 g can of peach slices in syrup, drained and syrup reserved
4 large egg whites, at room temperature
2 pinches of cream of tartar
115 g (4 oz) castor sugar
115 g (4 oz) icing sugar, sifted
lemon juice
500 g (1 lb 2 oz) vanilla ice cream, softened but not sloppy
10 glacé cherries
115 g (4 oz) angelica, cut into diamonds
½ orange, flesh scooped out carefully
castor sugar, to sprinkle

brandy, for lighting
double cream, to serve

serves 6–8

Preheat the oven to 200°C/400°F/Gas Mark 6. Lightly butter the inside of a 20 cm (8-inch) diameter x 7 cm (2¾-inch) deep cake tin, then chill.

Place the eggs and sugar in a bowl and whisk until thick and foamy, so the mixture holds its own weight (see the second paragraph of the method for Basic Light Sponge on page 256). Carefully fold in the sifted flour and then the melted butter. Pour into the chilled cake tin and place in the oven. Cook for 15 minutes or until the sponge is golden and risen and starts to shrink away from the side. Remove from the oven and cool.

Turn the sponge out of the tin and slice in half horizontally. Place the bottom half of the sponge on an ovenproof plate. Arrange the peaches on top and drizzle over a little syrup.

Increase the oven temperature to 230°C/450°F/Gas Mark 8. Whisk the egg whites with the cream of tartar in a food mixer using a medium speed, until thick and foamy (see 'Whisking egg whites' on page 127). Add the castor sugar and whisk again on a low speed until thick and glossy. Remove the bowl; fold in the icing sugar and a squeeze of lemon juice by hand.

Spoon the ice cream on top of the peaches and top with the second piece of sponge. Spoon half of the meringue on to the sponge and very quickly spread all over the top and sides to seal. Smooth with a palette knife. Place the rest of meringue in a large piping bag fitted with a 1 cm (½-inch) fluted nozzle. Pipe a nice design over the cake and decorate with glacé cherries and angelica. Place the half-orange shell on top and carefully stick down with a blob of meringue. Sprinkle with a little castor sugar. Put the whole thing in the hot oven for 2–3 minutes to brown lightly and then remove from the oven.

Heat a little brandy in a ladle and pour into the half orange. Light and hey presto! Cut into large wedges and serve with double cream.

GOOSEBERRY PAVLOVA

This is a simple and foolproof way of making pavlova. Much cooked and written about, this dessert now ranks alongside Poire Belle Hélène and Peach Melba in the famous pudding stakes.

A few years ago I went to New Zealand, the reputed home of pavlova, and probably ate this delightful pudding 30 times, and all, I might add were perfect examples. The Kiwis like to fill their pavlovas rather predictably with either kiwifruit or passion-fruit, the acidity cutting not only the sweetness, but also the richness of the cream.

I do like to use English raspberries, but my all-time favourite just has to be gooseberries. The acidity and flavour of this wonderful, and under-used, British fruit is absolutely perfect. Gooseberries are only around for a short while so make the most of them. I have two bushes, and they always crop heavily, so I bag the fruit up and freeze it, so even at Christmas we can have gooseberry pavlova.

500 g (1 lb 2 oz) ripe English
    gooseberries, topped and
    tailed
finely grated zest of 1 large lemon
55 g (2 oz) unrefined castor sugar
15–20 ml (3–4 teaspoons)
    cornflour, slaked (moistened)
    in a little water
1 quantity Basic Meringue
    (page 122) or a sachet of
    Supercook Whisk and Bake
    Meringue Mix
10 ml (2 teaspoons) cornflour
5 ml (1 teaspoon) white wine
    vinegar
5 ml (1 teaspoon) vanilla powder
600 ml (1 pint) double cream,
    very lightly whipped

serves 6–8

Heat the gooseberries in a pan with 15 ml (1 tablespoon) of cold water, the lemon zest and castor sugar. Cook until the fruit starts to soften and pop; this will take around 10 minutes. Add the moistened cornflour, stirring all the time, to thicken. Remove from the heat and cool completely.

Preheat the oven to 140°C/275°F/Gas Mark 1. Lightly grease a baking sheet, at least 30 cm (12 inches) square – the pavlova will spread when cooking. Mark out a 20 cm (8-inch) diameter circle on a piece of parchment or greaseproof paper (a plate is a good guide), turn upside-down and press on to the baking sheet. Re-grease very lightly.

Pour the meringue mix into the bowl of a food mixer and set the speed to medium. Whisk until glossy and firm – this will take about 10 minutes – then finish on the highest speed for a further 2 minutes. Add the cornflour, vinegar and vanilla powder and continue to whisk on high speed for 1 minute.

Spoon the meringue into the centre of the marked-out circle and, using a palette knife or the back of a large spoon, carefully spread the mixture to the edge of the circle. Try to keep the sides nice and high (remember, this will eventually hold a lot of gooseberry compote and cream) whilst creating an indentation in the centre – it sounds more difficult than it actually is, I promise. When you are happy, place the tray in the oven and cook for 1 hour. You will find the meringue will expand quite a lot, slightly colour and crack; this is normal.

After 1 hour, check the pavlova is cooked: it should be firm to the touch, yet crack if squeezed lightly, this ensures a soft marshmallowy inside, essential for a good pavlova (my mother just turns her oven off and leaves the pavlova to cool all night in the oven). Remove from the oven and cool. To serve, carefully remove the meringue from the paper and place in the centre of a large serving plate.

Gently fold three-quarters of the gooseberry compote into the whipped cream, do not over mix as the acid from the gooseberries will thicken the cream and it's also nice to see a swirled effect. Spoon into the pavlova straight away, then drizzle over the remaining compote. Chill for 45 minutes – by this time the cream will have thickened slightly and you will be able to slice a nice wedge. That's it, just enjoy.

PEPPERED CLOTTED CREAM MERINGUES

These meringues use the Italian method for making meringue, that is, pouring boiling sugar over egg whites and whisking until very firm. The result is a very smooth meringue that does not collapse and is used a lot in the production of frozen and chilled mousses. Alternatively, you can use a Packet Meringue (page 124).

The flavouring I am using here is Chinese Sichuan pepper, not normally used in sweet production. In fact, despite its name, this is not a pepper at all but rather the dried red berry from the ash tree. Its perfume is ideal not only for meringues but also for poached pears and peaches.

150 g (5½ oz) granulated sugar
100 g (3½ oz) egg whites
(about 3 egg whites), at room temperature
7.5 ml (1½ teaspoons) finely ground Sichuan pepper
5 ml (1 teaspoon) vanilla powder
clotted cream, to serve
unrefined icing sugar, to decorate

makes about 16 meringues

Preheat the oven to 120°C/250°F/Gas Mark 1/2. Cut two pieces of baking parchment to fit two large baking sheets. Fit a large piping bag with a 2 cm (¾-inch) piping nozzle.

Place the sugar and 100 ml (3½ fl oz) of cold water in a pan and bring to the boil. Place a sugar thermometer in the pan and then cook over a high heat until the syrup temperature reaches 120°C/250°F.

Start whisking the egg whites on high speed and gradually add the boiling sugar, pouring it down the inside of the bowl and trying to keep the sugar off the whisk itself. Once all the sugar syrup is in, whisk on a medium speed for about 12–14 minutes until very thick and glossy.

Stick the baking paper to the baking sheets with a small blob of meringue in each corner. Carefully fold the Sichuan pepper and vanilla powder into the meringue. Fill the piping bag with the meringue and proceed to pipe about 32 small blobs of meringue the size of a 10p piece; try to keep them all the same size if possible.

Place in the oven and cook for about 2 hours to dry out – Italian meringue will dry a lot quicker than normal Swiss meringue. They should be a pale coffee colour. When cooked, remove from the oven and leave to cool.

To serve, sandwich two meringues together with a blob of clotted cream. Place in small paper cases and then dust with a little unrefined icing sugar.

LIME MERINGUE PIES

These little pies make great finger food – the cornflour in the lime filling makes it set thickly which makes them easy to pick up.

½ quantity Shortbread Pastry
    (page 43)
3 large eggs, separated, plus 1
    additional egg white

FOR THE FILLING
115 g (4 oz) castor sugar
20 g (¾ oz) cornflour
40 g (1½ oz) unsalted butter
finely grated zest and juice of
    3 large limes

FOR THE MERINGUE
a pinch of cream of tartar
115 g (4 oz) unrefined castor
    sugar
115 g (4 oz) unrefined icing
    sugar, sifted
granulated sugar, to decorate

makes 12 pies

Preheat the oven to 190°C/375°F/Gas Mark 5 and grease a 12-hole patty tin. Roll out the shortbread dough to about 2.5 mm (¼ inch) thick and then cut out twelve discs slightly larger than the patty tins themselves. Press a disc into each patty tin and then chill the tray well.

Cut small discs of greaseproof paper to line each patty tin individually. Press in lightly and then fill with baking beans. Place the tray on a baking sheet and bake for about 15–20 minutes, or until lightly browned. Keep an eye on them as they can burn very quickly indeed. Once cooked, remove from the oven and leave to cool until set. Do not try to remove the beans and paper until cool or you will end up tearing the fragile pastry.

For the filling, heat 125 ml (4 fl oz) of water and the castor sugar and bring to the boil. Remove from the heat. Slake the cornflour in 50 ml (2 fl oz) of water and add to the pan. Stir well, place the pan back on the heat and stir until it comes back to the boil, so the mixture thickens. The mixture will be very thick now, but don't worry. Add the butter and mix well until melted, then add the lime juice and zest, and finally the egg yolks. Stir well.

Leave the cooked pastry tarts in the baking tray. Spoon the lime filling into the cooked pastry tarts to fill them right up then leave to set thoroughly, which will take about 30 minutes at room temperature.

Turn up the oven to 220°C/425°F/Gas Mark 7. Whisk the egg whites with the cream of tartar using a medium speed, until thick and foamy (see 'Whisking egg whites' on page 127). Then add the castor sugar and continue to whisk until thick and glossy. Fold in the icing sugar.

Fit a large piping bag with a 1.5 cm (⅝-inch) piping nozzle, spoon in the meringue mixture and pipe it on to each tart with a nice design. Sprinkle over a little granulated sugar and bake for about 5–6 minutes, or until lightly browned and set. Allow to cool slightly before serving.

MERINGUE 'ASPARAGUS'

Just a bit of fun and a great talking point. I promise, these little 'spears' are nice and elegant for a dinner party wrapped up in ribbons and served with ice cream, fresh fruit or for dipping in hot fudge sauce.

2 large egg whites,
    at room temperature
a pinch of cream of tartar
115 g (4 oz) castor sugar
2.5 ml (½ teaspoon)
    vanilla powder
60 ml (4 tablespoons)
    flaked almonds

makes about 16 'spears'

Preheat the oven to 120°C/250°F/Gas Mark ½. Lightly grease a baking sheet. Cut a piece of baking parchment to line perfectly.

Whisk the egg whites and cream of tartar on a medium speed for about 2 minutes or until thick and foamy (see 'Whisking egg whites' on page 127). Add half the sugar and continue to whisk for a further 10 minutes or until very thick. When thick and glossy, fold in the vanilla powder and the rest of the sugar.

Spoon the meringue into a large piping bag fitted with a 1.5 cm (⅝-inch) plain piping nozzle. Pipe a line of meringue 12 cm (4¾ inches) long, making sure to release the pressure at the end of the line, so you get an elongated, slightly tapered end. Repeat this until all the meringue has been used up (you should have about sixteen 'spears').

Carefully insert six to eight flaked almonds on alternate sides along two-thirds of each strip of meringue so it resembles the leafy bottom half of an asparagus spear. Next, cluster about six or seven flaked almonds around the tip to form the head of the asparagus. Repeat on all the meringue strips (it's a bit fiddly but be patient!).

Place in the oven and cook for about 2 hours or until crisp and dry. Remove from the oven and leave to cool completely before attempting to remove from the parchment. Slide a small knife underneath each meringue strip and slide off carefully. Wrap a brightly coloured ribbon around four spears to make a bundle and then serve.

APRICOT DAQUAISE

This pudding must be chilled before serving so the meringue starts to break down and take on a gooey texture. A great summer dessert.

6 egg whites, at room
  temperature
a pinch of cream of tartar
150 g (5½ oz) castor sugar
150 g (5½ oz) sifted icing sugar
125 g (4½ oz) ground almonds
finely grated zest of 1 large lemon
600 ml (1 pint) double cream,
  lightly whipped
8 fresh ripe apricots, halved and
  stoned then halves cut into
  four
icing sugar, to decorate
Caramelised Apricot Sauce,
  to serve (page 226)

serves 4-6

Preheat the oven to 140°C/275°F/Gas Mark 1. Fit a large piping bag with a 2 cm (¾-inch) plain nozzle. Lightly grease two baking sheets, then cut baking parchment to fit each sheet perfectly. Mark out three 18 cm (7-inch) diameter circles, two on one sheet and one on the other – a small plate is a perfect guide. Turn the paper over and press on to the trays.

Whisk the egg whites and cream of tartar together using a medium speed until thick and frothy (see 'Whisking egg whites' on page 127). Add the castor sugar and whisk on a high speed until you have a thick, glossy meringue. Carefully fold in the icing sugar and then the ground almonds.

Spoon the meringue into the piping bag and carefully pipe discs on the baking parchment, using the circles as a guide. The meringue can also be spooned out and then smoothed over with a palette knife if you don't fancy the piping.

Bake for 1½ hours, by which time the meringue should be set but still soft and a pale straw colour. When cooked, remove from the oven and leave to cool.

Carefully remove the meringues from the baking parchment and place one circle on the serving plate. Add the lemon zest to the whipped cream. Scatter half the apricots over one of the meringue circles, then top with half the cream. Place another meringue circle on top and repeat the process. Top with the last meringue disc and press down lightly. Chill for at least an hour. Dust with icing sugar, cut into wedges and serve with a little apricot sauce.

New Recipe

SUMMER FRUIT CHEESECAKE PAVLOVA

This recipe combines two of the favourite desserts in the UK: cheesecake and the pavlova. The secret is to get the two to set and soften at the same time. I use freeze-dried fruits – they have a great colour, and wonderful aroma. I bet you can't just have one spoonful of this decadent pudding.

4 egg whites, at room
    temperature
a pinch of cream of tartar
230 g (8 oz) castor sugar
5 ml (1 teaspoon) cornflour
5 ml (1 teaspoon) balsamic
    vinegar
5 ml (1 teaspoon) vanilla essence
35 g (1¼ oz) freeze-dried
    summer fruits, half-
    powdered in a blender
200 g tub of full fat soft cheese
½ x 397 g can Carnation
    Condensed Milk
85 g (3 oz) blueberries
85 g (3 oz) raspberries
85 g (3 oz) strawberries, sliced
finely grated zest and juice of
    2 limes
icing sugar, for dusting
Raspberry Sauce (page 227),
    to serve

serves 6-8

Preheat the oven to 120°C/ 250°F/Gas Mark ½. Place the egg whites and cream of tartar in a mixing bowl and whisk until light and foamy. Add half the sugar and whisk well on full speed and then add the rest of the sugar, whisking until very glossy. Remove the bowl from the machine and fold in the cornflour, vanilla and vinegar, dried fruit powder and mix well.

Use a small, plain nozzle (1 cm/ ½ inch) on a piping bag to pipe the meringue mixture on to baking parchment to make two 20 cm discs. Lift the discs and baking parchment on to baking trays and pop them into the preheated oven. Cook for 1¼ hours, or until just set. Peel off the paper and place on a serving plate.

Whisk the cream cheese and condensed milk together. Add the fruits and finally stir in the lime juice and zest and mix carefully. Spoon on to the meringue base and top with the other. Dust with icing sugar and chill for 1 hour. Cut and serve with the Raspberry Sauce.

FRUIT AND COMPOTES

Poached, bottled and compote fruit became very close to my heart, after I watched the brilliant BBC series, *The Victorian Kitchen Garden* in the eighties. Since then I have been fascinated by how the Victorians grew and preserved fruits for the out-of-season months. They went to extraordinary lengths so they could always have fresh or preserved fruit on their dinner tables.

Many wealthy families had a town house and a country house, both of which needed a supply of fresh fruit, vegetables and flowers all year round. The head gardener and cook had to work very closely together in the planning and growing stages, to make sure everything was used. In times of heavy cropping, the cook had to use the fruit immediately or preserve it.

Fruits poached in a heavy syrup will keep for a few days. If the fruit is to be kept any longer, it needs to be bottled and sterilized. The Victorians pioneered this and all manner of fruits were kept for the winter months.

I try not to play around too much with perfect, fresh, ripe fruit. There really is no point. I just enhance the flavour with a little sugar or a flavouring such as vanilla, elderflowers, fresh ginger, mint or alcohol. Nothing else is needed. The main thing is to serve all fresh fruit at room temperature.

In this chapter I explain how to poach, compote and bottle fruits. Some bottled fruits will keep for months, like the Bottled Kumquats or Preserved Clementines in Brandy. The latter are an ideal alternative to Christmas pudding. English greengages (just as good as the French mirabelles in my opinion) are another fruit with a short season and therefore an ideal candidate for bottling. All currants bottle well, especially with a dash of liqueur. I also touch on poaching quinces, cherries, figs, and even sweet pickled gooseberries for eating with vanilla ice cream. Soft fruits, such as strawberries and raspberries, are less successful when cooked: just enjoy them uncooked and in season.

POACHED PEACHES WITH LIME SABAYON AND SHORTBREAD

A simple but very nice pudding; it's best to start it the day before if you can, so the peaches have time to cool in the syrup. Not only does this help the removal of tough skins but it also adds flavour to the peaches, especially if they are slightly under-ripe. I always buy peaches by smell: if they smell good the chances are they will taste good. I also tend to batch-cook peaches so I have plenty in stock, as they will keep perfectly in the syrup for a week in the fridge.

350 g (12 oz) castor sugar

zest of 1 lemon, removed with
     a peeler

4 ripe peaches

3 large egg yolks

50 ml (2 fl oz) dry white wine

55 g (2 oz) castor sugar

a squeeze of lime juice

45 ml (3 tablespoons)
     double cream

½ quantity My Mum's
     Shortbread (page 278), to
     serve

serves 4

Place the sugar, 400 ml (14 fl oz) of cold water and lemon zest together in a pan and bring to the boil. Add the peaches and place a heatproof saucer on top to keep the peaches suspended under the syrup. Turn the heat down and gently simmer for 30 seconds, then turn the heat off and leave the peaches to cool in the syrup, preferably overnight. For this process to work the peaches have to be very ripe to begin with; if they are a little firm then just simmer for a couple of minutes instead of 30 seconds. When cool, take the peaches out of the syrup and peel off their skins. Cut each peach in half and remove the stone, then drain on kitchen paper.

To make the sabayon, place the egg yolks, wine and sugar in a heatproof bowl and whisk over a pan of gently simmering water until thick, hot and foamy. Take the bowl off the pan and whisk the mixture on a high speed, with a hand-held whisk or in a food mixer, until thick, cold and creamy.

Add a squeeze of lime and the cream and stir – you should end up with a thick dropping consistency. Sit the peach halves on plates, coat with sabayon and serve with the shortbread.

MARINATED PEACHES WITH VANILLA MASCARPONE

The secret here is to make sure the peaches are really ripe. I normally allow one and a half peaches per person.

6 ripe peaches or nectarines
unrefined icing sugar, to taste
30–45 ml (2–3 tablespoons)
    peach liqueur
juice of 1 lime
60–75 ml (4–5 tablespoons)
shredded fresh mint or
    lemon verbena

FOR THE VANILLA
MASCARPONE CREAM
250 g (9 oz) mascarpone cheese
icing sugar, to taste
1 vanilla pod
milk, to taste

serves 4

Slice the peaches into wedges and lay on a ceramic or glass tray or bowl. Sprinkle over unrefined icing sugar, drizzle over the liqueur and lime juice and finally sprinkle with the verbena or mint. Cover and leave to marinate for 2 hours minimum.

Beat the mascarpone with icing sugar to taste (it must not be too sweet). Split the vanilla pod, scrape out the seeds carefully, add them to the mascarpone and mix well. You may want to add a touch of milk to make the end result a little lighter.

Serve the peaches in dishes with the vanilla mascarpone cream.

POACHED DRIED APRICOTS IN ROSEMARY FLOWER SYRUP

This is a very simple, and very nice way to finish off a meal.

500 g (1 lb 2 oz) no-need-to-soak
    dried apricots
finely grated zest and juice of
    2 large limes
Rosemary Flower Syrup
    (page 218)
vanilla ice cream or beaten
    mascarpone, to serve

serves 4

Place the apricots in a heatproof bowl. Strain the flowers out of the syrup, then bring the syrup to the boil in a small pan. Pour the syrup over the apricots, stir in the lime zest and juice and then tightly cover the bowl with cling film and leave to cool. Chill thoroughly, preferably overnight.

To serve, spoon the apricots into deep bowls and pour over a little of the syrup. Top with vanilla ice cream or beaten mascarpone.

POACHED PEACHES WITH LEMON BALM AND BAY SYRUP

You'll find a picture of these peaches on page 219.

4 ripe peaches or nectarines
    (they must be ripe and smell
    beautifully sweet)
Lemon Balm and Bay Syrup
    (page 218)
clotted cream, to serve

serves 4

Place a small pan of water on the hob and bring to the boil and have a bowl of iced water ready. Once boiling, plunge the peaches, one at a time, into the water for 10–15 seconds – depending on the ripeness of the peach, the skin will come away very quickly indeed. Immediately remove from the water and place in the iced water to arrest the cooking. If the peaches are a little unripe then bring the water to the boil, add the peaches, top with a plate to keep the peaches suspended and leave to cool completely before you attempt to peel. Let the water come back to the boil, and repeat the process for the other three.

Carefully remove the skin from the peaches, discard the stones and slice into nice thick wedges. Arrange in a bowl. Strain the syrup, pour it over the peaches and chill for about 2 hours. Spoon over the syrup occasionally. Serve in separate bowls with clotted cream.

POACHED DRIED PEACHES WITH MASCARPONE

A quick but delicious dessert. The same recipe could be applied to any of the excellent semi-dried fruits now available.

2 lemons

350 g (12 oz) castor sugar

2 vanilla pods, split

250 g (9 oz) no-need-to-soak
    dried peaches

55 g (2 oz) unsalted butter

250 g (9 oz) mascarpone cheese,
    beaten, to serve

serves 4

Remove the zest from the lemons using a vegetable peeler and then squeeze the juice. Place the sugar and 600 ml (1 pint) of cold water in a saucepan, add the lemon zest and heat gently until the sugar has dissolved.

Add the juice to the syrup once it has dissolved and then simmer for 1 minute. Next add the vanilla pods and peaches and bring to the boil. Leave to cool and steep in the liquid, preferably overnight.

When you are ready to serve, gently warm through completely and then strain in a colander, reserving the syrup. Pour the syrup back into the saucepan and bring to the boil. Whisk in the butter until emulsified – the sauce should not be too thick and sugary so add a touch of water if necessary.

Divide the peaches between serving bowls and spoon over a little syrup. Serve warm, with a little beaten mascarpone.

AMALFI LEMON COMPOTE

We spent our honeymoon in Ravello, Italy, in the heart of the lemon-growing area. Everywhere we went we would come across huge amounts of Amalfi lemons and oranges. I was absolutely stunned at the size of the fruits when I first saw them – they are enormous! I'm not kidding, the smallest are the size of a small grapefruit and the largest can be the size of a small football; they are quite unbelievable. So, I decided I needed to get to grips with cooking them pretty quickly.

The thought did cross my mind that they may be all skin and pith and have no substance whatsoever: how wrong I was, they were stunning. They are sweeter than any other lemon I have ever tasted (some people say that you can eat them like an orange; I think I may draw the line there).

This compote is a real gem and I love it. It's great with raspberries, ice creams, meringues, pavlovas or even folded into crème fraîche.

1 large Amalfi lemon, or 3 large, normal, unwaxed lemons
100 ml (3½ fl oz) water, plus extra for blanching
heaped 30 ml (2 tablespoons) liquid glucose
115 g (4 oz) granulated sugar
2.5 ml (½ teaspoon) citric acid powder
5–10 ml (1–2 teaspoons) arrowroot, slaked (moistened) in a little water (optional)

Carefully peel the lemon(s) by hand using a sharp knife; remove all the pith, taking care not to pierce the flesh. Next, carefully remove as much of the white pith from the skin as possible and discard, then chop the zest into 5 mm (¼-inch) pieces. Chop the flesh, retaining as much of the juice as possible.

Put the zest into a pan, cover with cold water and bring to the boil. Once boiling, strain well through a sieve. Return the zest to the pan, cover with fresh cold water again and repeat the process.

Now put the blanched zest and lemon flesh into a clean pan, add 100 ml (3½ fl oz) of cold water, and the glucose, sugar and citric acid and bring to the boil. Gently simmer for about 20–30 minutes, or until the liquor has reduced and thickened slightly. I tend to thicken the mixture a touch with a little arrowroot or cornflour at this point – the secret is not to thicken it too much. Normally I would expect to use about a teaspoon of arrowroot or cornflour for the above amount.

Pour into a small, sterilised preserving jar (see Techniques opposite) and refrigerate for at least 2 weeks to mature.

TECHNIQUES

STERILISING JARS FOR PRESERVES

If you are re-using jars, check for any chips or cracks and then wash the jars and remove any old labels. Rinse the jars well in hot water and turn upside-down to drain.

METHODS FOR STERILISING JARS

1 Oven: put the jars on a rack or on a pad of kitchen paper on a tray. Heat in the oven at 150°C/300°F/ Gas Mark 2 for 10 minutes or until thoroughly dry. Leave to cool.

2 Dishwasher: put the jars through a wash cycle to sterilise them ready for use.

3 Microwave: half fill the jars with water and heat on full power until the water boils. Use oven gloves to remove the jars from the oven, swirl the water round inside them, and then throw away the water and stand them upside-down on kitchen paper to drain thoroughly.

4 Saucepan: place the jars in a deep pan and cover with boiling water. Bring to the boil and boil for 10 minutes. Carefully remove and allow to drain and dry.

NEW-SEASON RHUBARB POACHED IN DRY VERMOUTH AND CINNAMON

I really look forward to the 'forced' new-season rhubarb – it's about the only decent colour you can get in Britain in February and March (apart from Seville oranges). The forced variety is quite delicate and seems to need gentle handling and flavours, so light poaching in syrup marries perfectly. I also like the thick-stemmed reddy-green home-grown variety which has a slightly tarter flavour and is much nicer in pies, puddings, ice creams and sorbets

350 g (12 oz) new-season
    rhubarb
450 ml (16 fl oz) Noilly Prat
    or other dry white vermouth
350 g (12 oz) castor sugar
1 vanilla pod, split
1 cinnamon stick
10 ml (2 teaspoons) finely
    chopped fresh root ginger
Champagne Sabayon (page 22)
    or vanilla ice cream, to serve

serves 4

Wash, then top and tail the rhubarb and cut into 2.5 cm (1-inch) pieces. Pour the vermouth into a saucepan add the sugar, vanilla pod and cinnamon stick and bring to the boil. Gently simmer for 1 minute until the sugar has dissolved, then add the rhubarb and ginger and stir well. Simmer for 1 minute then remove from the heat.

Tip into a large bowl, cover with cling film and leave to cool. Serve with Champagne Sabayon or vanilla ice cream.

NEW-SEASON RHUBARB SOUP WITH HONEYCOMB

Yorkshire produces a third of the world's rhubarb. Forced rhubarb is grown in huge sheds in almost total darkness; this process produces pale pink, subtly flavoured, tender stems. This rhubarb is excellent for poaching with a little white wine or vermouth, for making a delicate sorbet or beautifully coloured jelly or it can be mixed with custard to make a gorgeous fool.

Maincrop rhubarb, grown outside and later on in the year, lends itself better to pies, crumbles, jams and pickles. Rhubarb marries very well with rich foods such as wild duck and, served in ketchup form, with scallops.

450 g (1 lb) forced rhubarb,
    cut into 3 cm (1¼-inch)
    pieces
finely grated zest and juice of
    1 lime
115 g (4 oz) golden,
    unrefined castor sugar, plus
    extra to serve if you wish
200 ml (7 fl oz) dry vermouth
1 comb of honey (Tiptree sell a
    340 g jar, with the comb set in
    acacia honey)
200 g (7 oz) crème fraîche,
    to serve

serves 4

Place the rhubarb, lime zest and juice and castor sugar in a stainless steel pan. Put the lid on and cook for about 5 minutes, so the juices start to run and the rhubarb begins to break down. Add the vermouth, bring to the boil and continue to cook for a further 10 minutes or until the rhubarb is cooked.

Liquidise the rhubarb and juice together until very smooth, then pass through a fine sieve. Keep warm. Meanwhile carefully cut the comb honey into small chunks, add to the crème fraîche and just gently stir together so you can still see the comb.

To serve, swirl some crème fraîche into the warm rhubarb soup. If you have a sweet tooth, then you may want to add a little more sugar.

BLACKCURRANT LIQUEUR COMPOTE

Great with lemon ice cream, hot sponge puddings or even egg custard tart.

350 g (12 oz) firm
    English blackcurrants
200 g (7 oz) golden castor sugar
100 ml (3½ fl oz) good-quality
    Cassis

makes about 500 ml (16 fl oz)

Pick over the blackcurrants and remove any stalks or damaged currants and then wash and drain well. Place in a pan with the sugar and 200 ml (7 fl oz) of cold water and bring to a gentle boil. Simmer gently until the fruit is soft and thick but not too broken up. Remove from the heat, stir in the liqueur and place in a clean, hot, sterilised preserving jar (see page 147). Seal.

Using a pan which is deep enough to allow the jar to be covered completely with cold water, put a folded tea towel in the bottom of the pan so the glass is not in direct contact with the metal and then put the jar in the pan and cover with cold water. Lay a sugar or cooking thermometer on top of the jar.

Gently heat the water so it takes 1½ hours to reach 90°C/195°F. Once up to temperature, turn the heat down and hold the temperature at 90°C/195°F for 15 minutes exactly.

Carefully lift the jars out using gloves or tongs (take care not to drop them as they are very slippery and hot) and place on a wooden chopping board or cloth, never on a metal or cold surface as the sudden change in temperature will make the glass crack. Leave to cool and then store in a cool, dark place. If sterilised correctly, the compote will keep for months.

POACHED DAMSONS

My love of damsons began when I worked in the Lake District in the early eighties. All our damsons came from an area just outside Kendal called the Lythe valley. We would buy huge amounts to convert into jam or jelly, for bottling and even for relishes to serve with ham baked in stout. I once recall reading a very old Lake District recipe for damson sauce with baked char, a beautiful fish only found in Windermere: damson is a wonderfully versatile fruit. This area has been growing damsons since about 1870 and in those days nearly all the picked fruit was transported to Yorkshire. Over the years, many of the original damson trees have disappeared but, thankfully, you can still buy damsons from the Lythe valley.

Lightly poached in a sugar syrup, damsons are delicious, with the added bonus that you don't have to stone them.

400 g (14 oz) ripe English
    damsons
250 g (9 oz) unrefined
    granulated sugar
a pinch of citric acid powder
    (optional)
juice and finely grated zest of
    2 large lemons
vanilla ice cream, Rich Lemon
    Curd ice cream (page 168) or
    thick double cream

serves 4

Wash the damsons well in plenty of cold water and remove any stalks. Place the sugar and citric acid with 450 ml (16 fl oz) of cold water in a pan and bring to the boil to dissolve the sugar. Once dissolved, add the damsons, bring back to the boil then gently simmer for 30 seconds. Transfer to a bowl, cover with cling film and leave to cool. Chill well.

Once chilled, stir in the lemon juice and zest. Serve with vanilla or Rich Lemon Curd Ice Cream or thick double cream.

BOTTLED GREENGAGES WITH LEMON

As apprentices, we would cook and bottle hundreds of greengages but, sadly, chefs these days don't use this delicious British fruit much. I say British fruit but it was actually brought back from France in the late eighteenth century by a certain Sir William Gage, and has been a favourite ever since. I love greengage jam, which is an essential part of Fern's Queen of Puddings (page 20). The same method can be applied to plums and apricots.

18 ripe, unblemished and
    firm greengages
250 g (9 oz) granulated sugar
4 thick slices of lemon
clotted cream, to serve

makes about 750 ml (1¼ pints)

Sterilise the preserving jars and rubber rings (see page 147) and have the jars wet so the gages slide down inside them easily. Pick over the fruit and remove any stalks. Cut the fruit in half and remove the stones. Bring the sugar and 250 ml (5 fl oz) of cold water to the boil together and then leave to cool.

Carefully pack the fruit into the jar, pour over the syrup to cover and finally add the lemon slices. Seal the jars. You now need to use a pan which is deep enough to allow the bottles to be covered completely with cold water – put a folded tea towel in the bottom of the pan so the glass is not in direct contact with the metal and then put the jars in the pan and cover with cold water. Lay a sugar or cooking thermometer on top of the jars.

Gently heat the water so it takes 1½ hours to reach 90°C/195°F. Once the temperature is 90°C/195°F, turn the heat down and hold at this temperature for 15 minutes exactly.

Carefully lift the jars out using gloves or tongs and place on a wooden chopping board or cloth, never on a metal or cold surface or the sudden change in temperature will make the glass crack. Leave to cool and then store in a cool, dark place; they will keep indefinitely.

To serve, spoon the fruit into deep bowls and top with clotted cream.

SWEET PICKLED GOOSEBERRIES

A very unusual thing to do with gooseberries, nevertheless, this is very nice with vanilla ice cream. Go on, try it.

800 g (1 lb 12 oz) golden castor
  sugar
600 ml (1 pint) white wine
  vinegar or cider vinegar
627.5 cm (3-inch) sticks of
  fresh lemongrass
12 black peppercorns
1.25 kg (2 lb 12 oz) firm English
  green gooseberries, plus extra
  to serve
good-quality ice cream, to serve

makes 750 ml (about 1¼ pints)

Gently heat the sugar, vinegar, lemongrass and black peppercorns in a pan until the sugar has dissolved. Add the gooseberries and gently poach for about 8–10 minutes, or until the fruit is soft but not falling to pieces (this is very important). Lift out of the juice with a slotted spoon and place in a colander to drain. Meanwhile, rapidly simmer the vinegar syrup until it is thick and very syrupy (this will take about 10 minutes).

Carefully spoon the fruit into a sterilised preserving jar (see page 147), add the lemon grass and a few peppercorns and then pour over the syrup to cover all the gooseberries. Seal well and leave in a cool, dark place for a minimum of 4 weeks before eating. It will keep indefinitely: I have some at home that I cooked a year ago. To serve, place a large scoop of ice cream in a deep dish and spoon over a few of the gooseberries (but not too many) then eat away.

WARM QUINCES WITH GRAPEFRUIT TEA BUTTER SAUCE

When cooking quinces, the syrup must simmer gently or the fruit will fall apart. It's a good idea to place a saucer on top of the fruit so they are kept covered in the syrup; this way they will all cook at the same time.

350 g (12 oz) granulated sugar

2 large quinces

55 g (2 oz) unsalted butter

ground Sichuan pepper

30 ml (2 tablespoons) unrefined castor sugar

125 ml (4 fl oz) very strong grapefruit tea, made using 6 tea bags

Caramel Pecan or Nutmeg Ice Cream (pages 170 or 164) or double cream, to serve

serves 4

Place the granulated sugar and 450 ml (16 fl oz) of cold water in a pan and heat to dissolve the sugar, then bring to the boil. Add the quinces, putting a heatproof saucer on top so they are completely covered by the syrup and so will cook evenly. Turn the heat down, cover the pan with a lid and gently simmer for about 1 hour, or until the flesh is very soft, but not falling apart. All quinces cook differently so keep an eye on them. There is a hard core to a quince that does not break down when cooked; take care not to be deceived into thinking they are not cooked. Once cooked, turn off the heat and allow to cool completely in the syrup.

Remove the quinces from the pan and drain well. Carefully take off the skin using a sharp knife and then cut the fruit in half. You can leave the skin on if you wish, it's not unpleasant to eat. Remove the hard inner core and seeds with a teaspoon and discard, then cut each half into three nice wedges. Pat dry with kitchen paper.

Heat half the butter in a non-stick sauté pan then add the quince slices and cook on each side for about 2–3 minutes, seasoning well with the ground Sichuan pepper. Add the sugar and tea and simmer to reduce slightly. Finally, add the rest of the butter and cook until the sauce thickens and emulsifies but do not overcook the quinces.

Serve straight away, with Caramel Pecan or Nutmeg Ice Cream or double cream.

PRESERVED CLEMENTINES IN BRANDY

These are a great Christmas treat. When you are fed up with lashings of turkey, pudding, trifles, nuts, the obligatory Quality Street and all the rest of it, these whole preserved clementines are just the ticket: they are quite tart and juicy and partner a large blob of home-made vanilla ice cream extremely well. They also keep well in a sealed jar in a fridge for weeks.

8 large sweet, juicy clementines
225 g (8 oz) castor sugar
2 vanilla pods, split
juice and finely grated zest of
    2 lemons
150 ml (¼ pint) brandy
vanilla ice cream, to serve

Preheat the oven to 160°C/325°F/Gas Mark 3. Pick over the clementines and make sure there are no blemishes or rotting skins. Place them in a pan and cover with cold water. Bring to the boil, then strain into a colander. Put the clementines back into the pan, refill with cold water then bring to the boil again. Repeat this process twice more and then, on the final time, gently simmer for about 10 minutes, then strain.

Carefully cut the clementines in half (they will be very hot indeed) and place, cut-side down, in a shallow, non-metallic baking dish. Bring 250 ml (5 fl oz) of water to the boil with the castor sugar until the sugar has dissolved. Add the vanilla pods and gently simmer for about 2–3 minutes. Pour over the clementines and loosely cover with foil, then place the dish in the oven and cook for about 35–40 minutes.

Carefully remove the dish from the oven and take the foil off, return to the oven and turn up the heat to about 200°C/400°F/Gas Mark 6. Cook until the syrup has reduced by about half to a quarter and is nice and thick. Remove from the oven, spoon some of the syrup over each of the clementines and leave to cool completely.

When cool, pack into a sterilised jar (see Techniques on page 147) along with the vanilla pods. Stir the lemon juice and zest and brandy into the syrup and pour over the fruit. Seal the jar and store in the fridge. Serve with vanilla ice cream.

BOTTLED KUMQUATS WITH ARMAGNAC

Most of the time I really don't know what to do with kumquats because they can be rather unpleasant actually – bitter, sour and hard. For me, the only way to cook them is to soften them in a jar with sugar and Armagnac, then at last they are edible, and very nice they are too!

They make a great Christmas present and are also very nice to eat in January and February when you're fed up with the cold, wet, rainy days. I eat mine with a large cappuccino after a heavy meal.

600 g (1 lb 5 oz) kumquats
350 g (12 oz) light brown soft
    sugar
juice of 1 lemon
45 ml (3 tablespoons) Armagnac

makes two 500 ml (18 fl oz) jars

Sterilise two 500 ml (18 fl oz) preserving jars and their sealing rings (see Techniques on page 147). Wash the fruits well and remove any stalks. Boil the sugar and 400 ml (14 fl oz) of cold water together until the sugar has dissolved and then leave to cool. Stir in the lemon juice and Armagnac. Wet the preserving jars, divide the fruit between them, then pour in the syrup. Seal the jars.

You now need to use a pan which is deep enough to allow the jars to be covered completely with cold water – put a folded tea towel in the bottom of the pan so the glass is not in direct contact with the metal then put the jars in the pan and cover with cold water. Lay a sugar or cooking thermometer on top of the jars.

Gently heat the water so it takes 1½ hours to reach 90°C/195°F. Once the temperature is 90°C/195°F, turn the heat down and hold the temperature at 90°C/195°F for 15 minutes exactly.

Carefully lift the jars out using gloves or tongs and place on a wooden chopping board or cloth, never on a metal or cold surface or the sudden change in temperature will make the glass crack. Leave to cool and then store in a cool, dark place. If bottled correctly, these will keep in a cool place indefinitely.

POACHED PEARS WITH SPICES AND CHILLI SYRUP

A nice way to end a heavy meal. Remember that the chilli is a seasoning, so a little goes a long way.

1 small red chilli
5 ml (1 teaspoon) whole cloves
5 ml (1 teaspoon) garam masala
½ cinnamon stick
350 g (12 oz) castor sugar
1 lime
6 ripe pears
thick cream, to serve

serves 6

To make the syrup, cut the chilli in half lengthways and discard the seeds, then place in a large pan with the cloves, garam masala and cinnamon stick. Add the sugar and 600 ml (1 pint) of cold water, bring to the boil and simmer until the sugar dissolves. Cut the lime in half, squeeze the juice into the pan and then add the lime halves. Simmer for 30 seconds and then remove from the heat.

Carefully peel the pears using a potato peeler. Using a small, sharp knife, work up from the base to make a narrow tunnel and remove the core, but leave the pears whole. Add the pears to the hot syrup and bring back to the boil, then remove the pan from the heat. Cover and leave the pears to cool in the syrup.

To finish, serve the whole cool pears in a bowl and spoon over some of the syrup. Serve with thick cream.

New Recipe

DAMSON JELLY PASTILLES

Pastilles have been around for many years; the idea originally came from the discovery that fruit could be preserved this way. I like them coated in crunchy sugar – the flavour and colour are amazing!

2 x 340 g jars damson jam

45 ml (3 tablespoons) lemon juice

30 ml (2 tablespoons) glucose syrup

60 ml (4 tablespoons) liquid pectin extract

4 pinches of citric acid (optional)

granulated sugar, for dusting

makes 300 g or about 18 jellies

Line an 18 cm (7 inch) square tin with baking paper. Put the jam into a medium-sized non stick pan with the lemon juice, glucose, citric acid and pectin. Gently heat the mixture, stirring all the time. Bring to a full boil and boil rapidly for 10 minutes, stirring frequently. The mixture reduces by about half, and thickens. Remove from the heat, spread into the prepared tin and when cool, put the tray in the freezer until set to a thick jelly.

When you take the tray out of the freezer, leave it for a few minutes so that the jelly becomes pliable. Peel the jelly sheet slowly away from the paper and fold it in half, to double thickness. Slice into strips, and then cut into 24 lozenges (2.5 cm/1 inch). Sugar your hands if it gets sticky. Roll each one in granulated sugar, and store in an airtight container in the fridge.

ICE CREAM

AND PARFAITS

Ice cream has been around for centuries, and was supposedly invented by the Italians. I'm not too sure about this, but they were certainly amongst the first to sell ice cream on street corners. In those days it was a sort of crunchy honeycomb ice cream, now very popular in New Zealand where it's called Hokey Pokey.

English cooks also made ice cream. Some of our great country houses had ice caves to store ice in the winter, so come spring and summer ice creams could still be made. The Victorians adored ice cream and sherbets and consumed huge amounts. It was the thing at the time to have a continental chef and these chefs brought new and exciting ice creams to the tables of the very rich. My old college lecturer, Brian, told me fascinating stories of how they used to cut ice from the lochs near Balmoral and store it, covered with ferns in caves, to make the Queen's ice cream in the summer months. Of course it was all churned by hand; it must have been really hard work.

In Britain we are one of the biggest producers of ice cream in the world, with thousands of flavours. We Brits eat an average of 15 kg each of it every year; only the Americans eat more.

I still have fond memories of Mr Whippy and his weird musical van. Though it's not what the purists call ice cream, there was something strangely comforting and delicious about the stuff. Even now I really like the creamy, soft texture with a couple of flakes; so do the kids.

Parfaits are close cousins of ice cream. There are two sorts: the boiled sugar version and the meringue variety. Parfaits lend themselves to an enormous range of interesting flavours and I've included some real winners here. The other great thing about parfaits is that you don't need an ice-cream machine to make them. For the recipes that need to be made in a machine, all are suitable for a 1.2-litre (2-pint) ice-cream maker.

CUSTARD BASE FOR ICE CREAM

Good ice creams need a good base and this is it; it's relatively simple. Make it and pop it in the fridge for up to four days and then just knock up the ice cream when you are ready.

250 ml (5 fl oz) whole milk
1 vanilla pod, split
4 egg yolks
55 g (2 oz) castor sugar

makes about 225 ml (8 fl oz)

Place the milk and vanilla pod in a pan and bring to the boil. Whisk the egg yolks and sugar together until fairly pale; there is no need to go mad! When the milk is simmering, pour it carefully over the whisked egg and sugar. Whisk well and return to the pan.

Cook over a low heat, stirring constantly, until thickened. This may take a few seconds or a couple of minutes so just keep an eye on the custard to make sure it does not get too hot and curdle. Remove from the heat and strain through a fine sieve to remove the vanilla pod and any pieces of over-cooked egg. Cover and allow to cool. Ready to go!

NUTMEG ICE CREAM

I started to make this ice cream way back in 1990; a lot of people have since made their own versions but to me this is the only way to do it. A slightly unusual ice cream but it works very well with baked egg custard tart, a combination that won me 'Dessert Chef of the Year'.

I like to eat this ice cream in autumn and winter, with apples, pears, quinces and plums. I think it's a little too strong for summer fruits.

The last thing I would say is always grate fresh nutmegs for this, as the delicate perfume of nutmeg deteriorates very quickly.

225 ml (8 fl oz) Custard Base
    for Ice Cream (above)
250 ml (5 fl oz) Stock Syrup
    (page 182)
250 ml (5 fl oz) double cream
heaped 10 ml (2 teaspoons)
    grated nutmeg (about 1
    whole nutmeg)

serves 6–8

Place a container in the freezer to pre-chill. Place all the ingredients in a bowl and mix well. Pour into an ice-cream maker and churn until thick. Remove, transfer to the pre-chilled container and store in the freezer for up to two weeks.

VANILLA ICE CREAM

This is a very smooth, sweet, velvety-rich, classic ice cream, perfect not only with warm summer strawberries or raspberries, or with sliced plums or peaches, but also with apple pie, or steamed hazelnut or sticky toffee puddings.

If you are going to eat this ice cream with any fruit, don't automatically sweeten the fruit but taste first: the ice cream will probably be sweet enough. If you like your ice cream a little less sweet, add only about 150 ml ($\frac{1}{4}$ pint) of stock syrup instead of the whole amount. This means the finished product will lose some of its velvety texture, though, so be careful not to reduce it too much.

225 ml (8 fl oz) Custard Base
    for Ice Cream (page 164)
250 ml (5 fl oz) double cream
250 ml (5 fl oz) Stock Syrup
    (page 182)

serves 4–6

Place a container in the freezer to pre-chill. Once the custard base is cool, add the double cream and stock syrup and whisk well. Pour into an ice-cream machine and churn following the ice-cream-maker's instructions until thick and creamy – this ice cream will not set too firmly, so remove it from the machine when very thick and velvety. Transfer to a chilled container. Store in the freezer for up to two weeks.

CHOCOLATE RIPPLE ICE CREAM

1 quantity Vanilla Ice Cream
    recipe (above)
115 g (4 oz) melted bitter
    chocolate (see 'Melting
    chocolate' on page 89)

serves 4–6

To make chocolate ripple ice cream, once the ice cream has been churned in the machine, carefully pour the melted chocolate into it in a thin, steady stream. The chocolate will set upon contact with the ice cream and break up. Churn for a further 10 seconds and then transfer to a container and store in the freezer for up to two weeks.

CARAMEL ICE CREAM

The thing to remember with anything to do with caramel is to make sure the sweetness is not too intense. Caramel by its very nature is sweet, but it's amazing how, as the sugar darkens, the caramel becomes less sweet. Years ago, almost black caramel known as 'black jack' was actually used to darken gravies and sauces – caramel can be extremely bitter. For this recipe, make sure the caramel is very dark (not black) and, coupled with a little salt – yes, salt! – this ice cream will have a nice sharp caramel flavour, and finish up as smooth as silk.

The recipe does need an ice-cream machine to get a perfect result but you will not taste a better caramel ice cream anywhere.

125 g (4½ oz) castor sugar
225 ml (8 fl oz) Custard Base
    for Ice Cream (page 164)
275 ml (9½ fl oz) double cream
225 ml (8 fl oz) Stock Syrup
    (page 182)
1.25 ml (¼ teaspoon) salt

serves 4–6

Place a container in the freezer to pre-chill. The first thing is to make the caramel (see 'Making caramel' on page 167). Place the sugar in a thick-bottomed pan and barely cover with cold water. Bring to the boil and cook rapidly until very dark, but not black. At this point add 75 ml (2½ fl oz) of cold water and stand back, the caramel will boil and splutter furiously, take care and don't panic, just let it bubble for a minute and then swirl the pan around to dissolve the caramel. Pour into a bowl or jug to cool; you will end up with a thick caramel syrup.

Place the cooled custard, cream, stock syrup, salt and caramel in a bowl and stir well together. Pour this mixture into an ice-cream machine and churn until thick and smooth. Transfer to the pre-chilled container and store in the freezer for a couple of weeks.

TECHNIQUES

MAKING CARAMEL

1 Place the sugar in a heavy-based, preferably non-stick pan and add just enough cold water to cover, or follow the recipe instructions as to whether to add water or not.

2 Using a pastry brush and a little more cold water, brush down any sugar crystals sticking to the side of the pan into the sugar water. This is very important as, if you do not do this, grains of sugar can fall back into the boiling sugar and cause the whole thing to crystallise. This might not matter for caramel but if you are attempting any kind of spun-sugar decoration or making sweets like humbugs, it's vital you avoid this, so get into the habit of brushing down the sides until the water and sugar have been boiling for at least 5 minutes.

3 Now place the pan over a fairly high heat and bring to the boil quickly. Keep washing down the edges and keep it at boiling point; the syrup will thicken gradually and start to turn a very pale amber. Keep watching it all the time.

4 Follow the recipe instructions for how dark a caramel you are aiming at. The rule is, the lighter the colour, the sweeter the taste will be.

5 If the recipe requires more water to be added to the finished caramel to dissolve it to make caramel syrup, put the water in a jug and tip it carefully into the hot caramel. There will be a lot of spluttering and splashing so stand back from it and don't worry. Bring the caramel syrup back to the boil to allow any pieces of caramel to melt, stirring occasionally. Pour into a jug and allow to cool a little or use as the recipe directs.

RICH LEMON CURD ICE CREAM

The wonderful thing about this ice cream is that you can really adapt it for any curd you want with a delicious result. This is a very simple and quick recipe, I promise.

I buy my lemon curd, purely because it's easier but, if you want to go the whole hog and make your own that is up to you. If not, make sure you buy a good-quality curd or see Tangy lemon Curd on page 71.

Passion-fruit, banana and orange curds all make great ice cream. Just remember that, if you are going to make a curd ice cream, you will need to add extra juice and zest of your chosen fruit to your ice cream. This will ensure a deep-tasting, powerful ice cream.

I like to serve this ice cream with Caramel Mousse (page 102) and candied orange zest.

225 ml (8 fl oz) Custard Base
   for Ice Cream (page 164)
300 ml (½ pint) double cream
310 g jar of good-quality
   lemon curd
finely grated zest and juice of
   1 large lemon

**FOR THE CANDIED
ORANGE ZEST**
2 large oranges
115 g (4 oz) granulated sugar
15 ml (1 tablespoon)
   liquid glucose
castor sugar, for sprinkling

serves 4–6

Place a container in the freezer to pre-chill. Pour the custard, cream and lemon curd into a clean bowl and whisk together. Add the lemon zest and juice and mix well.

Place in the ice-cream maker and churn according the instructions until very thick. Remove from the machine and spoon into the pre-chilled container. Freeze for 30 minutes and then eat or keep in the freezer for a up to a couple of weeks. To serve, decorate with candied orange zest.

To make the candied orange zest, remove the zest from the oranges using a sharp knife, taking great care not to include any pith. Slice finely and then cover with cold water in a small pan. Bring to the boil, strain well and repeat twice more. To the zest, add 115 ml (4 fl oz) of cold water, the sugar and the liquid glucose. Bring to the boil and then simmer very gently for about 25 minutes. The zest should be soft and succulent. Drain well, spread out on baking parchment and leave to dry in a warm place. Store in an airtight jar, sprinkled with a little castor sugar.

CHRISTMAS PUDDING ICE CREAM

If you are not too keen on Christmas pudding on its own, this may be for you. Not too rich, easy to make and can be made well in advance – plus, the kids will eat it.

If you really do not like Christmas pudding, a good fruit cake soaked in a little brandy is a good alternative.

185 ml (6½ fl oz) Stock Syrup
    (page 182)
1 cinnamon stick
2.5 ml (½ teaspoon)
    ground mixed spice
85 g (3 oz) Christmas pudding,
    chopped into small pieces
30 ml (2 tablespoons) brandy
225 ml (8 fl oz) Custard Base
    for Ice Cream (page 164)
150 ml (¼ pint) double cream

TO SERVE
large glass of brandy
Brandy Snaps (page 271)

serves 4–6

Place a container in the freezer to pre-chill. Warm the stock syrup in a small pan, add the cinnamon stick and mixed spice. Remove from the heat and leave to cool and infuse for 15 minutes. Meanwhile, soak the Christmas pudding in the brandy.

Mix the custard with the cream. Strain the stock syrup to remove the cinnamon and add to the cream mixture. Mix in the Christmas pudding and brandy.

Churn in an ice-cream-maker until thick and frozen and then transfer to the chilled container and store in the freezer for up to a couple of weeks. Serve with a large glass of brandy and Brandy Snaps.

CARAMEL PECAN ICE CREAM

One of the nicest ice creams, not just because I love to eat great bowlfuls, but also because it is good accompanying other desserts, such as cheesecakes, fruit compotes, pancakes, sponges, cakes and meringues with clotted cream.

The two things to remember are to roast the pecans first in a moderate oven to release their unique flavour, and the addition of salt. This balances the whole ice cream, cutting the sweetness amazingly. You would never notice the saltiness if I had not told you about it but it is vital to the balanced, finished product.

You will see that I have added gelatine: if this ice cream is kept in the freezer for more than a day or two, gelatine helps to set the weeping sugar whilst the ice cream is frozen and also helps stop the ice cream collapsing in a warm environment when serving.

115 g (4 oz) pecans
85 g (3 oz) granulated sugar
250 ml (5 fl oz) whole milk
1 vanilla pod, split
4 egg yolks
3 pinches of salt
55 g (2 oz) castor sugar
1 gelatine leaf, soaked in
    cold water
250 ml (5 fl oz) double cream
150 ml (¼ pint) Stock Syrup
    (page 182)

serves 4–6

Preheat the oven to 220°C/425°F/Gas Mark 7. Place a container in the freezer to pre-chill. Place the pecans on a metal baking tray and roast for 10 minutes until nicely browned all over. Remove and cool. Do use the oven: toasting under a grill tends to brown the nuts unevenly and burns them very quickly.

To make the caramel, place the granulated sugar in a shallow pan and cook over a moderate heat until light brown (see 'Making caramel' on page 167). Add the pecans and stir. Cook for 2–3 minutes and then tip out on to well-oiled greaseproof paper and leave to cool completely. Chop into chunks the size of a thumbnail (don't do this in the processor as this just turns the caramel pecans into powder). Place the milk and vanilla pod in a saucepan and bring to the boil gently.

Meanwhile, whisk together the egg yolks, salt and castor sugar until just pale (do not overdo it). Pour on the boiling milk, whisk and return to the pan. Cook over a low heat, stirring continuously, until thickened, and then add the soaked gelatine. Strain the mixture and cool.

Once cool, add the double cream and stock syrup, mix well and place in the ice-cream machine. Churn to the maker's instructions until the ice cream is soft and silky, then add the chopped pecan and caramel crunch and mix well. Spoon into the chilled container, cover and store in the freezer. This ice cream keeps for about 3–4 days but, after this time, the caramel will begin to weep, which spoils the appearance though it doesn't affect the taste.

New Recipe

PHIL'S VANILLA ARCTIC ROLL

I remember Arctic Roll when it first came out. I was a child and it was a real treat to have one; even now I love the texture and the simplicity of this ice cream pudding. I cooked this version on the telly this year and I had many lovely comments on this great pudding! In fact I think this could go down as one of the NEW British puddings, along with Sticky Toffee Pudding. You can make your own vanilla ice cream if you want to, or just buy good quality vanilla, not soft scoop though as it is too soft and won't keep its shape.

500 g (1 lb 2 oz) vanilla ice cream,
    about 1 litre (1¾ pint), not
    soft scoop, softened slightly
4 eggs
140 g (5 oz) castor sugar
40 g (1½ oz) plain flour, sieved
a pinch of salt (optional)
40 g (1½ oz) cornflour, sieved
70 g (2½ oz) unsalted butter,
    melted
6 tablespoons seedless
    raspberry jam
Raspberry Sauce (page 227),
    to serve

makes 8 slices

Preheat the oven to 200°C/400°F/Gas Mark 6. Lay out a 40 cm x 30 cm (16 x 12-inch) piece of cling film and then spoon the slightly softened ice cream down one edge of the cling film. Quickly roll up, then squeeze in both ends, and twist the ends over until you have a nice 6–7 cm (2½–2¾ inch) diameter cylinder, about 30 cm (12 inches) long. Freeze again until very firm.

Line a Swiss roll tin, about 37 x 28 cm (14 ½ x 11-inch), with baking parchment. Whisk the eggs and castor sugar together until they are thick and creamy and hold their own weight. Fold in the sieved flours, salt and then the melted butter, carefully. Spread on to the lined Swiss roll tray and then bake in the oven for about 12 minutes, until set and very slightly shrunken away from the sides of the tray.

Remove from the oven and immediately turn the tray out on to a clean tea towel: the sponge should fall out of the tray cleanly. Flick about 2–3 teaspoons of cold water over the back of the baking parchment and spread over lightly with your fingers. Carefully peel away the parchment, taking care not to rip the sides of the sponge away and then leave to cool. Spread the jam over the sponge evenly.

Take the ice cream out of the freezer and unwrap. Lay the ice cream on to the short edge of the sponge and carefully roll up the sponge until the edges meet. Press down well. Wrap in cling film and freeze again for about 10 minutes. Slice, and serve with raspberry sauce.

PUNCH PARFAIT

I got the idea for this dessert years ago when I was working for a German chef who used to love Glühwein when he was out skiing; when he came back to England, he used to make it in the kitchen on cold days. The smell of the warm red wine, cloves, cinnamon and citrus fruits is one of the most welcoming I know. Needless to say, we always had plenty left over, so, as I hate waste, I devised this parfait recipe. The added bonus is that you do not need an ice-cream machine, just a freezer and a plastic tub!

200 ml (7 fl oz) dry red wine

200 ml (7 fl oz) strong cold tea

200 ml (7 fl oz) freshly squeezed
    orange juice

juice of 2 lemons

200 ml (7 fl oz) castor sugar

1 cinnamon stick

6 cloves

6 allspice berries

2 large eggs, plus 2 large egg yolks

60 ml (4 tablespoons) dark rum

55 g (2 oz) castor sugar

250 ml (5 fl oz) double cream,
    lightly whipped

My Mum's Shortbread
    (page 278), to serve

serves 6–8

Firstly put a 2-litre (3½-pint) plastic container and lid in a freezer to chill well. Pour the red wine, tea, orange juice, lemon juice, castor sugar, cinnamon stick, cloves, and allspice into a measuring jug, and make a note of the total amount. Pour this mixture into a pan and bring to the boil, stirring to dissolve the sugar. Once boiling, turn down the heat and continue to simmer rapidly to reduce the liquid until you have only one-quarter of the original volume (make sure you measure it exactly). Do take care not to burn the liquid as it has quite a lot of sugar in it. Strain the reduced liquid and allow to cool.

Put the eggs, egg yolks, rum and castor sugar in a heatproof bowl and whisk over a pan of gently simmering water until thick and foamy. Transfer the egg mixture to a food-mixer bowl and whisk at high speed until cold and thick.

The rest is easy! Gently fold the cooled sugar reduction into the egg mixture with a whisk and then carefully fold in the whipped cream. Remove the ice-cold container from the freezer, fill with the parfait and freeze until set, overnight if possible. It can be kept frozen for up to two weeks. Serve with fingers of My Mum's Shortbread.

POPPY SEED AND CINNAMON PARFAIT

This unusual parfait is very simple to make and perfect with poached fruits such as cherries, plums, peaches and even Medjool dates. Its dense texture and distinct flavour are a real joy to eat and one of my favourites from years ago.

35 g (1¼ oz) poppy seeds
100 ml (3½ fl oz) whole milk
1 cinnamon stick
4 large egg yolks, plus 1 large egg
2 pinches of ground cinnamon
150 g (5½ oz) castor sugar
30 ml (2 tablespoons) dark rum
300 ml (½ pint) double cream,
    lightly whipped

serves 6–8

Wet a 450 g (1 lb) loaf tin and line it with cling film. Lightly grind the poppy seeds with a rolling pin on a chopping board or in a pestle and mortar. Alternatively, you could grind them in a spice grinder; take care, though, as all you want is to crush them enough to get the flavour out, not to reduce them to powder.

Place them in a saucepan and add the milk and cinnamon stick. Bring to the boil and cover and leave to simmer for 10 minutes. Strain through a fine sieve, reserving the seeds.

Place the egg yolks, egg, ground cinnamon, sugar and rum in a heatproof bowl and, using an electric hand-whisk, whisk over a pan of gently simmering water until thick, cooked and foamy (this will take about 10 minutes).

Pour the mixture into the bowl of a food mixer if possible, and whisk on a high speed until cold and very thick. Fold the egg mixture into the whipped cream, along with the poppy seeds.

Spoon into the lined loaf tin, cover with another piece of cling film and freeze overnight or keep in the freezer for up to a couple of weeks. The next day, turn the parfait out of the tin, remove the cling film and cut into thick slices.

RHUBARB PARFAIT

It's quite difficult to halve this recipe so I make two parfaits – and I can guarantee you that they won't stay in the freezer very long once you have tasted this very subtle and very easy parfait.

Forced (new-season) rhubarb is the best for this parfait, maincrop tends to be very green and doesn't have the subtlety of flavour, or the impact of colour, that new-season rhubarb possesses.

400 g (14 oz) new-season
  rhubarb, cut into 2 cm
  (¾-inch) pieces
juice of 1 large lemon
4 egg whites, at room
  temperature
2 pinches of cream of tartar
200 g (7 oz) unrefined castor
  sugar
300 ml (½ pint) double cream,
  lightly whipped

TO SERVE
poached rhubarb
Macaroons (page 122)

makes two 450 g (1 lb) loaf tins

Lightly wet two 450 g (1 lb) loaf tins and then line with cling film. Place the rhubarb and lemon juice in a pan and cook over a low heat for 10 minutes until you have a stringy purée. Remove from the heat and allow to cool.

Whisk the egg whites with the cream of tartar on a medium speed until thick and foamy (see 'Whisking egg whites' on page 127). Add the castor sugar and continue to whisk on a medium speed until firm and glossy, but do not over whisk.

Fold the cooled purée into the egg whites and then quickly fold this mixture into the double cream before the acid from the rhubarb curdles the cream. Spoon into the lined loaf tins, smooth out the top to flatten, then cover with cling film and freeze overnight or keep for up to two weeks.

To serve, unwrap and cut into thick slices. Serve with a little poached rhubarb and Macaroons.

MALT LOAF PARFAIT

As children we were often fed malt loaf, as it was cheap and very good for you. I really like it, it's great just sliced and spread with cold butter. Malt loaf has fallen out of fashion over the past few years and is one of those foods you see all the time in the supermarket but never really know what to do with. Well, look no further, here is a fantastic dessert, quick and very moreish.

This recipe makes a lot but it isn't really feasible to make it in a smaller quantity (for some reason, some recipes are like this). Just make it and freeze it in two containers; it keeps fine for a month.

175 g (6 oz) malt loaf

8 eggs, separated

250 g (9 oz) unrefined castor sugar

a very small pinch of cream of tartar

75 g (2¾ oz) unrefined icing sugar, sifted

600 ml (1 pint) double cream, very lightly whipped

biscuits or Macaroons (page 122), to serve

serves 6–8

Put the malt loaf into a food processor and blitz to make a fine crumb – it will stick together but don't worry. Place the egg yolks in the bowl of a food mixer. Put the castor sugar and 150 ml (¼ pint) of cold water in a pan and bring to the boil. Once boiling, leave to boil for 5 minutes exactly, no more no less – I use a small digital timer. Once the sugar and water have been boiling for 2 minutes, set the mixer to medium speed.

After 5 minutes, take the sugar and water off the stove, turn the mixer up to full speed and pour the syrup on to the egg yolks. Continue whisking until the mixture is thick, foamy and cold.

When the egg mixture is cold, lightly whisk the egg whites with the cream of tartar, until foamy but not grainy, and then add the icing sugar and whisk well. Remove the bowl from the machine, add the malt loaf and break up carefully with a spatula. Fold in the lightly whipped cream and, finally, the egg whites. Pour into two containers and freeze overnight or for up to two weeks. That's it. Serve with biscuits or Macaroons.

CARAMELISED CROISSANT PARFAIT

This is my variation of the very famous and much copied brown bread ice cream. It came about quite by chance, because I needed to use up the all-butter croissants left over from breakfast.

2 large all-butter croissants,
about 140 g (5 oz) total
weight
2.5 ml (½ teaspoon) grated
nutmeg
2.5 ml (½ teaspoon) ground
mixed spice
85 g (3 oz) dark brown
muscovado sugar

FOR THE MERINGUE
4 large egg whites
75 g (2¾ oz) castor sugar
75 g (2¾ oz) light brown soft
sugar
250 ml (5 fl oz) whipping cream
juice and finely grated zest of
1 lemon

Raspberry Sauce (page 227),
to serve

Preheat the oven to 180°C/350°F/Gas Mark 4. Lightly wet a 900 g (2 lb) loaf tin and then line with cling film (the water helps you line the tin more easily). Pop the croissants into a food processor and blitz to make fine breadcrumbs. Add the spices and muscovado sugar and blitz again very briefly, just to mix together.

Tip the crumbs on to a large baking sheet, spread out evenly and then bake for about 8–10 minutes, or until golden brown and producing a wonderful aroma – keep an eye on the crumbs as they can burn very quickly. Once browned, remove from the oven and cool.

Place the egg whites in a very clean bowl and whisk until they have a thick and creamy look to them but are not grainy (see 'Whisking egg whites' on page 127). At this point, add the castor sugar and continue to whisk on a high speed until glossy and shiny, then add the light brown sugar and whisk again until very thick. This will take about 5–6 minutes.

Whip the cream to soft peaks. Fold the whipped cream into the meringue, along with the croissant crumbs and lemon juice and zest. Spoon into the lined loaf tin and cover with a piece of cling film. Freeze overnight or for a couple of weeks.

When frozen, unwrap and cut the parfait into slices. Serve with a tart raspberry sauce.

FROZEN BLACKCURRANT MOUSSE

This is a good way of making ice cream without a machine – it's quick and easy. Make it with other summer berries, such as strawberries and raspberries, but for these you may need to reduce the sugar as they are sweeter than blackcurrants.

350 g (12 oz) blackcurrants

4 egg whites

a pinch of cream of tartar

125 g (4½ oz) golden
    castor sugar

250 ml (5 fl oz) double cream,
    lightly whipped, plus extra
    to serve

a few summer berries, to serve

serves 4–6

Blitz the blackcurrants in a food processor to make a purée and then sieve to remove the pips. Line a lightly oiled 1 kg (2 lb) loaf tin with cling film.

Next, whisk the egg whites with the cream of tartar until lightly foamy but holding their own weight. Add half the sugar and beat until firm and glossy, then add the rest of the sugar and whisk until very firm.

Fold the cream into the meringue, then add the purée and carefully fold together well, but do not over-mix. Pour the mixture into the lined loaf tin, cover with cling film and freeze overnight. Or keep in the freezer for a couple of weeks. Unwrap and slice with a hot knife. Serve with a few summer berries and a little whipped double cream.

SORBETS AND GRANITAS

The great chef Escoffier once wrote about sorbets: 'Sherbets and their derivative preparations consist of light, barely-congealed ices, served after the entrées; they serve in freshening the stomach; preparing it properly to receive the roast.' As an apprentice, no large meal I helped to prepare would be served without the obligatory sorbet course. This custom seems to have fallen by the wayside. The only time I would contemplate serving a sorbet course now is on Christmas day, as the menu is not only very large, but also very filling!

Nowadays most sorbets are eaten as puddings or desserts, and are one of the most pleasurable things to eat and make. No dish brings out the natural perfume and flavour of ripe fruit better than a sorbet. Not only that, but you always end up with stunning colours too. Yorkshire forced rhubarb makes the best-coloured sorbet by far.

Quinces are a very English fruit and I cook a lot of them. They seem to have been forgotten and it's a real shame. Once used in huge amounts by medieval cooks, they are a real joy to cook with and eat. One or two of these delightful fruit placed in a bowl will perfume the whole room. The only problem is they must be gently simmered or baked to render them suitable for a sorbet. Here I bake them first, which intensifies their unique flavour.

Not that sorbet-making is limited to fruit and syrup however. Nowadays chefs seem to make anything into a sorbet. Chocolate, coconut, tomato, and avocado, to name just a few, are all popular and can actually be quite nice if made correctly. A lot of professional chefs frown upon savoury sorbets. I'm not too sure about this. On the one hand they can taste frankly awful, but in skilled hands they can be very interesting. My colleague Heston Blumenthal from The Fat Duck at Bray has spent a lot of time experimenting with savoury sorbets and ice cream and has come up with some really different and startling concoctions such as bacon and egg ice cream. Escoffier would not be a happy man.

STOCK SYRUP

The reason why I make stock or sugar syrup is that it gives a wonderful finished texture to any ice cream or sorbet. The glucose helps the sugar chill in a more stable form; if you don't use glucose then the texture is grainy and the ice cream or sorbet is not velvety smooth.

There are a few commercial inverted sugars on the market, Staboline or Trimoline are two that I have used and still do, but good old-fashioned liquid glucose from chemists also does a satisfactory job. I find I have to add a little more liquid glucose to get a perfect result, just experiment and you'll soon get the knack.

125 g (4½ oz) granulated sugar
60 g (2¼ oz) Staboline,
    Trimoline or liquid glucose

makes 250 ml (8 fl oz)

Pour 150 ml (¼ pint) of cold water into a pan. Weigh the sugar out on to the tray of the scales and make a small indentation in the middle. Place the jar of liquid glucose in the microwave and heat on medium power for a few seconds or until the liquid is soft and runny. Pour the warmed liquid glucose on to the sugar, weighing out as much as you need by adding the desired weight to the weight of the sugar – this way the glucose stays on the sugar and not stuck to the scale pan, which can be a real pain.

Carefully add the sugar and liquid glucose to the water and then heat to bring to the boil. Remove from the hob, cover and allow to cool. Keep covered in the fridge, where it can be stored indefinitely.

TAMARILLO SORBET

This rather unusual fruit has been around for centuries, but only in the past few years has it become readily available – and quite trendy. Originally from South America, the tree tomato or tamarillo is now grown in East Africa and the North Island of New Zealand, to name just a couple of places. The fruit says 'eat me' when you look at it but, if you were to take a bite you would probably spit it out straight away. The flesh needs to be very ripe to be eaten, the best way to tell if a tamarillo is ready is by the colour, which turns from deep orange to deep purply crimson, and if the fruit is very soft to the touch.

Tamarillos can be poached or roasted in a hot oven, but are full of seeds; I'm not a great fan of them cooked this way. Married with rich meats such as venison, hare and game, a little tamarillo purée really livens up sauces, cutting strong flavours really well. But for me, there really is only one way to enjoy them and that's in a wonderfully coloured and deeply flavoured sorbet. Just great on its own or with a little poached or fresh fruit, such as pears or apricots, and a syrup.

6 ripe tamarillos, weighing about
  600 g (1 lb 5 oz) in total
500 ml (18 fl oz) Stock Syrup
  (opposite, make a double
  quantity)
5 ml (1 teaspoon) egg white
juice of 1 large lemon

makes 1.2 litres (2 pints)

Place a container in the freezer to pre-chill. Top and tail the tamarillos, then carefully pare away the skin with a sharp knife. Place the fruit in a liquidiser and add the stock syrup. Blitz until you have a thick purée but take care not to go on for too long so as to avoid splitting the seeds, as this sometimes makes the purée a little bitter.

Pour the purée into a fine strainer and push through into a bowl with a ladle. Add the egg white. (This helps to bind everything together and give a nice fudgy edge to the finished sorbet. I like to add a little egg white to all my sorbets, it really does make a difference especially to juice sorbets such as lemon or lime.)

Taste the mixture and add as much of the lemon juice as necessary. Pour into an ice-cream maker and churn according to the instructions until thick. Spoon into the pre-chilled container and store in the freezer, where it will keep well for a couple of weeks.

BRAMLEY APPLE SORBET

The unique taste of this recipe reminds me of the good old-fashioned stewed apples and custard we ate as children. My mother would always stew apples and leave them to cool, and make the custard far too early and leave that to cool also. So for years I never had hot stewed apples and custard! Even now I prefer them cold, but what a perfect combination.

Well, back to this recipe. Bramleys are a wonderful apple to cook with, contrary to some people's view, and the 'marmalade' they turn into, the technical term for the stewed apple, has a depth of flavour when stewed that no other apple seems to have. Howgate Wonder does run a close second but, for me, Bramleys are the best for stewing.

2 large Bramley apples,
    weighing about
    750–800 g (1 lb 10 oz–
    1 lb 12 oz) in total, peeled,
    cored and cut into 2 cm
    (¾-inch) pieces
juice of 1 large lemon
2 pinches of citric acid powder
250 ml (5 fl oz) Stock Syrup
    (page 182)
½ teaspoon egg white

Put a container in the freezer to pre-chill. Place the apples, lemon juice and citric acid in a pan with about 250 ml (5 fl oz) of cold water and bring to the boil. Turn down the heat and gently stew over a low heat until pulpy. You should end up with about 500 g (1 lb 2 oz) apples in total.

Remove from the heat, carefully pour into a liquidiser and blitz until smooth. Spoon into a bowl, add the stock syrup and whisk well then leave to cool.

When cool, add the egg white and whisk well again. Strain through a fine sieve then pour into the ice-cream maker and churn until firm and frozen. Transfer to the pre-chilled container and store in the freezer, where it will keep for a couple of weeks.

PINK CHAMPAGNE SORBET WITH DOUBLE CREAM

Most people think of sorbets as made with just water, flavouring and sugar. Well, that's right as far as it goes but you can also add a twist to sorbets by including cream, which makes the texture smooth, creamy and silky. Here is a very clever recipe from a chap called Allan Garth, a chef I used to work for years ago. It's very simple and very refreshing and a great way to end a heavy meal.

I like to serve coconut biscuits or Brandy Snaps (page 271) with this sorbet.

375 ml (13 fl oz) pink
    Champagne
375 ml (13 fl oz) freshly squeezed
    orange juice, strained
375 ml (13 fl oz) Stock Syrup
    (page 182) made with 185 g
    (6½ oz) granulated sugar,
    225 ml (8 fl oz) water and
    90 g (3¼ oz) liquid glucose
juice of 2 lemons
brandy
400 ml (14 fl oz) double cream,
    lightly whipped
coconut biscuits, to serve

makes 1.5 litres (2³/₄ pints)

Place a container in the freezer to pre-chill. Pour the Champagne, orange juice, stock syrup, lemon juice and a dash of brandy into a bowl and whisk together. Churn the mixture in an ice-cream maker until thick and frozen or just freeze until thick and slushy.

Remove the mixture from the machine and place in a cold bowl. Add the whipped cream and whisk together – the mixture might turn lumpy but that's quite normal. Spoon into the pre-chilled container, seal the lid and freeze overnight; any lumps will disappear. You can keep it in the freezer for a couple of weeks. Scoop the sorbet out and serve in glasses, with coconut biscuits.

MANGO SORBET

Made into a sorbet, mango takes on a dense, fudgy texture that no other fruit has. I'm not too sure why, but the result is fantastic. I have tried to replicate this glorious texture in other sorbets by using all sorts of tricks, including starches and egg white, but never really attained a good result. The closest is gelatine, melted and added to white chocolate sorbet; this not only helps the texture but also helps hold the sorbet in warm weather.

For this sorbet to taste its best, you must use very ripe, perfumed mangoes, you can also add a touch of medium white wine to the purée if you want, for an extra twist of flavour.

375 g (13 oz) fresh mango flesh (about 2 medium, ripe mangoes, free of skin and stone)

375 ml (13 fl oz) Stock Syrup (page 182), made with 185 g (6½ oz) granulated sugar, 225 ml (8 fl oz) water and 90 g (3¼ oz) liquid glucose

juice of 1 large lemon

serves 4–6

Place a container in the freezer to pre-chill. Place the mango in the liquidiser along with the stock syrup. Blitz until smooth and then add the lemon juice. At this point, remove the jug from the liquidizer, taste the purée and see what you think; it may need a touch more lemon juice to balance the sweetness. As there are about 1300 varieties of mango, all will taste slightly different, so it's good to check.

If you are happy, then churn the mixture in an ice-cream maker until frozen, thick and shiny. Transfer to the pre-chilled container and store in a freezer for a couple of weeks.

TECHNIQUES

MAKING THE PERFECT SORBET

INGREDIENTS FOR SORBET

Sorbets can be enriched with double cream, without losing their unique fruit flavour. Champagne mixed with fresh orange juice and double cream makes a surprisingly light, refreshing sorbet. Gin and tonic, Campari and grapefruit and white wine all work well too.

ADDING SYRUP TO SORBET

1 The best tip I can give people when it comes to making sorbet is to taste, taste and keep tasting. Different fruit, chocolate and so on have different levels of sweetness, so it's hard to give an exact recipe. I have tried and tested these recipes many times and I have come up with what I think is just right, but use your common sense and judge for yourselves. If you think a recipe needs a touch more syrup then add it.

2 The secret with sorbet is to get the perfect balance of flavour, sweetness and dead smooth, almost fudgy consistency. Far too often sorbet is too crystalline, almost crunchy. This is due to insufficient use of sugar or glucose syrup or, in some cases, alcohol. However if you use too much syrup, the sorbet will be too sweet – it's a fine line. Escoffier said that, 'Fruit sorbets are generally prepared from the juices and syrups of aqueous fruits. Fruit purées are scarcely suited to this mode of procedure and they are only resorted to in exceptional cases.' What he meant, in my view, is that a fruit syrup has a wonderful perfume and clarity of flavour and that it is easy to freeze, unlike a thick, grainy purée with added sugar.

MAKING GRANITAS

Granitas are a no-hassle type of sorbet. They can be made well in advance without an ice-cream machine and are extremely simple to do. Watermelon mixed with a little alcohol is probably my favourite. It's a wonderfully refreshing way to end a meal and to me is the only way to get the best flavour out of a watermelon without the pesky seeds.

CREAMY COCONUT SORBET

This is a little different from the normal smooth sorbets. I think it's sometimes nice to ring the changes and this sorbet has a nice coconutty, grainy texture. This is a deliciously rich accompaniment to Coconut Tart or Bitter Chocolate Tart (pages 60 and 80). It's also very good with fresh fruit.

200 g (7 oz) block of creamed
    coconut, cut into small cubes
300 ml (½ pint) boiling water
250 ml (5 fl oz) Stock Syrup
    (page 182)
100 ml (3½ fl oz) Malibu liqueur
100 ml (3½ fl oz) single cream
15 ml (1 tablespoon) egg white

Leave a container in the freezer to pre-chill. Place the creamed coconut in a heatproof bowl, pour over the boiling water and stir until dissolved. Leave to cool.

Mix together the cooled coconut cream, stock syrup, Malibu, cream and egg white. Pour into the ice-cream maker and churn until smooth and frozen. Transfer to the pre-chilled container and store in the freezer for a couple of weeks.

NEW-SEASON RHUBARB SORBET

This beautifully coloured sorbet is probably one of my favourites. New-season rhubarb is perfect for sorbets, poaching or oven-baking. It's only around for a few short weeks in the early part of the year so make the most of it. It will freeze well if blanched first, but I like to bottle mine in a light syrup.

The good thing about this recipe is that everything can be cooked together in one pan, liquidised and then churned in an ice-cream maker.

650 g (1 lb 7 oz) new-season
    rhubarb, cut into 2 cm
    (¾-inch) pieces
225 g (8 oz) unrefined castor
    sugar
juice of 1 large lemon
180 g (6 oz) liquid glucose

Put a container in the freezer to pre-chill. Place all the ingredients in a pan, mix well and gently heat until the sugar starts to melt. Turn up the heat until the fruit simmers and then cook with the lid on (this keeps all the moisture in the pan) for about 10 minutes or until the fruit is nicely puréed. Spoon into a liquidiser and blitz until you have a very fine purée. Leave to cool.

Spoon into the ice-cream maker and churn until thick and frozen. Transfer to the pre-chilled container and store in the freezer for up to two weeks.

WHITE WINE GRANITA WITH BLOOD ORANGES

Blood oranges always fascinated me as a child: they had such a beautiful colour and were only around for such a short time. Apart from mandarins, these are by far the finest dessert oranges. The two most common varieties are Moro and Tarocco and Sicily remains the best area for growing these heavenly little oranges.

The redness is due to a combination of cold nights and mild sunny days, which causes a chemical reaction in the skin. Blood oranges themselves make a great sorbet and the juice combines very well with a little butter and fish stock to make the most sublime sauce to serve with roasted scallops.

115 g (4 oz) castor sugar
30 ml (2 tablespoons) liquid
    glucose
350 ml (12 fl oz) dry white wine
juice of 1 lemon and 1 lime
8 blood oranges

serves 4

Put a container in the freezer to pre-chill. Place the sugar, glucose and 300 ml (½ pint) of cold water in a stainless-steel saucepan and dissolve over a low heat. (The glucose gives a crystalline finish to the granita.) Stir in the wine and lime and lemon juice and transfer to the container. Freeze overnight or for up to a week.

When ready to serve, peel and segment the oranges, removing every bit of pith and all the pips and reserving any juice that comes out. Pile the segments into four bowls. Remove the granita from the freezer and scrape off the top layer with a spatula, so you end up with a pile of fine crystals. Pile on top of the segments and add a little blood orange juice. Serve straight away.

WATERMELON GRANITA

Watermelon is one of those fruits that look and taste wonderful but is a real pain to eat – those blessed pips are very annoying. Here you get all the flavour without the pips.

350 ml (12 fl oz) white sweet
    dessert wine
45 ml (3 tablespoons) liquid
    glucose
120 g (4¼ oz) castor sugar
1 watermelon, weighing about
    3 kg (6 lb 8 oz)
juice of 1 lemon

serves 4

Place a container in the freezer to pre-chill. Place the wine, glucose and sugar in a stainless-steel saucepan and dissolve over a low heat. The glucose gives a soft crystalline finish to the granita.

Cut the watermelon in half. Scoop the flesh out of one of the halves and place it in a food processor. Blitz and then pass through a sieve to remove all the pips. Measure the purée, you should end up with about 600 ml (1 pint). If there is not enough, process a little more watermelon or top up with a little cold water.

Stir the melon purée and lemon juice into the white-wine syrup, pour into the pre-chilled container and freeze overnight or keep it in the freezer for a week. Cut the remaining melon into wedges or chunks.

Remove the granita from the freezer, scrape off the top layer with a spoon or spatula, so you end up with a pile of fine crystals. Serve straight away, in a glass bowl with the remaining fresh watermelon.

BAKED QUINCE SORBET

Baked quinces take on a beautiful pinky-orange hue, and although baking does take a little time it is well worth the wait. All the juices and flavour are kept inside the tightly wrapped foil and there is no need to skin them either; I think the skin gives the finished sorbet a nice speckled finish. I also like to bake quinces, scoop out the tough, grainy centres and serve then warm with clotted cream and a sprinkling of nutmeg or cinnamon.

Most supermarkets and grocers will start to stock quinces by late September and they are still around in late January, though by then they are imported from Turkey and Iran.

2 medium perfumed quinces,
    weighing about 600 g
      (1 lb 5 oz) in total
250 ml (5 fl oz) Stock Syrup
    (page 182)
juice of 2 large lemons

serves 6–8

Preheat the oven to 200°C/400°F/Gas Mark 6. Wrap the quinces in two layers of foil and place on a baking sheet. Pop in the oven and cook for about 1 hour. The reason I'm a bit vague here is that, having cooked this recipe four times, I have concluded that all quinces cook at different times. So I took the average of the four and it came out at about an hour; just use your common sense; when the quinces are cooked, there should be no resistance at all when they are squeezed. When ready, leave to cool completely.

Place an empty container in the freezer to chill. Cut the quinces in half and remove the grainy, tough core. Place the fruit in a liquidiser and add the stock syrup and lemon juice. Blitz until smooth and transfer straight into the ice-cream machine.

Churn until frozen – this will take about 15–20 minutes – then transfer to the pre-chilled container and store in the freezer, where it will keep for a couple of weeks.

New Recipe

BLACKCURRANT SORBET

This is one of the most intensely-flavoured sorbets you can make, with a rich colour and a deliciously refreshing flavour. The secret is to freeze the blackcurrants first - this releases the wonderful colour and taste. It's the perfect foil to a creamy rich pudding such as the Baked Mango Cream (page 23). You can buy good-quality blackcurrant sorbet, but this recipe is definitely worth a try.

650 g (1 lb 7 oz) frozen
    blackcurrants (or fresh
    then freeze yourself), then
    defrosted
200 g (7 oz) castor sugar
juice of 1 large lemon
180 g (6 oz) liquid glucose

**suitable for a 2-pint ice cream
machine, serves 4–6**

Spoon the defrosted blackcurrants into a liquidiser. Add the sugar and lemon juice and blitz to a very fine purée. Pass through a fine sieve into a bowl. You may need to repeat this procedure.

Put the glucose in a pan and warm over a very gentle heat, then add to the purée in the bowl. Mix well then spoon into the ice cream machine and churn until thick and frozen. Transfer to a pre-chilled container and freeze.

FRESH PINEAPPLE SORBET

The two points to remember about this sorbet are to use ripe, sweet pineapples to get a satisfactory result (Del Monte brand is usually reliable), and make sure to liquidise very well, or the finished sorbet will have a grainy texture.

500 g (1 lb 2 oz) cored, skinned
    sweet pineapple (prepared
    weight), roughly
    chopped
250 ml (5 fl oz) Stock Syrup
    (page 182)
a pinch of citric acid
5 ml (1 teaspoon) egg white

serves 4–6

Place a container in the freezer to pre-chill. Put the pineapple, syrup and citric acid in a liquidiser and blitz until very smooth. Pour into a bowl and whisk in the egg white.

Transfer to an ice-cream maker and churn until thick and frozen. Spoon into the pre-chilled container and store in the freezer for a couple of weeks.

QUICK PUDDINGS

I love quick puddings. They are a great way of getting a hit of sugar with the minimum of fuss. All the puds in this chapter are extremely simple and rely on ingredients that are widely available in a supermarket. It's amazing what you can achieve with a few bits and bobs and a little thought.

Knickerbocker glory is an anything-goes recipe – just as long as you include huge amounts of ice cream, chocolate sauce, sponge and lashings of cream. Another favourite, along the same lines, is banana split. As kids, we sometimes ate at a restaurant in Dover called The Britannia. It was a real treat. All the greats were on the menu: prawn cocktail with a tomato rose, steak au poivre (cooked at the table of course) and chicken Maryland, to name but a few. The dessert course was the best bit – banana split in all its glory. I can still recall looking forward to the pudding so much that by the time it arrived, it was almost an anticlimax. I remember the shape of the thick glass dish, and the two long-handled spoons were great fun. Nowadays banana split is frowned upon. I think that's a bit sad, so I've set to work re-inventing this classic.

A lot of these puds involve cooking fruit very quickly and adding a little cream and sugar. I have cooked the sautéed pears and apples in Calvados for some 25 years. It's always quick, easy and very tasty. More up to date are the Hot Plums on Toast, and the Fresh Pineapple with Chilli and Vanilla Syrup.

No quick puddings section would be complete without Angel Cake in there somewhere. The soft, crumbly, delicate sponge with its pastel colours is probably the most vivid of all my childhood memories. It can be used as a base for trifle instead of Swiss roll (most Swiss rolls, I'm afraid, don't taste like the old-fashioned ones). Nowadays I top Angel Cake with fresh raspberries and Bird's custard as a quick pud for the kids and they love it.

KNICKERBOCKER GLORY

There are so many varieties of this sweet that there really is no set format. You just need ice cream, raspberry sauce, chocolate sauce, chopped nuts, whipped double cream and Swiss roll. Vanilla ice cream is the best, perhaps with a touch of, say, fudge, to add a little extra twist.

The only way to serve this is in very tall glasses with very long spoons. This is fun and makes the whole eating experience even nicer.

4 x 1 cm (½-inch) slices of Swiss
    roll, cut into small pieces
2 scoops of fudge ice cream
55 g (2 oz) chopped walnuts
Bitter Chocolate Sauce (page
    225) or good-quality ready-
    made chocolate sauce
Raspberry Sauce (page 227)
4 scoops of good-quality
    vanilla ice cream
very lightly whipped
    double cream
a few 'cigarette' biscuits

serves 2

Put some of the chopped Swiss roll in the bottoms of two sundae glasses. Add a ball of fudge ice cream to each. Sprinkle over a few nuts and a generous slug each of raspberry and chocolate sauce. Add the rest of the sponge and two balls of vanilla ice cream to each glass.

Finally, top with whipped cream, more nuts and the rest of the two sauces. Pop in the cigarette biscuits and get stuck in! It really is as easy as that.

BANANA SPLITS

A classic pudding. In the late sixties and seventies, the banana split was the dessert to have in posh restaurants. Sadly it has become a bit of a joke, which I think is unfair because its combination of flavours and textures is very well balanced. Forget the calories and enjoy it!

If you don't want to use brandy-snap baskets, just serve in a dessert glass. Apple bananas are baby bananas the size of a small courgette, with a faintly ripe apple flavour. Ordinary bananas work just as well, of course.

125 g (4½ oz) granulated sugar

12 pecan or walnut halves

250 ml (8 fl oz) whipping cream, whipped

4 brandy-snap baskets (optional)

Raspberry Sauce (page 227)

8 scoops of good-quality vanilla ice cream

8 apple bananas

Bitter Chocolate Sauce (page 225)

icing sugar, to decorate

serves 4

To make the caramel, place the granulated sugar in a thick-bottomed pan. Add 45 ml (3 tablespoons) of water and heat to dissolve the sugar, then bring to the boil (see 'Making caramel' on page 167). Cook until the caramel starts to turn a pale golden-brown colour; then remove from the heat and drop in the nuts. Swirl around and then, using a fork, lift out the nuts one at a time and place on baking parchment or greased greaseproof paper. Leave to cool completely.

To serve, place a small blob of whipped cream on a plate and top with a brandy-snap basket, if you are using them. Spoon a little of the raspberry sauce around the biscuit and then scoop two balls of ice cream into the basket (be careful as the biscuits are very delicate). Cut the bananas in half lengthways and divide between the baskets. Decorate with more whipped cream, caramel nut halves and a drizzle of chocolate sauce. Dust with icing sugar and serve straight away.

HOT PLUMS ON TOAST

A different way to eat plums – the secret is to use the crust from the loaf and to leave the juices to soak into the bread once cooked. I use Victoria plums for this dish as they are slightly firmer and less sweet than ruby red ones.

25 g (1 oz) unsalted butter

25 g (1 oz) soft light brown sugar

juice of ½ lime

1 thick slice of bread, from
    crust end

3 Victoria plums, halved
    and stoned

serves I

Preheat the oven to 220°C/425°F/Gas Mark 7. Gently heat the butter and sugar together in a pan until melted. Increase the heat and bring to the boil. Add the lime juice, remove from the heat and stir well.

Sit the crust of bread on a baking sheet and arrange the plums on top. Spoon over half the lime and butter mixture and then place the tray in the oven and bake for 10 minutes. After this time, spoon over the rest of the mixture and cook for a further 10 minutes or until the plums are just soft and the bread is browning nicely.

Remove from the oven and allow to cool for 5 minutes. Carefully lift the plum toast off the tray using a fish slice and serve at once.

WARM PEARS WITH ALMONDS AND VANILLA SUGAR

Pears are a very versatile fruit – in Britain alone, there are something like 100 varieties, and apparently about 6000 varieties grown worldwide, although you only really see a couple of dozen or so used these days. By the sixteenth century, there were nearly 250 varieties available in Italy, and 1500 in America alone. Today, though, you will see only the occasional unusual variety – and I have to say that the supermarkets have done their bit here, in trying to get people to buy an alternative to the familiar ones you see day in day out. Good ones for this dish include Comice, Red Bartlett and Williams Bon Chretien. Do look out for Anjou, a very juicy variety, and Packham's Triumph, with sweet succulent flesh.

With this recipe, taste the fruit first and then adjust the amount of sugar to taste: there is nothing worse than an over-sweet dish

4 ripe Williams, Red Bartlett
    or Comice pears
40 g (1½ oz) unsalted butter
1 vanilla pod, split
about 55 g (2 oz) castor sugar
finely grated zest and juice of
    1 large orange
about 300 ml (½ pint) double
    cream
15 ml (1 tablespoon) finely
    chopped fresh mint
40 g (1½ oz) flaked almonds,
    lightly browned in a hot oven

serves 4

Remove the base from the pears, then carefully remove the skin with a sharp vegetable peeler, trying to keep to the natural shape of the pear. Cut each pear into six pieces and remove the core and seeds.

Heat the butter in a sauté or deep frying pan until it starts to foam. Scrape in the seeds from the vanilla pod, add the pod and sugar and then add the pears and gently brown in the butter on all sides.

Add the orange zest and juice and cook for 15–20 seconds, then pour in the cream and warm through; the cream will thicken straight away. Do not overcook the pears or they will disintegrate. Just as the cream and juice simmer, remove from the heat and add the chopped mint. Taste and adjust if necessary by adding more sugar or orange juice.

Spoon into warm bowls and sprinkle over the almonds. You can increase the amount of cream you use if you want to; I like the nice balance of this amount.

SAUTÉED APPLES IN CALVADOS

There are about 250 varieties of apple in Britain today. A lot of once out of favour, older varieties are now being grown again, which is good to see: George Cave, a crimson blush with sweet flesh; Laxton's Superb, with a yellow skin and deep sweet flavour that is great with cheese; Howgate Wonder, the best baking apple by far, are all being sold again and about time.

I use a lot of Granny Smith apples in my cooking: they are a tart, firm apple that can stand up to all sorts of harsh treatment – whether it's being plunged into caramel, baked in a pie or even roasted in the oven, a Granny Smith will fare well. Cox's are not only a superb eating apple but a great apple to cook lightly, or even to pickle, and hardly need any sugar at all. The only thing to take care with is not to lose the wonderful aroma that the Cox has by overcooking it. This pudding is a real favourite of mine and a great light ending to the meal.

4 large Cox's apples
55 g (2 oz) unsalted butter
20 ml (4 teaspoons) castor sugar
200 ml (7 fl oz) Calvados
60 ml (4 tablespoons) double
 cream
30 ml (2 tablespoons) chopped
 fresh lemon balm or mint

serves 4

Top and tail the apples and cut into quarters. Carefully remove the skin with a small paring knife and then cut each quarter into three or four thin slices. You will have to work quickly so the apples do not turn brown; remember that you cannot put them into water or add lemon juice to them or they will not brown in the butter.

Heat a large non-stick sauté or frying pan. Add the butter and, once it starts to foam, add the apples and sugar and toss around so they colour slightly; do not overcook. Pour in the Calvados – be aware that once the Calvados is hot it may ignite straight away so do take care. It looks good on the telly but believe me it can come as quite a shock. If it does ignite then do not panic, it will soon burn off.

Add the double cream and swirl around until fully incorporated and then cook until the apples are cooked but still have slight bite to them; do take care as they will turn into mush very quickly indeed. Finally pop in the chopped lemon balm or mint. Serve in deep bowls.

GRILLED FIGS WITH MULLED WINE SAUCE AND SABAYON

A strange combination but a very nice one. The secret is to use very ripe figs and just warm them through under a hot grill; do not overheat them or they will fall apart.

8 fresh, ripe figs

FOR THE SAUCE
600 ml (1 pint) full-bodied
    red wine
1 cinnamon stick
6 cloves
2.5 ml (½ teaspoon)
    freshly grated nutmeg
115 g (4 oz) castor sugar plus
    40 ml (8 teaspoons)
1 vanilla pod, split
finely grated zest and juice of
    1 lemon and 1 orange
40 g (1½ oz) cold unsalted
    butter, cubed

FOR THE SABAYON
3 large egg yolks
55 g (2 oz) castor sugar
50 ml (2 fl oz) white wine

serves 4

To make the sauce, place the wine, cinnamon, cloves, nutmeg, 115 g (4 oz) castor sugar, vanilla pod and lemon and orange zest and juice in a stainless-steel saucepan and reduce by two-thirds.

Whisk in the cold butter, cover and keep the sauce warm but not hot. Preheat the grill. Cut the figs in half lengthways and sprinkle 2.5 ml (½ teaspoon) castor sugar on to each half. Place under the hot grill and warm through for a maximum of 2–3 minutes. Meanwhile, place the sabayon ingredients in a bowl, and whisk over a pan of gently simmering water until thick and foamy.

To serve, place four fig halves in a bowl. Drizzle over some red wine sauce. Top with a spoon of the sabayon froth and eat straight away.

PASSION-FRUIT JELLY WITH SHORTBREAD

Passion-fruit basically fall into two categories, ripe and unripe. This small, intensely flavoured fruit is firm, and slightly green in appearance when under ripe, and when ripe starts to shrivel and loose its green hue. I prefer to use the fruit when they are older, you seem to get more juice out, and, the juice seems to be slightly sweeter.

A little juice from this fruit goes a long way and can overpower a dish very easily, so I add fresh orange juice to the passion-fruit to get a better balance.

3 gelatine leaves
8 passion-fruit
fresh orange juice (must be
    fresh), strained
about 115 g (4 oz) castor sugar

TO SERVE
8 fingers of My Mum's
    Shortbread (page 278)
clotted cream

serves 4

Soak the gelatine leaves in a little cold water until soft and pliable (see 'Dissolving gelatine' on page 99). Make sure the gelatine is soaked very well indeed: the smallest amount of un-soaked gelatine in the finished jelly is awful.

Cut the passion-fruit in half and remove all the seeds and juice with a teaspoon. Place in a food processor, not a liquidiser, which would purée the pips as well, leaving you with a black-speckled end product. Using a food processor on the pulse button will take the flesh from the seeds perfectly. Sieve the seeds and juice and take care to extract every last drop. Place the sieved juice in a measuring jug and top up to the 600 ml (1 pint) mark with fresh orange juice.

Place the gelatine in a small saucepan with a little of the juice mixture and melt gently over a low heat. Add castor sugar to taste to the juice (I've suggested 115 g/4 oz as a guideline, but taste and adjust to your own preference). Stir until dissolved; it's a bit of a pain but as we want to keep the taste as fresh as possible you should not warm any of the juice at all.

Add the dissolved gelatine to the juice, stir well and pour into a bowl to set. Chill well, preferably overnight. To serve, lightly break up with a spoon and spoon into tall glasses. Serve with shortbread and clotted cream.

DRY CIDER AND PERRY JELLY

A very simple and unusual dessert. I use perry, a traditional drink made from pears, with cider to give a very refreshing adult jelly.

It's also very nice to use two varieties of apple that are not normally spoken about, but which are now available in the supermarkets. They are slightly more expensive but well worth the extra cost.

300 ml (½ pint) dry cider
115 g (4 oz) castor sugar
3 gelatine leaves, soaked in
    cold water (see 'Dissolving
    gelatine' on page 99)
300 ml (½ pint) perry
1 Charles Ross apple
1 Russet apple
1 small, ripe mango
juice of ½ a lemon
a few autumn raspberries
    (optional)
clotted cream, to serve

serves 4-6

Pour the cider and sugar into a pan, heat until the sugar has dissolved and then bring to the boil. Remove from the heat and add the soaked gelatine. Once the gelatine has melted, add the perry and mix together, then pour into a shallow dish and allow to cool slightly.

Peel and core the apples and peel the mango. Cut the fruit into small pieces and stir into the cooled cider and perry. Finally, add the lemon juice and raspberries, if using, and stir well. Cover with cling film and chill until set. It's best to break the jelly up slightly before you serve it, so the fruit is dispersed when eaten. Spoon into glasses and top with a little clotted cream.

BLACKBERRY, PORRIDGE AND HONEY YOGURT

This is a great way to use up cold porridge. It is very refreshing and blackberries or any summer fruit will be delicious. Just try it!

140 g (5 oz) cooled, cooked
    porridge (made with no salt),
    broken up with a fork
100 g (3½ oz) Jordan's
    Original cereal
400 g (14 oz) sheep's milk yogurt
350 g (12 oz) fresh, very ripe
    blackberries
finely grated zest and juice of
    1 lime
85 g (3 oz) unrefined castor sugar
60 ml (4 tablespoons) runny
    honey

serves 4–6

Mix together the porridge, cereal and yogurt. Place the blackberries, lime juice and zest and castor sugar in a separate bowl then gently crush with a potato masher to break up the fruit very slightly. Carefully fold the blackberries into the porridge, so you end up with a 'ripple' effect.

Spoon into wide glasses or bowls, layering with honey. Chill for at least an hour and preferably overnight.

ANGEL CAKE WITH RASPBERRIES, MANGO AND CUSTARD

All kids love the taste and texture of angel cake. I adored it as a child. Here we surreptitiously add a little fruit by using canned mango. Fresh mangoes are fine, but a little expensive and sometimes not too ripe, so I always keep a can in the cupboard. You could also use leftover Saffron Cake (page 247), Chocolate Cup Cakes (page 81), Glazed Chocolate Cake (page 90) or Baby Bakewells (page 260) for this idea.

200 g can of mango slices,
    drained
1 angel cake, cut into 4 chunks
small punnet of fresh raspberries
two 150 g tubs of low-fat custard
sprinkles or silver balls,
    to decorate

serves 4 children

Divide the mango slices between four small bowls. Top each with a piece of sponge and then sprinkle over a few raspberries. Finally, spoon over the cold custard and dot with a few 'sprinkles' or silver balls. Who said kids' food is not delicious?

PANCAKES WITH BOTTLED BLUEB

*This is a nice way to serve pancakes and using bottled
dear grandmother used to cook with the fresh berries p
Trough of Bowland in Lancashire. I believe you could
Blackburn market some years ago. If anyone knows w
am desperate to find out if they are still around. They
very satisfactorily. Bottled blueberries are hard to mak
from the supermarket.*

FOR THE PANCAKES
2 eggs
100 g (3½ oz) plain white flour
a pinch of salt
a pinch of sugar
about 75 ml (2½ fl oz)
    whole milk
15 ml (1 tablespoon)
    vegetable oil

FOR THE FILLING
500 ml (18 fl oz) whole milk
4 egg yolks
150 g (5½ oz) castor sugar
75 g (3½ oz) plain white flour
finely grated zest of 1 lime
225 g (8 oz) bottled blueberries,
    drained well

FOR THE SABAYON
2 egg yolks
50 g (1¾ oz) castor sugar
60 ml (4 tablespoons) white wine

serves 4

First make the pan
sugar and half the
and whisk until yo

Heat the vegetable
smoking. Pour in
you have covered t
any small holes. C
brown the other si
pan and continue

To make the fillin
sugar together unt
Pour on the boilin
over a low heat, sti
lime zest. Pour int

When you come t
bowl. Add the set
quarter of the mix
sides and then the
with a small parce
the parcels in war
oven, or gently wa
the oven, cover th

Meanwhile, make
bowl, place over
and foamy. Spoo
with a blowtorch

SWEET SPICED NAAN BREAD WITH YOGURT AND ORANGES

*A great idea – it's different and unusual. Try it with all sorts of spices. The thicker greek-style yogurt
is best for this dish; if it's not available use a sheep's milk yogurt.*

300 ml (½ pint) dry cider
finely grated zest of 1 lime
10 ml (2 teaspoons) green
    cardamom pods
1.25 ml (½ teaspoon)
    ground cloves
1 vanilla pod, seeds removed
    and pod roughly chopped
115 g (4 oz) unsalted butter,
    softened
115 g (4 oz) unrefined dark
    muscovado sugar
2 large plain naan breads,
    about 150 g (5½ oz) each

TO SERVE
greek-style yogurt
orange segments

serves 4

Preheat the oven to 180°C/350°F Gas Mark 4. Place the lime zest, cardamom, cloves and vanilla seeds and pod in a spice grinder and blitz until smooth. (If you don't have a spice grinder, use the food processor or grind the spices with a rolling pin.) Tip into a bowl, add the butter and sugar and mix well.

Carefully slice the top layer off the top of the naan bread to reveal the spongy inside. Spread the spice and butter mixture right to the edges. Place on a non-stick baking sheet and bake for about 10 minutes, or until nicely browned. Remove from the oven and leave to cool and crispen. Cut into slices and serve with yogurt and orange segments.

209

LAVENDER SHORTBREAD WITH
AND FROMAGE FRAIS

I started experimenting with lavender when we started g
wonderful the smell is when fresh. I started to play arour
combination of strawberries, lavender and a very crumb

450 g (1 lb) small English
    strawberries
400 g (14 oz) fromage frais
juice of ½ lime
unrefined icing sugar, sifted
1 quantity of Lavender
    Shortbread (page 273)

serves 4

Hull and halve the str
fromage frais into and
taste with icing sugar.
just put all three item
themselves.

SABAYONS, SAUCES AND FROSTINGS

All the recipes in this section are essentially additions to spoon over, serve with or spread on a cake or pudding. They range from very light, perfumed sabayons (a frothy custard of egg yolk, sugar and wine which is related to the Italian Zabaglione and made by whisking the ingredients over simmerimg water and served warm or cold, as a dessert or a sauce) for poached fruits and hot puddings to cake coverings and frostings.

A lot of the time a great pudding or cake has one or two key elements that make the finished product sensational. Carrot cake without the fresh orange and cream cheese frosting is very dry and a bit boring. Twice-baked toffee sponge without toffee sauce is very nice – but add the sauce, and a little vanilla ice cream, and even a spoonful of thick double cream and you have one of the best puddings in the world. And this is the only exception to my rule of eating all fruit at room temperature – nothing could be nicer than very cold, beautifully ripe melon with a warm Beaumes de Venise sabayon on a hot summer's day.

Thinking up new and successful combinations of ingredients is very difficult and this is where the skill of professional chef comes in. Some of my own that I think are real crackers are: Cider Sabayon with warm apple puddings; fresh Rose-Petal Syrup with Almond Blancmange; and Baby Bakewells with Lime Water Icing.

Custards are a personal favourite of mine. I sometimes add flavourings such as maple syrup to good old-fashioned custard powder that I was brought up on and also to fresh custard made with fresh eggs and vanilla.

Syrups have always been a firm favourite with the British. A lot of the cordials you see now started many years ago. Syrups were not only made to preserve fruit juice, they were also turned into jellies and sherbets. Escoffier used syrups for his sorbets, dismissing fruit purées.

Various cake coverings are also touched on. I had actually forgotten how nice butter cream was – and I've adapted the recipe for this book. Just remember the golden rule: it's not what you eat...it's how much!

LEMON BALM AND BAY SYRUP

Pictured opposite is Poached Peaches with Lemon Balm and Bay Syrup (see page 144 for the Poached Peaches).

225 g (8 oz) granulated sugar
10 x 10 cm (4-inch) sprigs
    of fresh lemon balm, picked
    on a bright sunny day
3 small bay leaves, bruised
juice of ½ fresh lime

To make the syrup, place the sugar and 275 ml (9½ fl oz) of cold water together in a saucepan and dissolve over a low heat. Put the lemon balm and bay in a sealable jar and pour on the hot syrup. Stir in the lime juice and seal. Leave for a minimum of two days or up to one month in a cool place.

ROSEMARY FLOWER SYRUP

Rosemary flowers are normally in full bloom by the end of March for about two weeks and make the most delicate syrup. The golden rule when using all flowers in cooking is to make sure you pick them on a sunny day, when the pollen is dry and most fragrant; otherwise the syrup will taste dull.

150 g (5½ oz) granulated sugar
40 g (1½ oz) light brown
    soft sugar
about 25 rosemary flower heads

Place 350 ml (12 fl oz) of cold water and the two sugars in a pan and bring just to the boil. Place the flower heads in a heatproof, screw-top jar and pour on the syrup. Seal the jar and leave in a cool place for about a week.

CRÈME ANGLAISE

No pudding book could be complete without a recipe for crème anglaise, a simple and tasty accompaniment to every kind of sweet. Though purists frown on the addition of cornflour, I think it's worth doing as cornflour helps to stabilise the sauce and make it smoother. Serve this warm with puddings, pies and crumbles or cool with poached fruits or flans.

300 ml (½ pint) whole milk
1 vanilla pod, split
6 egg yolks
70 g (2½ oz) castor sugar
a pinch of cornflour

makes about 400 ml (14 fl oz)

Place the milk in a saucepan, scrape in the vanilla seeds, add the pod and bring to the boil. Meanwhile, whisk the egg yolks, sugar and cornflour together until thick and pale. Pour on the boiling milk, whisk well and return to the pan. Cook over a very low heat until the sauce has thickened and is coating the back of the spoon. Immediately remove from the heat and strain through a sieve, pushing all the vanilla seeds through as well.

FRESH COFFEE SAUCE

A good sauce not only for mousses but also ice creams, and great with chocolate cake.

500 ml (18 fl oz) whole milk
75 g (2¾ oz) freshly
    ground coffee
5 large egg yolks
100 g (3½ oz) castor sugar

makes about 600 ml (1 pint)

Heat the milk and coffee together and bring to the boil, then remove from the heat and allow to infuse for 10 minutes. Whisk the egg yolks and sugar together until very thick and foamy – the whiter and thicker the eggs and sugar are at this stage, the thicker the sauce will be.

Pour the hot-milk mixture on to the egg yolks and sugar, whisk well, and then return to the pan. Cook over a low heat, stirring continuously, until the mixture is thick and glossy. Strain the sauce through a fine sieve and then allow to cool. Chill before serving.

BITTER CHOCOLATE SAUCE

If you like a dark, extra-bitter chocolate sauce, this is the one for you. It makes a great change from the sweet, sickly sauces you can buy. It is easy to make and will keep for two weeks in the fridge, in a sealed container. You can reheat this in the microwave if necessary.

175 g (6 oz) good-quality
    cocoa powder
600 ml (1 pint) double cream
40 g (1½ oz) cold unsalted
    butter, cubed
175 g (6 oz) castor sugar

serves 4

Place the cocoa powder and cream in a saucepan and bring to the boil. Allow to bubble for 1 minute. Whisk in the butter, bring back to the boil and cook for a further 1–2 minutes. Strain into a jug or container and cover tightly.

CARAMELISED APRICOT SAUCE

This sauce is very good with ice cream.

250 g (9 oz) castor sugar
420 g can of apricots in syrup,
    drained

makes about 450 ml (16 fl oz)

Place the sugar in a pan, add 150 ml (¼ pint) of cold water and then bring to the boil. Cook until it becomes a dark caramel colour. Pour in another 150 ml (¼ pint) of cold water and stand back: the mixture will splutter and splash. Let the syrup come back to the boil and then remove from the heat and swirl the pan around to dissolve the caramel. Allow to cool.

Liquidise the drained apricots and then add cooled caramel syrup until you end up with a nice caramel-flavoured sauce. Cool completely.

BRANDY SAUCE

A very simple sauce but nevertheless very good with Christmas pudding. I like to serve double cream as well; why not, after all it's Christmas!

600 ml (1 pint) whole milk
25 g (1 oz) cornflour, slaked
    with 60 ml (4 tablespoons)
    cold water
55 g (2 oz) unrefined
    granulated sugar
55 g (2 oz) unsalted butter,
    cut in small cubes
brandy, to taste

makes about 600 ml (1 pint)

Bring the milk to the boil and then stir in the slaked cornflour. Bring back to the boil, stirring, to thicken. Remove from the heat and stir in the sugar and butter, until dissolved. Finally, stir in brandy to taste. Cover and keep warm (I keep mine in a Thermos flask).

RASPBERRY SAUCE

Surprisingly, frozen raspberries are sometimes better than fresh ones for making a sauce; the freezing process seems to draw out the juices better, making a thicker sauce.

225 g (8 oz) fresh or good-quality
    frozen raspberries
about 100 g (3½ oz) castor sugar
15 ml (1 tablespoon) lemon juice

makes 300 ml (½ pint)

Put the raspberries in a liquidiser along with the sugar and lemon juice. Blitz until smooth; you may need to add a touch of cold water to let the sauce down, if it's too thick. Pass through a fine sieve and check the sweetness; add more sugar or even a touch more lemon to get the right balance. Chill well before serving.

LIME WATER ICING

This can also be made with lemon or orange juice but lime has the most powerful flavour.

juice of 1 lime
60–75 ml (4–5 tablespoons)
    icing sugar

Sift the icing sugar into a small bowl. Put the lime juice in another small bowl. Gradually mix the icing sugar into the lime juice to make a thin icing.

CREAM CHEESE FROSTING

Incredibly easy and so delicious.

300 g (10½ oz) cream cheese,
    softened
70 g (2½ oz) icing sugar, sifted
finely grated zest of 1 orange and
    juice of about half an orange

Beat the cream cheese and sugar together until soft. Add the orange zest and then gradually add enough of the orange juice to give a soft consistency. That's it!

CREAM CHEESE AND MERINGUE FROSTING

This idea just seemed to come out of the blue: it's an alternative to butter-cream icing, which is a thing you either love or hate. With that in mind, I thought it would be nice to create a slightly different icing that would have wider appeal. Everybody seems to like meringue in one way, shape or form – that was the reason I dedicated a whole chapter to this delicious confection – coupling this with the 'afternoon tea' cake idea, this was the result. I make no bones about the fact I use a sachet of meringue mix (all the reasons for this explained on page 124).

1 quantity Basic Meringue
    (page 122) or a 245 g sachet
    of Supercook Whisk and
    Bake Meringue Mix
25 g (1 oz) castor sugar
150 g (5½ oz) cream cheese,
    whisked until soft
2.5 ml (½ teaspoon) ground
    mixed spice

**makes enough to cover a 24 cm
(9¹⁄₂-inch) diameter cake**

Whisk the meringue until very stiff and then add the castor sugar. Whisk again until firm and glossy but still smooth and silky. Whisk the cream cheese and mixed spice together in a separate bowl. Slowly and gently beat the meringue and cream cheese mixtures together.

Spread on to the cake, covering it completely so you end up with a fluffy-looking cake. Chill for 1 hour or longer (overnight if possible); this will firm up the meringue and set the cream cheese perfectly.

ROYAL ICING

For instructions on how to cover a cake with marzipan and royal icing, see Techniques on pages 235–237.

1.5 kg (3 lb 5 oz) icing sugar,
   sifted
40 g (1½ oz) 'Meri White'
   (powdered egg white)
about 15 ml (1 tablespoon)
   glycerine (available from
   chemists)

**makes enough to coat a 30 cm
(12-inch) cake twice**

Make sure the icing sugar is sifted at least twice just to be on the safe side. Place the dry egg white powder in a clean mixing bowl, add 275 ml (9½ fl oz) of cold water and stir with a fork until frothy. Pour into the bowl of a food mixer or use a hand-held whisk.

Add half of the icing sugar to the egg mixture. Set the machine to a medium speed and beat slowly until you have a smooth paste – if you beat it too fast you will end up with lots of air bubbles in the finished icing and, once it has dried, there will be tiny holes, so be patient. Add the rest of the icing sugar and beat to a firm paste. The icing should fall off a spoon when tapped slightly. Add a little extra water if too thick or a little more icing sugar if the icing is too thin.

Finally, add the glycerine and mix carefully and well. Keep covered with cling film until needed, up to 2 hours.

REAL BUTTER CREAM

As children, we always had butter-cream-filled cakes. Sadly, these days butter cream has fallen from grace, basically due to our obsession with healthy eating. Most butter-cream recipes just use butter or even margarine beaten with sugar to form a sweet greasy stodge but adding egg yolks makes the icing light and very creamy.

This recipe was used by the Queen's pastry chef, an old college lecturer of mine by the name of Brian Gilham, probably the best 'old-school' pastry chef I have ever met. His attention to detail was second to none; I owe this man a great deal. This recipe is light and not at all greasy, a real treat. Use it to pipe or spread over cakes, or to fill Brandy Snaps (page 271).

280 g (10 oz) unrefined icing
    sugar, sifted
6 large egg yolks
450 g (1 lb) softened but not
    runny unsalted butter, cut
    into small cubes
squeeze of lemon juice

**makes enough to cover a
23 cm (9-inch) diameter x 3 cm
(1¼-inch) deep Victoria sponge**

Whisk together the sugar, egg yolks and 150 ml (¼ pint) of cold water in a heatproof bowl over a pan of gently simmering water until thick, foamy and cooked – this will take about 10 minutes. I find it's best to use an electric hand-whisk.

Remove the bowl from the heat and whisk at high speed until cool and very thick (transfer it to a food mixer at this point, if you like). Whisk in the soft butter a little at a time so you end up with a light, creamy icing. Finally add the lemon juice and it's ready for piping or spreading.

coffee butter cream
Add 30 ml (2 tablespoons) of strong coffee to the egg yolks.

vanilla butter cream
Add a few drops of vanilla extract to the yolks.

hazelnut butter cream
Add 115 g (4 oz) chopped browned hazelnuts.

TANGERINE SHERBET TOPPING

Everything you use for this recipe must be absolutely dry or the sherbet will not work.

Orange oil can be bought from good kitchen shops or online; citric acid can be purchased from your local pharmacy. This is a simple but different topping with a intense orange kick – kids love it. It's ideal for sprinkling over ice creams, cream or custard tarts and cheesecakes.

peel from 6 fresh tangerines,
   satsumas or mandarins
orange oil (optional)
60–75 ml (4–5 tablespoons)
   icing sugar
5 ml (1 teaspoon)
   sodium bicarbonate
5 ml (1 teaspoon)
   citric acid powder

Spread the lemon peel on to a sheet of baking parchment and dry it in a very low oven, (50°C/120°F/ Gas Mark ¼) for about 1 hour, or until completely dry. Allow to cool completely.

Then finely grind it in a spice grinder or with a pestle and mortar, and add a couple of drops of orange oil, if using.

Sift the icing sugar and the remaining ingredients into the orange powdered zest. Mix well, grinding the contents to a fine powder with the back of a spoon.

CAKES

When we were growing up, my mother cooked a huge number of cakes and biscuits. Our first real taste of other cakes started when Grandma Vickery used to buy us what we termed 'shop cakes' every Tuesday. Suddenly we had wonderful cakes, such as cream horns with their crunchy, sugary tops, large Viennese whirls with their buttery, crumbly texture, chocolate Swiss rolls and giant fresh cream meringues. The only trouble was that there were three of us – all boys – and we could never agree on who got what.

There was a time when I was at college when I really wanted to become a professional confectioner. I bought French cookery books and marvelled at their pâtisserie photos. Spurred on by the photograph of a beautiful strawberry gâteau in the book, *Great Chefs of France* by Anthony Blake and Quentin Crewe, I got an unpaid job in a bakery on my day off to learn the trade. The chap was very nice and said I could have a lie-in and start at 4 am (he

started at 1 am!). It was invaluable experience and I really enjoyed the time with him. In my next job I met a French pastry chef called Jean who was close to retiring. One day we got chatting over staff lunch and I asked him about France and the pastry shops. He told me he used to work in a pâtisserie and said if I wanted him to show me, I had to come in at five in the morning. So I did exactly that for the following year. He taught me so much and I can never thank him enough. It was a great start for a 19 year old.

My love of cakes and bakery has never waned. Recently I made a small film in Pâtisserie Valerie in Soho and I realised that, after 25 years in the trade, I still got a buzz from watching Robert, the larger-than-life owner, and his head baker producing wonderful wedding and celebration cakes. They produce an average of 15 wedding cakes on a Saturday, all hand-finished, delivered and perfect. Thank goodness this unique art is still alive and well.

RICH CHRISTMAS FRUIT CAKE

This classic cake is based on my mum's recipe; I have just added honey, whisky and mixed peel.

500 g (1 lb 2 oz) unsalted butter,
    softened
500 g (1 lb 2 oz) soft brown sugar
8 eggs
500 g (1 lb 2 oz) plain white flour
450 g (1 lb) currants
450 g (1 lb) fat sultanas
450 g (1 lb) raisins
225 g (8 oz) whole natural
    coloured glacé cherries
175 g (6 oz) candied peel
10 ml (2 teaspoons) ground
    mixed spice
10 ml (2 teaspoons) ground
    allspice
10 ml (2 teaspoons) vanilla
    powder
85 g (3 oz) ground almonds
85 g (3 oz) slivered almonds
20 ml (4 teaspoons) black treacle
60 ml (4 tablespoons) malt whisky
30 ml (2 tablespoons) heather
    or other clear honey
finely grated zest and juice of
    1 large lemon
finely grated zest of 1 large orange
    and juice of ½ the orange

TO DECORATE
1.25 kg (2 lb 12 oz) natural-
    coloured marzipan
Royal Icing (page 229)
glazed candied fruits

makes a 28 cm (11-inch) cake
serves 10–12

Preheat the oven to 140°C/275°F/Gas Mark 1. Line a 28 cm (11-inch) round cake tin with at least two layers of greaseproof or silicone paper, leaving at least 4 cm (1½ inches) sticking up above the sides of the tin. Wrap two layers of brown paper around the outside of the tin and tie with heatproof string to secure.

Add the sugar to the softened butter and beat well until very light, pale and creamy. Whisk the eggs together and gradually add to the butter mixture in small amounts, taking care to beat well after every small amount of egg. Take care towards the end as the mixture will separate very easily; if it does curdle, add 55 g (2 oz) of the flour before continuing to add the rest of the egg.

Chop the candied peel and when the egg has been fully incorporated, fold in the flour, dried fruits and all the rest of the dry ingredients carefully; do not overwork. Finally, stir in the treacle, whisky, honey and fruit zests and juices, and that's it. Carefully spoon into the tin, cover loosely with greaseproof paper and bake for about 5½ hours, removing the greaseproof paper from the top after about 4½ hours.

To test whether the cake is cooked, insert a metal skewer or the blade of a small, sharp knife in the centre; it should be clean when removed with no mixture sticking to it. When cooked, remove from the oven and leave to cool for 30 minutes before turning out on to a cooling rack. Leave to cool overnight.

To decorate
Decorate to your own design then add ribbons and bits and pieces once dried. Cover with marzipan, at least 2 cm (¾ inch) thick and ice with royal icing, giving it at least three coats (see Techniques, opposite), or ready-made, ready-to-roll icing. You can decorate with glazed candied fruits and a thick ribbon, for a different Christmas look.

TECHNIQUES

HOW TO COVER A CAKE WITH MARZIPAN AND ROYAL ICING

Remove any paper from the cake and place on a chopping board. With a sharp serrated knife, carefully cut the top of the cake off evenly, so you have a perfectly crisp edge. It looks like you are wasting a lot of cake but this makes the end-product much easier to marzipan and ice and also looks a lot neater.

Heat 90 ml (6 tablespoons) of apricot jam with 45 ml (3 tablespoons) of cold water and stir together until smooth.

Unwrap all the marzipan blocks and knead well together until soft and supple; you may need to use a little cornflour to prevent the marzipan from sticking. Cut off about one-third of the marzipan and roll into a ball, then flatten to roughly the diameter of the cake, trying to keep the marzipan as thick as possible.

Brush what will be the top of the cake (actually the bottom) with apricot jam and then invert the cake on to the marzipan and press down well. The marzipan should fit well; trim off any excess. Add the excess to the rest of the marzipan and knead well. Leave the cake inverted so it sits on top of the marzipan.

Cut a piece of string long enough to go around the circumference of the cake and allow an extra 4 cm (1½ inches) roughly. Roll the marzipan out to a long sausage, roughly the length of the string. Then carefully, using a rolling pin, roll the sausage flat and as evenly as possible to the depth of the cake, plus the marzipan already on the top of the cake. I find it's easier to use another piece of string as a guide. Trim the marzipan with a sharp knife on both sides so it's the exact width of the cake.

Lightly brush the side of the cake with apricot jam and then carefully roll up the marzipan like a large Swiss roll. Place the end of the marzipan on the side of the cake so it's flush with the board or work surface, and stick well, then very carefully unwrap the roll around the cake, taking care to press it evenly, until you reach the point you started from. Finally roll over the top of the other marzipan from where you started, then cut straight through both pieces and remove the excess, gently push together, you should have a perfect seal.

Turn the cake over and seal the top edge of marzipan; you should now have a totally even and covered cake. Re-roll the top and sides with a rolling pin to really smooth out the marzipan. Then 'polish', basically, rubbing your hand all over the marzipan quickly; this warms the oils in the marzipan and brings out a nice shine and smoothness.

Place 15 ml (1 tablespoon) of royal icing on a silver cake board and smooth out slightly. Place the cake on the board and press down; check that it's central and leave to dry, preferably overnight in an airing cupboard or warm kitchen. This part is quite important if you plan to keep the cake for any length of time, as the drying process stops the oils from the almonds spoiling the royal icing on the cake. Some bakers brush the marzipan with lightly beaten egg white to seal and dry, but that's up to you.

I find the best way to ice a cake is to do it in four stages. Firstly, spoon a thick layer of icing around the outside of the cake trying to make it as even as possible. Then, with a palette knife, even out further still. Using a large stainless-steel scraper and a turntable, place the scraper at exactly 90° to the cake, carefully turn the turntable and a smooth edge will start to appear. Carry on until you end up at the point you started, then pull the scraper away at an angle. Don't worry too much at this point about getting it perfect, just aim to get it even and fairly smooth. With a wet cloth, wipe any icing off the board. Trim all the icing from the top of the cake with a palette knife and leave to dry for at least 36 hours.

Once it has dried, you can ice the top. Spoon over the icing to the same thickness as before and even out with a stainless-steel ruler or palette knife. Gently spin the cake around on the turntable and gently paddle the icing, by this I mean make small indentations keeping the palette knife flat to the cake to remove any air bubbles.

Take a stainless-steel ruler or long, sturdy knife and, starting at one side of the cake, as evenly as possible, draw the rule across the cake towards you, so you end up with a completely smooth top to the cake. Again, do not worry too much about getting the top too smooth, this will get easier as you add more coats. Trim the edges and leave to dry again for 36 hours.

Once dried, lightly sand with sand paper and shave with a sharp knife to remove any bumps and spare icing. Repeat both processes again so you end up with a very smooth, finished cake. I sometimes do this three or four times to get it right. It does take a bit of practice but is well worth it.

You can of course use the ready-rolled icing. I do rather think it's cheating but, having said that, I admit that it's much, much quicker to use ready-rolled, which is a very good product and extremely versatile.

TWELFTH-NIGHT CAKE

This version is based on a recipe sent to me from my good friend and colleague Mary Cadogan, a very clever and informative writer. She got the original from a French nanny who used to work for her. Like many good food ideas that were invented in Britain, however, the French seemed to have hijacked it from the Victorians originally. I have a suspicion that the history of this lovely cake goes even further back: it was traditionally eaten at Epiphany (6th January). Anyway, it's good fun and very tasty indeed. In Victorian England, the cake would have been served with brandy butter and/ or cream.

The tradition is to hide a gold king charm and a dried pea or bean in the sponge. When the cake is cut, the person who gets the charm is king for the day, and will have good luck for the rest of the year. The person who gets the bean or pea gets to do all the washing-up or, if adults are playing, gets to buy the next bottle of bubbly. No doubt we will soon have some sort of Brussels directive, saying that there is a danger of choking if the king is swallowed and dishing out huge fines and jail sentences to people who dare to cook this cake! So, I suggest you cook it while you still can.

500 g (1 lb 2 oz) Puff Pastry
(page 40)
125 g (4½ oz) unsalted butter
125 g (4½ oz) castor sugar
1 large egg, plus 1 large egg yolk,
lightly beaten
40 g (1½ oz) plain white flour,
sifted
125 g (4½ oz) ground almonds
30 ml (2 tablespoons) brandy
finely grated zest of 1 orange
and 1 lemon
45 ml (3 tablespoons) apricot
jam
king charm and dried bean
beaten egg, for glazing
icing sugar, to decorate

serves 8

Cut the puff pastry in half, and roll out both pieces nice and thinly, to make two circles about 23 cm (9 inches) in diameter. Place one piece of pastry on a greased baking tray and then the other on a plate, chill both for about 20 minutes.

Preheat the oven to 200°C/400°F/Gas Mark 6. Beat the butter and sugar together until thick and white and then add the beaten egg a little at a time. Carefully fold in the flour and ground almonds; finally, add the brandy and zests.

Mark an 18 cm (7-inch) diameter circle on the puff pastry on the baking sheet. Spread the apricot jam on the chilled pastry, keeping it inside the marked circle.

Pipe or spoon the almond mixture on top of the jam in a slight mound, again keeping within the inner circle. Press the king charm and bean into the mixture, keeping them apart. Brush beaten egg over the edge of the pastry, lay the other piece of pastry on top and press the edges together firmly. Cut out a scalloped edge. Using the back of a knife, draw in the sides at frequent intervals so the edge is neat and well sealed. Brush beaten egg all over.

Using the back of a knife, mark a crown design in the middle of the pastry for decoration, but only cut about halfway through the pastry; don't go all the way. Make a small incision in the top to allow steam to escape. Bake for about 40 minutes, or until well risen and golden (the oven must be hot for this to work, or the pastry will fall away).

Remove the cooked cake from the oven, dust lightly with icing sugar and return to the oven for a further 15 minutes or so, until golden brown and glazed – take care as the cake can catch and burn.

Cool, then serve in large slices, remembering to let your guests know about the hard bits.

CARROT CAKE WITH CREAM CHEESE AND ORANGE FROSTING

I love this cake, it's so moist and delicate. I normally coat mine in tempered bitter chocolate, but here I'm using cream-cheese icing, a twist on passion cake. Be careful to squeeze any juice out of the carrots very well, and then weigh them after that. The only thing to serve with this is Caramelised Apricot Sauce, a great foil to the rich sponge.

85 g (3 oz) madeira cake crumbs

55 g (2 oz) plain white flour, sifted

15 g (½ oz) baking powder

250 g (9 oz) skinned hazelnuts, chopped

300 g (10½ oz) grated and well-squeezed-out carrot

15 ml (1 tablespoon) rum

5 large eggs, separated

240 g (8½ oz) castor sugar

2 large pinches of ground cinnamon

grated zest of 1 large lemon

5 ml (1 teaspoon) vanilla extract or powder

60 ml (4 tablespoons) apricot jam

500 g (1 lb 2 oz) natural-colour marzipan

FOR THE FROSTING

400 g (14 oz) cream cheese

finely grated zest of 1 orange, plus the juice from ½ the orange

85 g (3 oz) icing sugar, sifted

1 quantity Caramelised Apricot Sauce (page 226), to serve

makes a 25 cm (10-inch) cake

Preheat the oven to 190°C/375°F/Gas Mark 5. Grease and line a 25 cm (10-inch) diameter x 6 cm (5½-inch) deep, loose-bottomed cake tin.

Mix the madeira crumbs with the flour and baking powder. Add the hazelnuts and carrot and mix well. Next, whisk the rum, egg yolks and 125 g (4½ oz) of castor sugar together until thick and foamy. Fold in the cinnamon, zest and vanilla.

Whisk the egg whites until they are thick and foamy, add the remaining 115 g (4 oz) of castor sugar and whisk until firm and glossy. Fold the madeira crumb mixture into the egg yolks, then finally add the meringue. Spoon into the tin and bake for 30 minutes.

Check to see if the cake has set, using a skewer or small, sharp knife. You should be able to withdraw it without any uncooked mixture clinging to it. If so, reduce the heat to 160°C/325°F/Gas Mark 3, and cook for about a further 15 minutes or until nicely browned and firm to the touch. If not, cook for a few minutes more and test again before reducing the oven temperature. Allow to cool.

Remove the cake from the tin. Warm and sieve the apricot jam. Spread the top and sides of the cake all over with jam. Roll out the marzipan as thinly as possible so it is about 6 cm (5½ inches) bigger than the cake all around and then place centrally on top of the cake. Press on to the sides and top and leave to dry slightly.

To make the cream-cheese frosting, beat the cream cheese with the icing sugar and orange zest, adding the juice to loosen the mixture slightly. Spread frosting evenly on to the cake. Cut and serve with the Caramelised Apricot Sauce.

SIMNEL CAKE

This is the traditional Easter Cake – the marzipan balls represent the number of disciples…

500 g (1 lb 2 oz) natural-colour
  marzipan
225 g (8 oz) unsalted butter,
  softened
225 g (8 oz) unrefined castor
  sugar
4 eggs, beaten
225 g (8 oz) self-raising white
  flour
25 g (1 oz) ground almonds
2.5 ml (½ teaspoon) ground
  allspice
2.5 ml (½ teaspoon) ground
  mace
2.5 ml (½ teaspoon) ground
  cinnamon
2.5 ml (½ teaspoon) freshly
  grated nutmeg
225 g (8 oz) currants
115 g (4 oz) sultanas
100 g (3½ oz) glacé cherries,
  washed and chopped
55 g (2 oz) candied peel,
  chopped very finely
finely grated zest of 2 lemons
30 ml (2 tablespoons) brandy
30 ml (2 tablespoons) apricot
  jam, to glaze
1 small egg, beaten, to glaze

FOR THE ICING
about 60 ml (4 tablespoons)
  golden icing sugar, sifted
juice of 1 lime, strained

makes a 20 cm (8-inch) cake

Preheat the oven to 160°C/325°F/Gas Mark 3. Butter a deep 20 cm (8-inch) diameter cake tin and line with a double layer of greaseproof paper. Cut an 85 g (3 oz) piece off the marzipan and reserve, then cut the remaining marzipan in half.

Cream the soft butter and sugar together until thick and creamy. Beat in the eggs one at a time, then fold in the flour, almonds and spices. Finally, stir in the dried fruit, cherries, peel, lemon zest and brandy. Use half the mixture to fill the bottom of the prepared tin.

Roll out one of the larger pieces of marzipan into a circle just large enough to fit into the cake tin. Lay carefully over the cake mixture, pressing down to expel any air bubbles. Spoon in the rest of the cake mixture and level out. Bake for about 1 hour 40–1 hour 50 minutes, or until set and nicely browned. Test with a skewer in the normal way; if the skewer comes out clean, the cake is cooked. Remove from the oven and allow to cool.

Warm and sieve the apricot jam. Take the cooled cake out of the tin and remove the paper, then trim the top flat if necessary and turn the cake upside-down. Brush a little jam over what is now the top. Roll out the remaining larger piece of marzipan to fit the top of the cake perfectly, press down on top with your hands and roll flat with a rolling pin. Decorate the edge of the marzipan using a 'pinching' effect. Divide the reserved 85 g (3 oz) marzipan into eleven, twelve or thirteen balls. Brush a little beaten egg on the marzipan on top of the cake and stick down the balls along the edge.

Place the cake on a baking sheet and brown under a hot grill.

Gradually mix enough icing sugar into the lime juice to give a runny consistency. Pour into the middle of the cake and allow to set. Wrap a large ribbon around the side of the cake so you can just see the cake and marzipan.

MUM'S BOILED FRUIT CAKE

This recipe could not be easier: just boil it up and leave to cool, add the eggs and bake in the oven. Its very dense, very moist texture will keep very well indeed without drying out. This recipe is a good way to get kids involved in the kitchen, as the processes are extremely easy. It is my mum's recipe, so I can't take the credit for this clever, unusual cake.

900 g (2 lb) mixed dried fruit (I prefer more sultanas than any other fruit)

100 g (3½ oz) chopped glacé cherries

450 g (1 lb) unsalted butter, cubed

500 g (1 lb 2 oz) unrefined castor sugar

4 large eggs, beaten

575 g (1 lb 4½ oz) self-raising flour, sifted

5 ml (1 teaspoon) bicarbonate of soda

10 ml (2 teaspoons) ground mixed spice

ice cream, to serve (optional)

serves 8–10

Place the dried fruit, cherries, butter, sugar and 500 ml (18 fl oz) of cold water in a pan and bring to the boil. Cover and leave until cold. Preheat the oven to 190°C/375°F/Gas Mark 5. Grease a 25 cm (10-inch) square cake tin and dust with a little flour.

Place the cooled fruit mixture in a large bowl. Add the eggs, flour, bicarbonate of soda and mixed spice, mix well and spoon into the prepared baking tin. Bake for 35–45 minutes, or until well risen and dark brown. Remove from the oven and cool completely before trying to cut. Wrap in foil to store. This cake is very nice with vanilla ice cream, served as a dessert.

FRESH STRAWBERRY MILLE-FEUILLE

The best things about the English summer, I believe, are strawberries and raspberries. Having been a pastry chef for more years than I can remember, there is nothing I like better than making these wonderful berries into all sorts of glorious sweets, tarts and puddings. Most of the strawberries and raspberries grown commercially these days are devoid of real colour and flavour and are frankly not worth the effort but, if you are lucky enough to pick your own or, better still, grow your own, I can assure you that you'll never touch a tasteless impostor again. The recipe here is the only way to eat strawberries, apart from just with cream.

about 200 g (7 oz) Puff Pastry
    (page 40) or a 28 x 23 cm
    (11 x 9 inch) sheet of frozen
    puff pastry
10 ml (2 teaspoons)
    vanilla extract
30 ml (2 tablespoons) icing sugar,
    plus extra for dusting
300 ml (½ pint) double cream,
    lightly whipped
60 ml (4 tablespoons) strawberry
    preserve or good-quality jam
300 g (10½ oz) fresh English
    strawberries, hulled and
    halved
flaked almonds, toasted,
    to decorate (optional)

serves 4–6

Preheat the oven to 200°C/400°F/Gas Mark 6. Unwrap the puff pastry carefully, place on a non-stick baking sheet and prick really well with a fork. Bake for about 15–20 minutes or until nicely risen and golden brown. Take care with puff pastry because it tends to burn very quickly once you take your eye off it. Once cooked, remove from the oven and transfer to a cooling rack to allow to cool.

Next, add the vanilla and icing sugar to the cream and stir together; do not over beat or the cream will separate. Keep as cold as possible.

Cut the pastry into three equal pieces. Spread the strawberry jam over two of the layers (this is a novel idea but not only does it sweeten the dessert but it also brings out the flavour of the strawberries). Place the halved strawberries on top of the strawberry jam. Using a palette knife, spread a thick layer of the cream mixture on top of the strawberries and jam.

Use the palette knife carefully to lift one of the covered pieces of pastry on top of the other and nestle it down nicely. Top with the final piece of puff pastry and then lay the cooling rack on top of that and press down lightly (this is quite important because if you don't it can be extremely difficult to cut; don't worry too much about the cream that oozes out). Take the palette knife again and, using any excess cream from the bowl and from the edge of the pastry, carefully fill in the gaps around the layers of pastry and strawberries so you end up with a solid-looking pastry.

Dust the top heavily with icing sugar. If you really want to go the whole hog then lightly toast some flaked almonds and stick them to the side of the finished mille-feuille.It's best to eat this dessert within an hour or the pastry will start to soften; and the easiest way to cut it is to use a serrated bread or carving knife in a sawing motion.

STOLLEN

I used to cook this cake years ago for afternoon teas. The texture is a little different from most normal cakes – it's very similar to a rock bun, but delicious. I also rather like the marzipan centre.

The good thing is that you can make it in advance, then brush with butter and dredge well in icing sugar. The cake uses Quark, a sort of soft cheese, to bind, which is used a lot in German cakes, flans and tarts. If you cannot find Quark, substitute thick crème fraîche or yogurt.

500 g (1 lb 2 oz) plain white flour, sifted

2 pinches of salt

125 g (4½ oz) unsalted butter, softened

15 ml (1 tablespoon) baking powder

200 g (7 oz) unrefined castor sugar

a few drops of vanilla extract

a few drops of almond extract

30 ml (2 tablespoons) dark rum

finely grated zest of 1 large lemon

10 ml (2 teaspoons) ground mixed spice

50 g (1¾ oz) suet

125 g (4½ oz) currants

125 g (4½ oz) raisins

125 g (4½ oz) ground almonds

40 g (1½ oz) chopped mixed candied peel

250 g (9 oz) Quark, or thick crème fraîche or greek-style yogurt

2 large eggs, beaten

250 g (9 oz) natural-colour marzipan

TO FINISH

25 g (1 oz) melted butter

icing sugar, sifted

serves 6-8

Preheat the oven to 180°C/350°F/Gas Mark 4. Grease a baking sheet. Place the flour, salt and butter in a bowl and rub in carefully. Add the baking powder, sugar, vanilla and almond extracts, rum, lemon zest, mixed spice, suet, dried fruits, almonds and peel and mix well. Add the Quark and eggs and mix well to form a nice firm dough.

Place on a floured surface and gently roll out with a rolling pin to form an oblong about 30 x 45 cm (12 x 18 inches), leaving the dough about 2 cm (¾ inch) thick. Take the marzipan and form into a sausage shape the length of the dough. Fold the top of the dough over the marzipan, and seal well, then fold under the ends.

Place on the baking sheet and bake for about 35–40 minutes, or until well risen and golden brown. The cake will spread slightly; don't worry, this is quite normal.

Once cooked, remove from the oven and place on a wire rack with a piece of foil underneath. Brush liberally with melted butter and dust with plenty of icing sugar; then allow to cool. Wrap tightly in foil to store; it will keep for 2–3 weeks in a cool place. Cut into large slices.

SAFFRON CAKE

Saffron used to be grown in England years ago, believe it or not, and the town of Saffron Walden actually took its name from this precious spice. Saffron was even used to dye fabrics and later hair, until Henry VIII banned its use by any ladies of the court. It remains a really big part of modern-day cooking but use it sparingly: not only is it very, very pungent, but also very expensive. A 4 g jar of saffron is a perfect quantity for this recipe.

100 ml (3½ fl oz) milk
3 pinches of saffron strands
200 g (7 oz) unsalted butter, softened
175 g (6 oz) castor sugar
3 large eggs, lightly beaten
225 g (8 oz) plain white flour
7.5 ml (1½ teaspoons) baking powder
finely grated zest of 1 large lemon

makes a 675 g (1½ lb) loaf

Preheat the oven to 160°C/325°F/Gas Mark 3, and then butter a 675 g (1½ lb) loaf tin well, or line with a bought made-to-measure paper case. Gently warm the milk and saffron together and leave to infuse for a few minutes until deep and golden coloured, then cool.

Beat the butter and sugar together until pale and very creamy. Gradually add the beaten eggs, and beat again until light and very creamy. Fold in the flour, baking powder and lemon zest until incorporated. Add the saffron milk and mix well but lightly.

Spoon into the prepared loaf tin and bake for 40–45 minutes. The top will crack slightly but this is quite normal, and the cake will be well risen, golden and have a beautiful aroma. Remove from the oven and cool slightly, then turn out on to a wire rack and cool completely. Wrap in cling film and store in an airtight container.

PUMPKIN AND POPPY SEED LOAF

A good all-round afternoon tea cake – simple and quick.

175 g (6 oz) self-raising
    white flour
¼ teaspoon baking powder
¼ teaspoon bicarbonate of soda
7.5 ml (1½ teaspoons)
    ground mixed spice
½ teaspoon grated nutmeg
15 ml (1 tablespoon) poppy seeds
50 g (1¾ oz) unsalted butter
140 g (5 oz) castor sugar
200 g (7 oz) canned
    pumpkin purée
45 ml (3 tablespoons) whole milk
1 large egg, beaten
55 g (2 oz) castor sugar
thick cream, to serve

makes a 900 g (2 lb) loaf

Preheat the oven to 180°C/350°F/Gas Mark 4. Line a 900 g (2 lb) loaf tin (about 21.5 x 11 x 6 cm deep/8½ x 5½ x 2½ inches) with greaseproof paper and grease well.

Mix together the flour, baking powder, bicarbonate of soda, mixed spice, nutmeg and poppy seeds, then add the butter and rub in. Add the castor sugar and mix well.

Mix together the pumpkin, milk and beaten egg. Add to the flour mixture and fold in but do not overwork. Spoon into the prepared tin and bake for 35–40 minutes or until well risen.

Meanwhile, make the syrup. Place the sugar in a small saucepan and add enough water to moisten. Cook over a high heat until the sugar is a dark caramel and then add 45 ml (3 tablespoons) of water and stand back, as it will splutter. Swirl the pan to dissolve any lumps and, when the caramel has dissolved, allow to cool.

Once the cake is cooked, remove from the oven and prick well with a skewer. Pour over the hot syrup and leave to cool completely in the tin before turning the cake out. Serve with thick cream.

PARKIN

This is my mum's recipe and I'm assured it's very good indeed by my dad (I can't stand ground ginger so, unfortunately, it's out for me). Lancashire and Yorkshire both have recipes for this, but I'm not telling you which side of the Pennines this came from. I like to serve this either with a cup of strong tea, or warm with custard, flavoured with 5 tablespoons of golden syrup.

225 g (8 oz) plain white flour

2 pinches of salt

5 ml (1 teaspoon) ground ginger

5 ml (1 teaspoon) ground
    mixed spice

225 g (8 oz) oatmeal

280 g (10 oz) black treacle

225 g (8 oz) unrefined golden
    castor sugar

175 g (6 oz) unsalted butter

5 ml (1 teaspoon) bicarbonate
    of soda

125 ml (4 fl oz) whole milk

serves 8

Preheat the oven to 180°C/350°F/Gas Mark 4. Grease and line a deep baking tray, about 20 x 25 cm (8 x 10 inches).

Sift the flour, salt, ginger and mixed spice together. Add the oatmeal and stir well. Gently heat the treacle, sugar and butter together in a pan until melted and nice and runny. Dissolve the bicarbonate of soda in the milk.

Pour the melted butter mixture into the dry ingredients and then add the milk mixture too. Carefully stir together and pour into the prepared baking tray. Bake for about 45 minutes, or until well risen and firm. Cool, then cut into large squares.

TUTTI-FRUTTI ICE-CREAM CAKE

A few years ago I worked with a chef who asked me to come up with an idea for an ice-cream cake or gâteau. I did look at him with an air of suspicion, but got down to work and eventually came up with a bitter chocolate and tangerine ice-cream cake that was delicious. In fact, it went on to be one of the best sellers on the sweet menu. It was a real pain to prepare, though, as we had to make all the ice cream from scratch.

Here is a version using good-quality bought ice cream that is far easier and quicker to make – and the end product is stunning. It is still a bit time-consuming though, so when you're going to make this, start early in the day and remember to soak the fruit the day before. The finished cake needs to be frozen overnight.

60 ml (4 tablespoons) brandy

200 g (7 oz) mixed candied fruits
   or peel, roughly chopped

3 eggs

100 g (3½ oz) castor sugar

100 g (3½ oz) plain white flour,
   sifted

2.5 ml (½ teaspoon)
   grated nutmeg

2.5 ml (½ teaspoon) ground
   mixed spice

1 litre (1¾ pints) good-quality
   vanilla ice cream, softened
   but not melted

500 ml (18 fl oz) good-quality
   cherry ice cream, softened
   but not melted

100 g (7 oz) natural dyed glacé
   cherries, roughly chopped

icing sugar, for dusting

whipped cream, to serve

serves 6–8

Pour the brandy over the candied fruits and leave overnight to soak.

The next day, preheat the oven to 190°C/375°F/Gas Mark 5. Lightly grease a 39 x 29 cm (15½ x 11½ inches) non-stick baking sheet. Line an 18 cm diameter x 10 cm deep (7-x 4-inch) soufflé dish with cling film – rub the dish first with a little vegetable oil, to prevent the cling film from freezing to the porcelain.

Whisk the eggs and sugar until pale and very thick: you should be able to lift the whisk and drizzle a figure of eight with the mixture on its surface (see the second paragraph in the method of Basic Light Sponge on page 256). Carefully fold in the flour and spices. Spread out evenly on the greased baking sheet. Bake for 15–20 minutes, or until well risen and springy to the touch. Allow to cool.

When cool, use a sharp knife to cut two 9 cm (3½-inch) strips from one of the shortest ends of the sponge. Sit the soufflé dish on the remaining sponge and cut around the base to make a circle. Remove the dish and trim off 1 cm (½ inch) from all around the circle, so it fits snugly into the base of the dish. Sit the circle inside the lined dish, making sure the browned side is facing outwards to ensure a nice neat finish. Line the sides of the dish with the cut strips of sponge, trimming the ends where necessary so they fit snugly.

Strain the brandy from the fruit and sprinkle the brandy on to the sponge. Freeze the lined dish for 30 minutes or until firm. When frozen, carefully spoon about two-thirds of the vanilla ice cream into the dish, pressing it to the sponge with a palette knife to make a circle of ice cream – you should end up with a 3 cm (1¼-inch) thick wall of ice cream; try to make it as even as possible. Press in the chopped candied fruit and then re-freeze until very firm, about 30 minutes. You must work quickly so the ice cream does not melt.

When frozen, repeat the process using the cherry ice cream and this time press in the glacé cherries. This will leave a centre hole that you can fill in with the rest of the vanilla ice cream. Flatten off the top. Cover the ice cream with the remaining sponge to seal; you will need to trim it to fit, but don't worry too much about the shape. Freeze overnight. The cake can be made well in advance to this stage.

To serve, remove from the freezer and leave in the fridge for about 30 minutes to soften slightly. Turn out of the dish and dust with icing sugar then cut into wedges and serve with a little whipped cream.

New Recipe

CORNISH CIDER CAKE

I think the success of this recipe is down to the use of Stork margarine; my mother swears by it for making cakes. It is a very old recipe given to me by a lady kitchen porter who worked for me many years ago. It's very tasty, topped with Cornish clotted cream.

85 g (3 oz) raisins

85 g (3 oz) sultanas

85 g (3 oz) currants

75 ml (5 tablespoons) cider or
    Scrumpy, the rougher
    the better

170 g (6 oz) Stork margarine, soft

170 g (6 oz) light brown sugar

3 eggs, beaten

225 g (8 oz) self-raising flour,
    sifted

10 ml (2 teaspoons) mixed spice

clotted cream, to serve

makes 1 loaf

Soak the fruit in the cider; it's best to do this overnight. Preheat the oven to 180°C/ 350°F/Gas Mark 4. Line a 23 cm x 13 cm x 7 cm (9 x 5 x 2¾-inch) deep loaf tin with baking parchment. Cream the margarine and sugar together until fluffy and light. Add the eggs slowly, adding a little flour as you go along.

Fold in the rest of the flour and spice and mix well. Add the soaked fruit and then spoon into the loaf tin. Pop into the oven and cook for 50–60 minutes, or until well risen and light brown. Cool and turn out. Serve with clotted cream.

SMALL CAKES
AND FANCIES

This chapter is the one with all the cakes we can't resist – especially when they're served as part of the great British afternoon tea. Present-day life is more hectic than ever before and unfortunately afternoon tea is now only really served and eaten in posh hotels and at weekends. My grandmother would always say things were tough in 'the old days' and from what she told me they were, but people always made time for a cup of tea and a piece of cake. Even cricketers, whether they're playing on the village green or at a test match, all stop for afternoon tea.

This great tradition really took off with the Victorians; they loved their afternoon tea. In fact they loved all food, from hearty six-course breakfasts, through long lunches and afternoon tea, to huge multi-course suppers. Tea would be served from four o'clock, but five was the best time and the range of food was staggering. Gentlemen would escort their wives or lady friends to the tea room, where they could choose from an array of beverages: wine, claret, tea, coffee, sherry or Champagne. Water ices were often served. Tea sandwiches would be tongue, ham, beef and sometimes cheese. Also on offer would be potted and cold meats, fish, sardines, crumpets and Madeira, seed and all manner of small cakes. Over the years a whole array of tea-time fancies has been created and become very popular.

There are some great British cakes in this chapter (Baby Bakewells with Lime Water Icing and Caramel Custard Buns), but you'll also find some continental delicacies like baby éclairs and warm madeleines. Apart from scones with cream and jam, my favourite cakes for tea are Strawberry Splits and meringues in any shape or form. Fresh, perfumed English strawberries with thick cream wrapped in a delicate soft sponge are sensational. And meringues with thick or clotted cream and frankly any filling whatsoever are divine.

BASIC LIGHT SPONGE

This is the basic recipe we use for all our birthday cakes: quick, simple and with a good texture. The addition of butter will help to keep the sponge from going stale too quickly and also gives the crumb a lovely buttery edge. You can make this sponge well in advance and freeze it.

4 large eggs, at room temperature

75 g (2¾ oz) castor sugar

75 g (2¾ oz) plain white flour, sifted

55 g (2 oz) unsalted butter, melted

makes a 25 cm (10-inch) cake

Preheat the oven to 200°C/400°F/Gas Mark 6. Brush the inside of a 25 cm diameter x 6 cm deep (10 x 5½inch), loose-bottomed cake tin with a little butter. Dust with a little flour and tip out any excess.

Whisk the eggs and castor sugar together using a medium speed until very thick and glossy. The mixture should hold its own weight when the whisk is lifted out, that is, a visible trail of mixture on top should stay visible, not sink down to blend with the rest of the mixture. You can use a food mixer, which takes about 15 minutes, or a hand-held whisk, which will take longer.

Carefully fold in the sifted flour, with a metal spoon or a rubber spatula and then finally fold in the butter. Pour into the prepared tin, place in the oven and cook for 15–18 minutes or until well risen and golden. Remove from the oven and cool, then remove from the tin.

STRAWBERRY SPLITS

These cakes look almost like soufflé pancakes – delicate sponge bursting open with lightly whipped cream and strawberries. A great afternoon tea cake.

The secret is the sponge. I use a combination of normal flour and cornflour – along with the butter this helps to make the sponge pliable and very soft, and so easy to fold.

70 g (2½ oz) plain white flour

70 g (2½ oz) cornflour

8 eggs

a pinch of salt

280 g (10 oz) castor sugar

140 g (5 oz) unsalted butter, melted

500 g (1 lb 2 oz) small, sweet English strawberries, hulled, plus a few extra to serve

2.5 ml (½ teaspoon) vanilla powder or extract

30–45 ml (2–3 heaped tablespoons) unrefined icing sugar, plus extra to dust, sifted

300 ml (½ pint) double cream, very lightly whipped, plus extra to serve

strawberries, to serve

makes 4 splits

Preheat the oven to 220°C/425°F/Gas Mark 7. Line two Swiss roll tins, about 38 x 28 cm (15 x 11 inches) with baking parchment. Sift together the plain flour and cornflour. Whisk the eggs, salt and castor sugar together until they are thick and creamy and hold their own weight (meaning that when the whisk is lifted and drawn across the top of the froth, the trail stays on top for at least 10 seconds). Fold in the sifted flours and then the melted butter.

Spread on to the lined Swiss roll trays and then bake for about 6–8 minutes, until set and very slightly shrunken away from the sides of the tray. Immediately turn the trays out on to clean tea towels; the sponge should fall out of the trays cleanly.

Flick about 10–15 ml (2–3 teaspoons) of cold water over the back of the baking parchment and spread over lightly with your fingers. Carefully peel away the paper, taking care not to rip the sides of the sponge away, and then leave to cool.

Meanwhile, cut the strawberries in half lengthways and lightly fold about three-quarters of them, together with the vanilla and icing sugar, into the lightly whipped cream (the cream must be whipped only to soft peaks; take care or it will 'turn' very quickly).

Using an 18 cm (7-inch) diameter saucer or a plate as a guide, cut two circles out of each of the sponges (the trimmings can be used for trifles, tiramisù or ground up and used in my favourite Fern's Queen of Puddings (page 20); they will freeze perfectly). Half-fill the sponge circles with the cream and strawberry mixture, fold over to make a nice full split, and dust with unrefined icing sugar. You can, for extra effect, heat up a skewer and brand the icing sugar in a criss-cross fashion. Serve any extra cream and strawberries separately.

BABY COFFEE ÉCLAIRS

Serve these classic treats piled high.

1 quantity Choux Pastry
    (page 42)
1 egg, beaten

FOR THE COFFEE
PASTRY CREAM
300 ml (½ pint) whole milk
10 g (¼ oz) freshly ground coffee
4 large egg yolks
60 g (2¼ oz) unrefined castor
    sugar
60 g (2¼ oz) plain white flour,
    sifted
300 ml (½ pint) double cream,
    lightly whipped

FOR THE ICING
25 ml (5 teaspoons) instant
    coffee
45 ml (3 tablespoons)
    boiling water
about 250 g (9 oz) Tate and Lyle
    Fondant Icing Sugar

makes 60–70 baby éclairs

Preheat the oven to 220°C/425°F/Gas Mark 7. Very lightly grease two baking sheets. Spoon the choux pastry into a large piping bag fitted with a 1.5 cm (⅝-inch) nozzle. Pipe the pastry on to the baking sheets to make 4 cm (1½-inch) long éclairs. Brush with beaten egg and re-shape at the same time. Bake for 15–20 minutes, or until well risen and golden.

Once they are fully formed and golden, turn the oven down to 160°C/325°F/ Gas Mark 3 and cook the éclairs for a further 5–10 minutes to dry them out until they are very crisp. This is very important as, the crisper they are, the easier they are to pipe and ice. It also ensures that you do not end up with raw choux pastry inside. Remove from the oven and cool completely – don't store them in an airtight container as this makes the pastry soggy.

Meanwhile, make the pastry cream: bring the milk and ground coffee to the boil in a pan, stirring all the time. Remove from the heat and leave to infuse for 10 minutes. Meanwhile, whisk the egg yolks and sugar together. Add the flour and mix well. Strain the milk through a fine sieve on to the egg and sugar mixture and stir well. Return to the pan and bring to the boil very slowly, stirring all the time in a figure of eight so it doesn't catch. Once boiling, remove from the heat and pour into a clean bowl. Cover with cling film and leave to cool.

Whisk the cooled coffee pastry cream to loosen and break it down, then add the whipped cream and whisk together. Spoon into a piping bag fitted with a 5 mm (¼-inch) nozzle. Using a small knife, make small incisions in the base of each éclair large enough to fit the nozzle. Pipe the coffee cream into the éclairs one by one, until they feel full.

Mix together the instant coffee and boiling water, then gradually add enough fondant icing sugar to make an icing of coating consistency. Dip each éclair into the icing one at a time and smooth off with your finger. Leave to set for 15 minutes and then serve.

BABY BAKEWELLS WITH LIME WATER ICING

Most people have eaten bakewell tart at some time in their lives but the trouble with most bakewells is that they are flavoured with almond essence, which, frankly, tastes nothing like real almonds. I would sooner eat the real thing: the taste is completely different. These are great as an afternoon tea or an autumn pudding.

Just use good-quality almonds and make sure to beat the butter and castor sugar for the sponge filling until the mixture is really pale.

250 g (9 oz) Shortbread Pastry
    (page 43)

FOR THE SPONGE FILLING
125 g (4½ oz) unsalted butter,
    softened
125 g (4½ oz) castor sugar
1 large egg, plus 1 large egg yolk,
    beaten
125 g (4½ oz) ground almonds
40 g (1½ oz) plain white flour,
    sifted
15 ml (1 tablespoon) Crème
    Pâtissière (optional) (see
    page 220)
45 ml (3 tablespoons) raspberry
    jam or jelly
about 30 flaked almonds

TO SERVE
Lime Water Icing (page 227),
    to decorate
clotted cream

**makes about 30 baby
bakewells**

Preheat the oven to 220°C/425°F/Gas Mark 7. Grease two mini muffin tins. Only rolling out half the mixture at a time so the dough does not get too warm, roll out the shortbread dough until the pastry is about 5 mm (¼ inch) thick. Cut out circles with a pastry cutter approximately 2 cm (¾ inch) larger than the diameter of the muffin cups and press the dough carefully into the tins. Repeat until you have lined all the tins and then chill for 30 minutes before use. There is no need to bake the pastry blind as it will cook very quickly; also it's nice to eat these tarts slightly undercooked.

Beat the soft butter and castor sugar together until soft and white. Gradually add the beaten egg until the mixture is thick and creamy. Fold in the almonds and sifted flour carefully and add the crème pâtissière, if using (this just makes the finished sponge richer). If you're not ready to cook the tartlets, you can chill the mixture now.

Spoon the mixture into a piping bag fitted with a medium nozzle (if the mixture has been chilled pop it into the microwave just to warm it through enough to be able to pipe easily). Spoon a little raspberry jam into each lined muffin tin and then pipe in the sponge mixture so it comes about three-quarters of the way up. Top each with a flaked almond. Bake in the oven for 12–15 minutes, or until well risen and golden brown. Allow to cool.

Mix together the lime juice and icing sugar to make a thin icing and drizzle over the top of the tarts; then leave to set. Serve with a large blob of clotted cream

MADELEINES

I love these small sponges. I have been cooking these little beauties for the best part of 20 years and they still are my favourite sponge, whether served warm with afternoon tea or ice cream, or as a petit four after dinner.

The best thing to do is to make up the mix and then chill it for 2 hours (I reckon the sponges are then much nicer). All you need to do then is pipe the mix, cold and straight from the fridge, into well-buttered madeleine moulds and bake in a hot oven. The mixture will keep perfectly, covered, in a fridge for a couple of days.

One word of warning, though: these little sponges will burn very quickly indeed due to the amount of sugar and honey, so take care.

2 large eggs, at room temperature

70 g (2½ oz) unrefined castor sugar

85 g (3 oz) plain white flour

7.5 ml (1½ teaspoons) baking powder

85 g (3 oz) unsalted butter, melted

15 ml (1 tablespoon) clear honey

unrefined icing sugar, sifted, to decorate

bitter chocolate, melted (see 'Melting chocolate' on page 89), for dipping (optional)

makes 12 large or 24 small sponges

Preheat the oven to 190°C/375°F/Gas Mark 5. Butter 12 large madeleine moulds, or 24 small moulds well (if you don't have madeleine moulds you can use patty tins).

Place the eggs and sugar in a mixing bowl and, using an electric whisk, beat on a moderate speed until thick and foamy (see Basic Light Sponge on page 256). Sift together the flour and baking powder and then sprinkle over the egg mixture and carefully fold in – do not overwork! Mix together the butter and honey and carefully fold in.

Spoon the madeleine mixture into a large piping bag, fitted with a 1 cm (½-inch) plain nozzle and then pipe into the moulds. Dip your finger into a little cold water and slightly press the mixture down.

Bake in the oven for about 8 minutes for the small moulds or 10 minutes for the large ones, or until well risen and golden brown. You may find that the centres rise up a little; don't worry this is quite normal. Turn out on to a cooling rack and dust with a little unrefined icing sugar. You can even dip the ends into some bitter melted chocolate, if you wish.

SMALL CAKES & FANCIES

CARAMEL CUSTARD BUNS

I have always liked cold custard buns: my grandfather worked as a bakery driver for a long time and would always come home with vanilla slices, still one my dad's favourite cakes. There is something wonderful about the combination of cooked puff pastry, custard and thick fondant icing.

Custard buns seem to be a northern idea, especially a Lancashire one, and it's a shame you don't really see them 'down south' or, if you do, they are not a patch on the northern variety. The use of unrefined sugar here intensifies the flavour of the caramel.

6 large egg yolks
175 g (6 oz) unrefined
    castor sugar
85 g (3 oz) plain white flour,
    sifted
500 ml (18 fl oz) whole milk
1 quantity Choux Pastry
    (page 42)
icing sugar, for dusting

makes about 25 buns

Whisk the egg yolks and 100 g (3½ oz) of the sugar together, until thick and creamy (see Basic Light Sponge on page 256). Add the flour and mix well.

Place the milk in a pan and bring to the boil, stirring all the time. Pour the hot milk on to the eggs and sugar and stir well. Return to the pan and bring to the boil very slowly, stirring all the time in a figure of eight fashion and paying particular attention to the bottom edge of the saucepan. Once boiling, cook for 30 seconds over a low heat, then remove from the heat and pour into a clean bowl. Cover with cling film and leave to cool.

To make the caramel syrup, place the other 75 g (2¾ oz) of unrefined castor sugar in a pan with 50 ml (2 fl oz) of cold water (see 'Making caramel' on page 167). Bring to the boil and cook for about 10 minutes, until you have a very dark caramel. (This is quite important: caramel by its very nature is sweet, but the longer the sugar is cooked, not only the darker it will become, but also the less sweet it will become. So, to get the right balance, you will need to cook the sugar until it is quite dark in colour – strong tea without milk is about right.)

Turn off the heat and, taking care, add another 50 ml (2 fl oz) of cold water – stand back as the caramel will spit and splutter. Give the pan a quick swirl and you should end up with a nice thick syrup. Pour the caramel into the custard and mix well. Cover again and leave to cool completely.

Preheat the oven to 200°C/400°F/Gas Mark 6. Very lightly grease two baking sheets (if you grease them too heavily the choux pastry will not stick to the baking sheet when you are trying to pipe them out). Using a large piping bag fitted with a 1 cm (½-inch) plain nozzle, pipe out 25 small blobs the size of a 50p piece. Using a wetted finger, lightly pat down each of the blobs.

Cook in the oven for 25 minutes or until well puffed up and golden. (Take care as these buns are quite deceptive: the outside might look cooked but the inside has a habit of being still undercooked, so do test one by sticking in a small knife, which should come out clean. The same rule applies as with Yorkshire pudding: once you think they are cooked just give them 10 minutes extra.) When cooked, remove from the oven and leave to cool.

Make a small hole in the bottom of each bun, just big enough to be able to pipe in the mixture. Using a piping bag, again fitted with a 1 cm (½-inch) plain nozzle, fill the little buns with the cold caramel custard, until they feel heavy. Stack in a pile and dust with icing sugar.

New Recipe

EASY TOFFEE CHOCOLATE MUFFINS

These gooey muffins are really easy to make and look and taste stunning. Just remember not to mix in the caramel too much, to ensure you end up with little pockets of delicious caramel in the muffins.

250 g (9 oz) self-raising flour

100 g (3½ oz) soft brown sugar

40 g (1½ oz) cocoa powder

15 ml (1 tablespoon) baking
    powder

1 egg

1 egg yolk

150 ml (¼ pint) milk

75 ml (5 tablespoons)
    vegetable oil

5 ml (1 teaspoon) vanilla extract

397 g can Carnation Caramel

makes 12

Preheat the oven to 190 °C/375 °F/Gas Mark 5. Place the flour, sugar, cocoa powder and baking powder into a bowl and mix well. In a separate bowl, mix the eggs, milk, oil and vanilla. Add the wet mixture to the dry ingredients and stir until just combined, without beating. Drop spoonfuls of the caramel into the mixture. Gently swirl through, but don't mix it in – it's nice to see little caramel bubbles in the finished muffins.

Place muffin cases in a 12-hole muffin tin or fold the 12 cm square pieces of greaseproof paper into the tin. Spoon the mixture into the cases until quite full. Bake in the preheated oven for 20 minutes and enjoy fresh and warm.

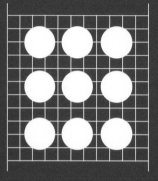

BISCUITS AND COOKIES

I can remember, at the age of six or seven, driving on our annual family holiday to Blackpool. Once we had reached the outskirts of the town, the two things to look for were the tower (of course) and the station where Uncle Frank was the station master. On the way we always passed the Symbol biscuit factory – a large building with the logo on the front. My father always used to say that all the fig rolls came from there, and for years I really believed him. I'm sure we could smell the freshly baked biscuits from the factory as we drove past.

Sweet biscuits are the original comfort food. A digestive with a cup of tea in the morning is a real joy (my mother would disagree). A custard cream in the afternoon is a simple pleasure, but very enjoyable. Some of the old varieties I really enjoyed were Garibaldi (or squashed fly as my dad called them), Malted Milk, Bourbon Creams, Nice and Raspberry

Wafers. Then you had the more up-market Iced Gems and even Wagon Wheels (though these are definitely smaller than they were when I was a child).

Biscuits have become a huge business and every imaginable combination of ingredients and flavours is now produced. Britain has a fantastic history when it comes to traditional biscuit-making. You only have to look in *Traditional Foods of Britain* by Laura Mason and Catherine Brown to see such lovely biscuit names as blackburn cracknel, fatty cake, aberffraw cake, easter, grantham, bath, heckle, shrewsbury and Scottish oatcakes.

I'm a great fan of the American-style cookie with its soft pliable texture and I've come up with a custard cookie that is rather different. Shortbread is my all-time favourite and my mum makes a no-fuss shortbread that is in this chapter. All in all this was a great section to cook, research and write.

CHOCOLATE CHIP COOKIES

I spend quite a bit of time in America, and have come to the conclusion that two things Americans can cook better than all of us are cookies and muffins.

It has taken a bit of time but I think I have come up with a cookie that comes close to the American varieties. The secret is condensed milk: not used much these days in British cookery apart from gypsy tart and toffee, it gives the finished cookie a soft, fudgy texture with a creamy taste.

The good thing about this recipe is that the dough can be made and stored in the freezer; then defrosted, sliced and baked whenever you want some cookies.

225 g (8 oz) unsalted butter, softened,

225 g (8 oz) castor sugar

350 g (12 oz) self-raising flour, sifted

175 g (6 oz) bitter chocolate, chopped

100 g (3½ oz) condensed milk

makes about 20 cookies

Cream the butter and sugar together and then stir in the flour, chocolate and condensed milk – it's as simple as that. Roll the mixture into a sausage shape, about 30 cm (12 inches) long, wrap in foil or cling film and then chill for 30 minutes (this mixture also freezes really well in the rolls).

When ready to bake, preheat the oven to 180°C/350°F/Gas Mark 4. Cut off slices of the mixture, the size is up to you, then peel off the cling film or foil. Place on a greased baking sheet, spacing well apart, and bake for about 12–14 minutes or until just browned. Take the baking sheet out of the oven and allow the biscuits to cool before trying to lift them off the baking sheet. The cookies will keep for up to a week in an airtight container.

CRUMBLY PECAN BISCUITS

These biscuits are very moreish. They are very crumbly indeed and make ideal after-meal nibbles, or an accompaniment to ice creams and parfaits. I devised the recipe after a dinner party some 10 years ago, for which the host made these delicious biscuits. The biscuits can be made by substituting any nut for the pecans, but pecans are the best.

125 g (4½ oz) unsalted butter, softened
70 g (2½ oz) unrefined castor sugar
150 g (5½ oz) plain white flour, sifted
150 g (5½ oz) pecans, ground
2.5 ml (½ teaspoon) vanilla powder or extract
unrefined icing sugar, to dredge

makes about 30 biscuits

Preheat the oven to 150°C/300°F/Gas Mark 2. Grease a baking sheet. Cream the butter and castor sugar together until pale and creamy. Mix in the flour, ground pecans and vanilla and mix to a firm paste. Wrap in cling film and chill for 30 minutes.

Break off small amounts of the chilled mixture and roll into small balls the size of a large marble. Place on the greased baking sheet and bake for 30 minutes. The biscuits will spread only very slightly, but will burn if overcooked, because of the amount of sugar and oil from the nuts.

Remove the tray from the oven, dust the biscuits liberally with icing sugar. Leave to cool completely before trying to lift them as they are very fragile. Store in an airtight container for up to a week.

ROASTED HAZELNUT SHORTCAKES

This is an unusual shortbread but simple to make; the secret is to make sure that the nuts are cold when added to the mixture, or the oil that is released will make the shortbread very difficult to roll out and it won't hold its shape once in the oven (the shortbread is already fairly high in butter).

Sandwich larger discs of this shortbread with fresh and ripe white peaches, and double cream sweetened slightly with icing sugar and vanilla, to make a great summer dessert.

175 g (6 oz) blanched hazelnuts
175 g (6 oz) unsalted butter,
    not too cold
115 g (4 oz) castor sugar
225 g (8 oz) plain white flour
a pinch of salt

makes about 18 shortcakes

Preheat the oven to 200°C/400°F/Gas Mark 6. Place the hazelnuts on a baking tray and cook in the oven for about 5–8 minutes, shaking occasionally, until the nuts are lightly brown. Remove from the oven and leave to cool completely.

Chop the cooled hazelnuts with a large knife or in a food processor, not too finely or too much oil will be released (but if they are too large it will be difficult to roll the dough out thinly enough!). Aim for pieces the size of coarse breadcrumbs.

Place the butter and sugar in a mixing bowl and beat until soft and blended – it shouldn't be too whipped and creamy. Add the flour, salt and hazelnuts and then mix together to form a soft dough. Roll into a sausage shape (this makes it much easier to roll out when chilled), wrap in cling film and for about 30 minutes.

When chilled, roll the dough out quickly to about 5 mm (¼ inch) thick and use a 7 cm (3-inch) diameter cutter to cut out the biscuits. Place the biscuits on a greased baking tray and cook in the oven for about 8–10 minutes or until just golden brown.

Allow the biscuits to cool on the baking sheet before attempting to move them, as they are very fragile. If you find they have stuck to the tray once cooled, just pop the tray back in the oven for 30 seconds to release them. Store in an airtight container, layered with paper napkins or greaseproof paper, for up to a week.

BRANDY SNAPS

These are nice filled with thick cream flavoured with a little vanilla, or shape them over an upturned small bowl to make decorative baskets in which to serve ice cream or sorbets, especially Pink Champagne Sorbet with Double Cream (page 185). The recipe makes a large quantity but can easily be halved.

225 g (8 oz) castor sugar
2 pinches of ground ginger
125 g (4½ oz) unsalted butter,
    softened
115 g (4 oz) plain white flour
115 g (4 oz) golden syrup

makes about 70 brandy snaps

Slightly cream together the sugar, ginger and butter. Add the flour and golden syrup and mix to a firm paste. Roll into a long sausage about 3.5 cm (1½ inches) in diameter and then wrap tightly in cling film, making sure not to catch the cling film inside the roll. Chill well (overnight is best).

Preheat the oven to 180°C/350°F/Gas Mark 4. Lightly grease a baking tray. Remove the cling film and cut off 5 mm (¼-inch) thick slices. Arrange on the baking tray, spacing them out well. Bake for about 8–10 minutes, or until well spread out and golden.

Remove from the oven and leave to cool for a few seconds to firm up slightly. Using a spatula or fish slice carefully remove one brandy snap at a time from the baking sheet and then straightaway loosely wrap it around the handle of a wooden spoon to shape into a roll (if the brandy snaps cool too quickly and start to break, a good tip is to replace the baking tray in the oven for a minute or so to soften them up again slightly). Once shaped, leave to cool. Slide the cooled brandy snaps off the spoon handles and store in an airtight container for three or four days.

ALMOND BUTTER CRISP

This is similar to the Greek baklava – sweet, sticky and delicious. Once you start eating it, it's difficult to stop and, as well as being a tea time treat, it makes a great pudding.

8 sheets of filo pastry
55 g (2 oz) unsalted butter,
    melted
about 50 ml (10 teaspoons)
    golden icing sugar, sifted
finely grated zest of 1 lemon
100 g (3½ oz) slivered almonds

serves 6

Preheat the oven to 160°C/325°F/Gas Mark 3. Grease a non-stick baking sheet. Lay the filo pastry sheets on top of one another on a chopping board and, with a very sharp knife, cut out 20 cm (8-inch) circles, using a plate as a guide. Cover with a slightly damp tea towel.

Place one sheet of pastry on the baking sheet and brush over some of the butter. Sprinkle with about 7.5 ml (1½ teaspoons) of icing sugar and all of the lemon zest and then add a layer of almonds.

Place another layer of pastry on top, brush over more butter, sprinkle with 7.5 ml (1½ teaspoons) of icing sugar and some of the almonds. Repeat this process using another five circles of pastry. Place the remaining pastry circle on top of the layered cake, brush a little butter over the top and loosely cover with cling film. Chill well for 15 minutes.

Remove the cling film and bake the chilled cake for 15–20 minutes, or until crisp and lightly browned all over. Cool slightly and cut into six wedges, then allow to cool completely. This will keep for a day, left uncovered.

LAVENDER SHORTBREAD

Lavender is a flavour that you either love or hate; there doesn't seem to be any middle ground. I didn't really cook much with it until recently, because it reminded me of drawers of winter clothes.

Fern planted several varieties of lavender in the garden but, to be honest, I didn't pay much attention to them at first. Then one hot day I happened to walk past the bushes and, as I brushed against them, the heady perfume that came from the plants was staggering. So, with this in mind, I started to play around with the flavour. I'm still not too sure about using lavender in savoury dishes as it has too perfumed an aroma; still, perhaps that's what some people would say about rosemary?

500 g (1 lb 2 oz) Shortbread
    Pastry dough (Pâte Sablé,
    page 43)
10 fresh lavender heads

makes 10–12 shortbreads

Cut off the top 5 cm (2 inches) of the lavender heads. Discard the stems. Finely chop the lavender tips and flowers and then add to the flour as you make the pâte sablé and chill for 20 minutes.

Preheat the oven to 190°C/375°F/Gas Mark 5. Lightly grease a baking sheet. Roll out the dough to no more than 1 cm (½ inch) thick and then use an 8 cm (3½-inch) cutter to cut out 10–12 discs; the mixture is quite unstable so take care. Transfer to the baking sheet. Bake the shortbreads for 15–20 minutes or until lightly browned.

Take the shortbreads out of the oven and allow to cool for about 10 minutes, to allow the butter to set. Then carefully take them off the baking sheet and transfer to a cooling rack to cool completely. Store in an airtight container for up to a week.

SOFT CUSTARD COOKIES WITH WHITE CHOCOLATE

I nicked this idea from a friend of mine in America; all I did was add the custard and chocolate. The taste of white chocolate really brings out the flavour of the custard – just remember to chop the chocolate finely or the dough will be difficult to cut. The mixture can be frozen and cut off as needed. The cookies will be soft and moist.

115 g (4 oz) unsalted butter,
  softened
115 g (4 oz) castor sugar
90 g (3¼ oz) white chocolate,
  finely chopped
200 g (7 oz) self-raising flour
100 g (3½ oz) cold Bird's
  custard, made to packet
  instructions

makes about 20 cookies

Cream the soft butter and sugar until white and creamy. Add the chocolate, flour and custard and mix well. Form into a sausage shape, roughly 5 cm (2 inches) in diameter. Roll in cling film or baking parchment and chill or freeze for about an hour.

Preheat the oven to 180°C/350°F/Gas Mark 4. Make sure the sausage is very cold before you attempt to cut it, then cut off 1.5 cm ($\frac{5}{8}$-inch) thick slices, peel off the cling film or paper and place on a greased baking sheet, spacing them out well as they will spread as they cook. Bake for about 12–15 minutes or until the edges are golden and the tops are a pale creamy colour.

Remove from the oven and allow to cool slightly before trying to lift off the hot tray. Store in an airtight container for up to a week.

GLACÉ CHERRY SHORTBREADS

A nice, very rich, shortbread biscuit that also makes an easy petit four.

175 g (6 oz) unsalted butter,
    softened
115 g (4 oz) castor sugar
2 egg yolks
225 g (8 oz) plain white flour
about 100 g (3½ oz) glacé
    cherries, halved

makes about 28 small rosettes

Preheat the oven to 190°C/375°F/Gas Mark 5. Lightly grease two baking trays. Beat the butter and sugar together until very pale and creamy. Add the egg yolks and mix well, then add the flour and bring together to form a soft mixture – the softer the mixture, the easier it will be to pipe out. Spoon into a large piping bag fitted with a 1 cm (½-inch) fluted nozzle.

Carefully pipe 4 cm (1½-inch) diameter rosettes on to the baking sheets, spacing them out to allow for spreading. Top each with a cherry half and press down gently. Bake in the oven for about 10 minutes, or until a light golden brown. Allow to cool slightly on the baking sheets before transferring to a cooling rack. Store in an airtight container for up to a week.

MY MUM'S SHORTBREAD

A good shortbread biscuit for eating with tea; my father thinks it's too rich, but I think it's great, mum! This recipe is good for biscuits but unsuitable for lining tins and moulds, as it is very fragile.

225 g (8 oz) plain white flour
115 g (4 oz) cornflour
225 g (8 oz) unsalted butter, softened
55 g (2 oz) castor sugar
55 g (2 oz) icing sugar, sifted
a couple of drops of vanilla extract or a large pinch of vanilla powder

makes about 20 biscuits

Sift the flour and cornflour together. Beat the butter and sugars together in a bowl until soft and fluffy. Add the vanilla extract or powder to the butter and sugar mixture along with the flour and cornflour then knead well to make a dough. Shape into a ball then flatten and wrap in cling film. Chill for about 30 minutes.

Preheat the oven to 180°C/350°F/Gas Mark 4. Grease two baking sheets. Roll out the dough to about 5 mm (¼ inch) thick and then use a 7 cm (3-inch) diameter cutter to cut out the biscuits. Place on the baking sheets and then bake for about 12–15 minutes, or until pale golden brown.

Allow to cool slightly on the baking sheets before putting on a rack to cool completely. Store in an airtight container for up to a week.

EASTER BISCUITS

My mum used to make these biscuits all year round, not just at Easter, when we were kids. They are simple and delicious.

280 g (10 oz) plain white flour
2.5 ml (1 teaspoon) baking
    powder
140 g (5 oz) cold unsalted butter,
    cubed
140 g (5 oz) castor sugar
finely grated zest of 1 lemon
55 g (2 oz) currants
1 egg, beaten

makes about 12 biscuits

Preheat the oven to 200°C/400°F/Gas Mark 6. Lightly grease a baking sheet. Sift the flour and baking powder together into a bowl or process them together for a few seconds, to mix. Carefully rub the butter into the flour or add the butter to the processor bowl and pulse until the mixture looks like fine breadcrumbs. Transfer to a bowl if using a processor and then stir in the lemon zest, currants and egg. Mix well until it forms a dough.

Roll out on a lightly floured surface to about 5 mm (¼ inch) thick. Use an 8 cm (3½-inch) cutter to cut out the biscuits. Re-roll the trimmings to make more biscuits. Place on the baking sheet and bake for 10–12 minutes or until golden brown all over.

Remove from the oven. Leave to cool slightly before moving to a wire rack to cool completely. Store in an airtight container for up to a week.

New Recipe

CHOCOLATE BUTTON CARAMEL PECAN TRAY BAKE

Tray bakes are very fashionable now – they are so simple, cook quickly and are great for coffee mornings or large gatherings. I like the unusual look of the square cake when it's ready to be cut up. Toppings can vary but this is a good one for the kids.

375 g (13 oz) sweet pastry
150 g (5½ oz) butter
150 g (5½ oz) brown soft sugar
397 g can condensed milk
100 g (3½ oz) chopped
    pecan nuts
50 g (1¾ oz) white chocolate
    buttons, roughly chopped
50 g (1¾ oz) milk chocolate
    buttons, roughly chopped
6 Hob Nobs, roughly chopped

serves 4-6

Preheat the oven to 190°C/ 375°F/Gas Mark 5. Line a 20 cm x 20 cm (8 x 8-inch) baking tray with baking parchment. Roll out the sweet pastry to fit the tin size and then leave slightly thicker than usual, say 5 mm (¼ inch). Just cover the base; there is no need to cover the sides. Press down well, and then dock with a fork. Cook for 20 minutes until nicely crisp.

Place the butter, sugar and condensed milk into a saucepan and cook carefully until the mixture boils, bubbling all over, then immediately turn on to the cooked pastry and set.

Mix the nuts, buttons and Hob Nobs together well. Once the caramel has cooled slightly, top with the button and nut topping. Cover with cling film, then press in slightly. Chill really well. Cut and serve.

FRUITY FLAPJACK-GRANOLA

One thing I really hate is a flapjack that is not moist; overcooked flapjacks are awful, too crunchy and jaw-breaking. This recipe is a cross between a flapjack and a granola, the breakfast cereal you get in America. It can be eaten on its own or broken up slightly and eaten with cold milk for breakfast.

175 g (6 oz) porridge oats
55 g (2 oz) raisins or currants
2 pinches of salt
55 g (2 oz) unrefined castor sugar
finely grated zest of 1 lemon,
    plus juice of ½ a lemon
140 g (5 oz) unsalted butter,
    melted
55 g (2 oz) runny honey
30 ml (2 tablespoons)
    golden syrup

serves 6-8

Preheat the oven to 160°C/325°F/Gas Mark 3. Lightly oil a 22 cm (8¾-inch) square baking tin. Mix together the oats, raisins or currants, salt, sugar and lemon zest. Add the butter, honey, golden syrup and lemon juice and mix well.

Spoon into the baking tin and press down lightly and then bake for about 25–30 minutes, or until set and slightly browned around the outside. Allow to cool before breaking up into pieces.

CHRISTMAS GINGERBREAD

I love this recipe. The fact that the biscuits are dual purpose – for eating and for decorating – makes it good fun. Don't be tempted to crush the boiled sweets up; otherwise when you add them to the gingerbread, they will go opaque and bubbly.

125 g (4½ oz) butter
95 g (3¼ oz) dark soft
    brown sugar
60 ml (4 tablespoons)
    Carnation Condensed Milk
325 g (11½ oz) plain flour
5 ml (1 teaspoon)
    bicarbonate of soda
10 ml (2 teaspoons)
    ground ginger
10 ml (2 teaspoons) mixed spice
20 boiled sugar sweets
coloured icing tubes,
    for decoration

makes 20–25 biscuits

Preheat the oven to 180°C/350°F/Gas Mark 4. Heat the butter and sugar in a saucepan, stirring until the sugar has dissolved. Add the condensed milk and stir together. Sift the flour, bicarbonate of soda, ginger and mixed spice into a bowl. Pour over the condensed milk mixture. Start by working the ingredients together with a spoon and then, with clean hands, bring the mixture together into a soft dough.

Roll the gingerbread out on a floured surface to the thickness of 0.5 cm (¼ inch thick). Cut rounds out and place on a baking sheet. Use a very small cutter or knife to cut out circles in the centre of the biscuits (about the size of a pound coin). Make a small hole in the top of the biscuit with a skewer or cocktail stick. Bake the biscuits for about 4 minutes until just golden. Then add the whole boiled sweet to the cut-out hole and cook for a further 5–6 minutes. Do not overcook or the sweets will boil and not set clear. Remove the biscuits from the oven and check that the small holes for hanging the biscuits are still open. Leave to cool completely before decorating with icing. Allow the icing to dry before hanging on the tree.

CONVERSION TABLES

The tables below are only approximate and are meant to be used as a guide only.

Approximate American/ European conversions

	USA	Metric	Imperial
brown sugar	1 cup	170 g	6 oz
butter	1 stick	115 g	4 oz
butter/ margarine/ lard	1 cup	225 g	8 oz
castor and granulated sugar	2 level tablespoons	30 g	1 oz
castor and granulated sugar	1 cup	225 g	8 oz
currants	1 cup	140 g	5 oz
flour	1 cup	140 g	5 oz
golden syrup	1 cup	350 g	12 oz
ground almonds	1 cup	115 g	4 oz
sultanas/ raisins	1 cup	200 g	7 oz

Approximate American/ European conversions

American	European
1 teaspoon	1 teaspoon/ 5 ml
½ fl oz	1 tablespoon/ ½ fl oz/ 15 ml
¼ cup	4 tablespoons/ 2 fl oz/ 50 ml
½ cup plus 2 tablespoons	¼ pint/ 5 fl oz/ 150 ml
1¼ cups	½ pint/ 10 fl oz/ 300 ml
1 pint/ 16 fl oz	1 pint/ 20 fl oz/ 600 ml
2½ pints (5 cups)	1.2 litres/ 2 pints
10 pints	4.5 litres/ 8 pints

Liquid measures

Imperial	ml	fl oz
1 teaspoon	5	
2 tablespoons	30	
4 tablespoons	60	
¼ pint/ 1 gill	150	5
⅓ pint	200	7
½ pint	300	10
¾ pint	425	15
1 pint	600	20
1¾ pints	1000 (1 litre)	35

Oven temperatures

American	Celsius	Fahrenheit	Gas Mark
Cool	120	250	½
Very slow	140	275	1
Slow	150	300	2
Moderate	160	320	3
Moderate	180	350	4
Moderately hot	190	375	5
Fairly hot	200	400	6
Hot	220	425	7
Very hot	230	450	8
Extremely hot	240	475	9

Other useful measurements

Measurement	Metric	Imperial
1 American cup	225 ml	8 fl oz
1 egg, size 3	50 ml	2 fl oz
1 egg white	30 ml	1 fl oz
1 rounded tablespoon flour	30 g	1 oz
1 rounded tablespoon cornflour	30 g	1 oz
1 rounded tablespoon castor sugar	30 g	1 oz
2 level teaspoons gelatine	10 g	¼ oz